Date Due

BRODART, INC.   Cat. No. 23 233   Printed in U.S.A.

DEMCO

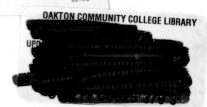

Updating Content in Secondary Business Education

NATIONAL BUSINESS EDUCATION YEARBOOK, NO. 19

Editors: CHARLES A. NEWMAN
Missouri State Department of Education
Jefferson City, Missouri

JOYCE J. CATON
Hazelwood West High School
Hazelwood, Missouri

Published by:

National Business Education Association
1914 Association Drive
Reston, Virginia 22091

UPDATING CONTENT IN SECONDARY BUSINESS EDUCATION

Copyright 1981 by

NATIONAL BUSINESS EDUCATION ASSOCIATION
1914 ASSOCIATION DRIVE
RESTON, VIRGINIA

$12.00

LIBRARY OF CONGRESS CARD NO. 81-81238
ISBN 0-933964-21-8

Any views or recommendations implied in this book do not necessarily constitute official policy of the National Business Education Association. References to and quotations from this publication are encouraged; however, no part of this book may be reproduced without permission of the National Business Education Association.

Contents

PART III
IMPLEMENTING CONTENT CHANGES

    Counselors, Students, Parents, and
    Community About Curriculum Revisions 156
        ROBERTA N. STEARNS
        Westbrook High School
        Westbrook, Maine

        TED D. SPRING
        Thomas College
        Waterville, Maine

**PART IV
CHANGING SECONDARY BUSINESS EDUCATION CONTENT
TO MEET SPECIAL NEEDS**

PART I
TRENDS AFFECTING SECONDARY BUSINESS EDUCATION CURRICULUM

CHAPTER 1

Career Education

WILLIE O. PYKE and WILLARD L. CAMPBELL, JR.

Southern Illinois University, Edwardsville

Since its formal recognition in 1971, the career education movement has had considerable impact on all levels of American education. Extensive publicity, discussion, and federal funds have been devoted to efforts to redesign public education around the career education concept. National, state, and local agencies have invested enormous amounts of money, time, and energy toward the establishment of pilot projects. In 1976, fifty-four percent, or 9,200 of the nation's school districts, reported the existence of some type of career education program.[1]

While the career education movement has generated substantial support, enthusiasm has not been universal. Career education continues to be under careful scrutiny and critical attack. Disagreements on the topic permeate a wide spectrum of American society. The dialogue between both proponents and opponents has been considerable. No doubt the debates will continue, and the outcome of such interaction is not known. What is evident, however, is that career education appears to be moving toward a status of permanence. The federal government has issued a strong mandate for the integration of career education into total school systems, and it continues to allocate millions of dollars to assure that this mandate is carried to fruition. It would seem, then, that despite some of the furor over career education, educators must come to grips with the realization that the movement continues to gain momentum, and it is indeed a viable trend that affects contemporary education in general, and business education in particular.

THE CAREER EDUCATION CONCEPT

National attention was first focused on career education in January 1971 when Sidney P. Marland, Jr., then U.S. Commissioner of Education, addressed the convention of the National Association of Secondary School Principals. Dr. Marland deplored the tendency toward dividing public education into academic and vocational components. He recommended an emphasis on career education that would be designed to redirect the total

---

[1]Heyneman, Stephen P. "The Career Education Debate: Where the Differences Lie." *Teachers College Record* 80:650; May 1979.

public education system. Under the Marland plan, all high school students would be qualified to enter either higher education or some type of useful and rewarding employment. Marland viewed the traditional curriculum as being inadequate. He also thought that the general education provided was irrelevant for the over one-half of high school students who were being prepared neither for employment nor college and who often leave school before graduating. Commissioner Marland pledged the full support of his office in the implementation of the new system.[2]

Defining career education. The U.S. Office of Education defines career education as follows:

> The total effort of public education and the community aimed at helping all individuals to become familiar with the values of a work-oriented society, to integrate these values into their personal value systems, and to implement these values in their lives in such a way that work becomes possible, meaningful, and satisfying to each individual.[3]

Since the Marland initiative, numerous other definitions of, and descriptive statements about, career education have emerged. In fact, Woolschlager and Harris, when researching this topic, concluded that the meaning of career education could be considered an issue in itself.[4]

Several states have developed career education models that are based upon the national plan. These states have also developed objectives that are designed to coincide with national goals. For example, the Illinois Office of Education describes career education as:

> . . . the total effort by educational agencies and communities in presenting organized career-oriented activities and experiences to all persons from nursery school through adulthood, and orients the entire educational plan into one unified career-based system.[5]

The Illinois model is designed to achieve four major goals:

1. Acquaint individuals with career opportunities and options.
2. Assist individuals to make career preferences and/or choices.
3. Provide the vehicle for developing skills and abilities needed by individuals for the achievement of career goals.
4. Assist individuals to develop realistic self-concepts.

This model calls for an emphasis upon *career awareness* in grades K through 6. In grades 7 through 8, the emphasis is upon *career exploration.* The *career orientation* emphasis is recommended at grades 9 and 10, and *career preparation* is emphasized in grades 11 and 12. The model is based on the premise that because career education is a developmental process,

---

[2]Calhoun, Calfrey C., and Finch, Alton V. *Vocational and Career Education: Concepts and Operations.* Belmont, Calif.: Wadsworth Publishing Co., 1976. pp. 107-08.

[3]U.S. Department of Health, Education and Welfare, Office of Education. *Career Education: A Handbook for Implementation.* Washington, D.C.: Government Printing Office, 1972.

[4]Woolschlager, Ruth B., and Harris, E. Edward. "Issues in Career Education." *Business Education Yesterday, Today, and Tomorrow.* Fourteenth Yearbook. Washington, D.C.: National Business Education Association, 1976. Chapter 20, p. 226.

[5]"Career Education . . . for All Students." Springfield: Illinois Office of Education, Department of Vocational and Technical Education. (brochure)

different types of learning experiences should be planned at various grade levels.

The major thrust of this chapter will be on career education at the secondary level, specifically grades 9 through 12. However, in order to place career education in the proper perspective, a brief overview of the role of career education at grades K through 12 will be provided, with subsequent discussions focusing upon grades 9 through 12.

Career education emphasis at grades K-12. In grades K-6, where the emphasis is on career awareness, it is recommended that experiences be provided that would enable elementary students to realize that through careful planning and decision making, they can exercise control over their future careers. The study of occupational groupings and their relationship to one another is an integral part of the awareness stage. Other activities suggested for this level include the analysis of self and the process of defining work and play.

During the career exploration stage in grades 7-8, students continue the analysis of their abilities, interests, and goals. It is at this level that individuals begin to explore various occupational areas.

The career orientation phase in grades 9-10 should be designed so that students can learn about the wide range of career opportunities available and the entrance requirements for these occupations. At this level provisions should be made for an in-depth exploration of various occupations. Learning experiences should include simulated work tasks or actual work activities related to specific occupations. Provision should be made for each student to exercise the decision-making process in preparation for career choices in grades 11-12.

In grades 11-12 career preparation should be emphasized. It is at this level that skills, knowledge, and attitudes for specific groups of occupations are developed. This later stage calls for the exploration of the responsibilities and requirements of specific occupations.[6]

The role of business education in career education at the secondary level (9-12). Since the career education emphasis at grades 9-12 is upon career orientation and career preparation, many business teachers will argue that they have always been involved in career education. This argument is certainly valid; one only has to consider that the vocational objective of business education is to prepare individuals for meaningful jobs. Teachers will also point out that they have been involved not only in career preparation but in career orientation as well. They are quick to show how these two phases are intermingled, and will, therefore, argue that it is difficult to be involved in one phase without focusing attention on the other.

It is not the intent of the writers to dispel any notions about the involvement of secondary business teachers in the career education process. Nor will an attempt be made to delineate the specific role of the business teacher in career education: Woolschlager and Harris provide impressive

[6]Nelson, Robert, and Clow, John. "Orientation Materials for Business, Marketing, and Management Careers." *Career Education Activated by Business Educators in Illinois.* Monograph. Illinois Business Education Association, 1973. p. 9.

suggestions in this regard.[7] Rather, the intent is to discuss three areas considered essential for the success of secondary career education programs, and to provide some practical suggestions. Focus will be upon (1) bridging the gap between vocational and nonvocational education, (2) involving business and industry in career education, and (3) developing personal attitudes and skills. Due to its critical nature, major attention will be given to the last area.

BRIDGING THE GAP BETWEEN VOCATIONAL AND NONVOCATIONAL EDUCATION

For years, there has been a curious illusion that the nonvocational, or so-called *academic*, courses are superior to the vocational courses. While there is ample evidence to show that this antithesis between vocational and liberal education is fallacious, the belief persists. There is still some resentment on both sides. Career education is a *joint* venture that calls for cooperation between teachers, counselors, administrators, parents, and the public. Traditional academic snobbery must cease, or career education implementation efforts will be impeded.

Business educators have an obligation to assist in bridging the gap between vocational and nonvocational education. Moreover, career education can be used as a vehicle for doing so. Some progress has been made in this direction, for various schools have initiated activities that have been designed for this purpose. Unfortunately, while commendable, these efforts are not as widespread as they should be. There still is a need for increased cooperation and participation among those individuals who are considered crucial to the success of career education endeavors.

Business teachers can help satisfy this need by working closely with counselors, teachers from other disciplines, and other pertinent individuals for the purpose of creating better understanding and appreciation of business education. Some teachers will argue that many counselors have been somewhat biased against business education; in too many instances counselors have tended to focus their attention on students who are "academically" inclined. Teachers are also critical of the caliber of vocational guidance that is provided. Many students, especially females and minorities, are advised into tracks that lead to low-level or unavailable positions. These arguments certainly have merit. Yet, there are some indications that counselors are becoming more receptive toward business education. The rationale for this belief is based on the extensive participation of the professional counseling organizations in the career education movement. Many position statements have emerged that indicate that there is now a recognized need among counselors to band together teachers from all disciplines and to work collectively in achieving career education goals.

Business teachers must help counselors learn about job requirements, the job market, job availability data, future projections, and job placement.

---

[7]Woolschlager and Harris, *op. cit.,* pp. 231-33.

Steps should be taken to change attitudes toward race and sex stereotyping.

Beyond this elementary orientation, however, there must be some types of participatory experiences that will allow for interaction between counselors and business educators. Many activities and experiences already initiated by business educators have resulted in increased understanding and cooperation between counselors and business teachers. For example, there are some counselors who are now serving as liaisons between the counseling and business education departments. Through workshops and committee work, counselors have become more involved in job placement activities, as opposed to focusing merely on traditional college placement. Counselors have joined with co-op coordinators in visits to training stations, resulting in increased counselor-employer contacts. Counselors have become involved in workshops and research projects devoted to sex and role stereotyping.

Business teachers must also work with teachers of different disciplines in order to create a better understanding among individuals from various academic areas. Without such understanding and cooperation, career education simply will not work. Marland realized the seriousness of this problem; in fact, this separation of academic and occupational programs helped to stimulate the career education movement. Marland considered this practice an "ugly by-product" of the general curriculum found in contemporary schools. He felt that if career education was to be effective, efforts had to be made to break down the barriers that divide the educational system into parochial enclaves. Curriculums and students must be blended into one flexible comprehensive system.[8]

The concerns outlined above point to the need for some sharing and caring between teachers of varied disciplines. All should work together toward the achievement of career education objectives. At the secondary level, business teachers can contribute to the goals of career education by lending their expertise through working with teachers from other areas in cooperative ventures designed to achieve this purpose. These practices will not only help to bridge the gap, but will contribute to the specific goals of career education as well. Samples of activities that have been used for this purpose, and have been considered successful, include:

1. Business teachers have discussed opportunities for entrepreneurship in art and music classes.
2. Business teachers have worked with school curriculum committees to assure that all students receive information about securing and maintaining employment.
3. Specific courses, such as a computer literacy course, have been designed for the total student population.
4. Business teachers have made presentations at faculty in-service institutes to discuss related topics; one topic focused on the role of business education in school and society.

---

[8]Marland, Sidney P. *Career Education*. New York, N.Y.: McGraw-Hill Book Co., 1974. pp. 18-20.

5. Business teachers have visited mathematics classes to discuss career opportunities in accounting. They have also cooperated with mathematics teachers through team teaching the data processing course.

6. Visits have been made by business teachers to foreign language classes to discuss career opportunities in international corporations and the benefits of foreign language study in such work.

7. Social studies and business teachers have joined together to team teach the consumer economics course in order to integrate business and economic concepts in the course.

INVOLVING BUSINESS AND INDUSTRY IN CAREER EDUCATION

The discussion in the preceding section emphasized the importance of cooperative participation between business teachers and other school personnel. However, the success of the career education program also requires that cooperative participation exist between school personnel and individuals from business and industry. The business community should not be considered as a mere market for business education graduates. Rather, it should also be viewed as an integral part of the learning process.

It is recognized that many business-related experiences are already included in several business education courses. Typical activities are visits to industry, guest speakers, and work experience. These efforts are certainly commendable and complement career education implementation efforts. However, based upon the literature, there appear to be some indicators to suggest that this participation is not as extensive as it should be.

Jewett, in 1930, recognizing the need for business and industry involvement in education, recommended that industry exert a lively interest in secondary education. He proposed that the results of such efforts would have a beneficial influence on business.[9]

Yet in 1971, there was still concern about the need for cooperative efforts between educators and industry. This concern was strong enough to result in a policy declaration from the U.S. Chamber of Commerce. This statement cited the need for businessmen and chambers of commerce to cooperate with various educational agencies in providing more relevant and authentic career education programs. The declaration further specified that potential business employers should provide technical advice on career programs, curriculum materials, equipment, and cooperative work programs.[10]

In 1973, the American Vocational Association issued a policy resolution that cited the need for increased involvement between educators and business and industry leaders.[11] Campbell, when examining the level of business and industry involvement in career education in Chicago metropolitan area firms, found that business and industry were *moderately* involved in career

---

[9]Jewett, Frank B. "Modern Business Looks at Secondary Education." *Schools and Society* 31:415-23; March 29, 1930.

[10]Chamber of Commerce of the United States. "Policy Declarations 1971/72." Washington, D.C.: the Chamber, 1971.

[11]American Vocational Association. *Convention Proceedings Digest.* Proceedings of the National Convention, Chicago, Ill., December 1-6, 1972. Washington, D.C.: the Association, May 1973.

education activities and generally desired involvement in the career education process.[12]

The above statements and research point to the need for increased cooperation and participatory experiences between educators and business leaders. Business teachers should assume the leadership to assure that appropriate experiences will be provided for all business education students.

The types of cooperative experiences that are offered should also be a major consideration for business teachers. They should be planned so that the outcome will result in increased awareness and appreciation among students, teachers, school administrators, and business leaders of the linkage that exists between education and the world of work in American society. The experiences should also be beneficial in helping students to make the transition from school to work with a greater degree of facility.

There are several volunteer services that are available through business firms that will enhance cooperative partnerships between business teachers and future employers. Business teachers should take the initiative in soliciting support from the business sector in this endeavor. Business leaders can cooperate with business educators by—

1. Allowing students to visit business installations.
2. Serving as classroom and assembly speakers.
3. Sponsoring and participating in student club programs.
4. Providing on-the-job opportunities in cooperative education programs.
5. Providing specialized business trade magazines.
6. Sponsoring city and statewide contests in various subject areas.
7. Providing information to teachers and counselors concerning desirable aptitudes and educational and experience backgrounds needed for entry-level jobs so that educators may properly plan their student recruitment, educational, training, and job placement programs.
8. Assisting in the development and evaluation of course content to assure its currency in meeting the changing skill and knowledge needs of industry and business.
9. Providing free audiovisual aids for use in a variety of instructional programs.
10. Assisting in the development of apprenticeship and on-the-job training-related educational courses.
11. Providing sample kits of raw materials, finished products, charts and posters, et cetera, for exhibit and instructional purposes in classrooms.
12. Compiling and publishing directories of community resources and personnel available to teachers, schools, and the school system for various volunteer services.[13]

The activities listed above are not to be considered comprehensive; they are samples that are offered for consideration.

---

[12]Campbell, Wilbur L., Jr. *The Career Education Involvement of Chicago Metropolitan Area Business and Industry with Secondary Schools.* Doctor's thesis. DeKalb: Northern Illinois University, 1976.

[13]*Ibid.*

DEVELOPING PERSONAL ATTITUDES AND SKILLS

The ultimate goal of career education at the secondary level is to prepare individuals for meaningful careers. After students have learned about the various career options available and have explored them in depth, learning experiences should be provided to ensure that they will be given opportunities that will allow them to become proficient in selected areas of specialization.

Teachers generally agree that the learning of specific facts, principles, and skills is a major purpose of classroom activities. While these activities aid in the development of efficient job-related competencies, it must be rendered that attitude formation is another vital area of the learning process. The learning of attitudes is important not only for the future goals of students but for their current motivation in classroom performance as well.[14]

Attitudinal development has been a persistent problem for many business teachers. Enormous amounts of time and energy have been devoted to this area. Yet, the evidence shows that the direct correlation between job failure and improper attitudes still exists.

Any individual who attempts to approach this area of inquiry will immediately sense the problems inherent in attitudinal formation. Philosophers, psychologists, and sociologists have offered different views on this complex topic. Further, societal and economic forces continue to have an effect on attitude formation and modification. Yet, despite all of the complexities, business teachers must somehow guide learners to develop the types of attitudes that will help them to succeed in society in general and the work environment in particular.

Fundamental problems. When students enter secondary school, they often bring with them an array of attitudes that are based on past experiences. Some of these attitudes, if left unattended, will have an adverse effect on efforts to create desirable work attitudes. In some cases, the problem has been so severe as to affect general school enrollment. For instance, many students have found their high school experiences so unpleasant and unrewarding that they have dropped out of school as soon as it was legal to do so. To the surprise of many educators, this dropout population is comprised of both slow and gifted youth, and the increase among gifted students has been substantial. Some failure in the teaching-learning process led these students to the formation of negative, rather than positive, attitudes toward education.[15]

There are various reasons for negative attitudes, and they are usually associated with unpleasant experiences. Some students see school as a failure experience that continually threatens their self-esteem. These failures often lead to decreased interest and motivation, a situation that results in further failure. Since much school learning is contingent upon having learned related material earlier, students who have not profited from past school experiences are often at a double disadvantage. They possess negative attitudes and they also exhibit a lack of readiness.

---

[14]Kuethe, James L. *The Teaching Learning Process.* Glenview, Ill: Scott, Foresman and Co., 1968. p. 8.
[15]*Ibid.*

Other students develop attitudes in previous classrooms toward particular subjects. Examples of this negativism are often found in subjects like mathematics where the learner is faced with the logical dependence of each step on the last, whereas in other subjects it is possible to be perplexed about one topic but fully understand the next.

Further, many of the attitudes that are important to the teaching-learning process are learned in the home. The attitudes in the home toward education and intellectual activities indeed exert a strong influence.

There is a cumulative interaction between school experiences and individual differences in ability, attitudes, and motivation. There is also a cumulative interaction between attitudes and classroom performance. Negative attitudes lead to inferior performance, which results in additional frustration and the strengthening of negative attitudes.[16] It would seem, then, that despite the multifaceted approaches scholars have used to find solutions to some of the problems cited above, one should not underestimate the role of individual differences and motivation in attitudinal formation and modification.

With regard to the principle of individual differences, three major factors should be considered. First, individuals differ not only physically, but in interests, ability, aptitude, home background experience, previous training, attitudes, and goals. Second, individuals learn in their own ways and at their own rates. They differ with regard to the method used to attain knowledge and in the degree of efficiency attained. Third, each individual's learning is influenced by interest, physical makeup, past experiences, and future goals. Just as the physician seeks the right treatment for each malady, the teacher must seek the right training procedure for all learners, and the proper remedial procedures for each deficiency in performance.[17]

Since individuals differ in intellectual abilities, often it is not possible to rely solely on the adopted text or upon mass teaching methods. In such instances, instructional strategies and materials must also be varied. Provision should be made for the average students, and special provision should be made for the slower and gifted learners. One possible strategy is differentiated assignments, wherein the amount of work and the difficulty of the assignment would be tailored to meet the needs of average, lower ability, or gifted learners. Another alternative is to have instruction on a totally individualized basis.

Several affective factors, such as motivation, fear of making mistakes, and expectancy of success, often are influential in determining the learner's success. These motives exist in a hierarchy, and six basic motives usually operate in any given classroom: (a) the desire for teacher approval; (b) the desire to be similar to the teacher; (c) the desire for mastery; (d) the desire to resolve uncertainty; (e) the desire for control, power, and status; and (f) the desire to gratify hostility. Hence, it is the teacher's role to ascertain each learner's hierarchy of motives, tailor individual programs, direct instruction

---

[16]*Ibid.*

[17]West, Leonard. "Five Major Learning Principles." New York: City University of New York. (Mimeographed)

carefully to each learner's anxiety, and generate mild uncertainty.[18] These techniques are valuable in aiding the learner to develop positive attitudes toward learning, which should ultimately result in efficient learning outcomes.

The motives of learners will determine what they choose to learn. Motivation is a crucial feature in learning; it is the condition inside and outside learners that causes them to try. Motivation takes on two basic forms—intrinsic and extrinsic. Intrinsic motivation, which is considered superior to extrinsic, comes from *inside* the learner. It is an integral part of the learning situation. The individual seeks to learn not for any external reward but because of a love for learning. This type of learning builds and grows. Extrinsic motivation comes from outside the learner, is established artificially, and is created by rewards or prizes that have no real connection with the learning situation. This form of motivation has some value, but must be widely distributed. It is of little benefit to reward only a few students.

Individuals are motivated when they reveal by words or actions that they desire ·to reach some goal. To motivate students is to increase their needs to reach a goal, or to create a need where there is no goal. The goal is the *incentive* for motivated behavior, and the specific need is the *motive* for this behavior.[19] The teacher's role is to manipulate anxiety states by creating dissatisfaction with the learner's present status. This can be achieved by working with the learner to formulate a definite goal. Next, the teacher assists the learner to remove that dissatisfaction through the use of teaching methods that lead to the learner's success. He or she achieves the goal, the teacher again creates dissatisfaction (new goal), and the process continues. The teacher should give praise and incentives, and should create in the learner the desire to discover.

Developing attitudes toward work. The transfer learning principle should be of utmost concern to business teachers. Knowledge gained in the classroom should be applicable to the duties performed in real work situations. Transfer of training results when the outcome of a learning situation can be used in an actual situation. Therefore, the content of the business education curriculum should consist of situations wherein students can develop the types of responses that will be needed on the job. This implies that teachers must be able to identify the specific tasks found in actual offices, and to use this information as a basis for selecting instructional content and procedures. It also implies that teachers must be able to identify the types of attitudes and behaviors that are needed for success in these jobs, and to guide learners in developing the traits that are necessary.

It has been pointed out that negative attitudes are usually associated with unpleasant experiences. It would follow, then, that if individuals are to achieve job satisfaction, the actual work encounter must be generally perceived as a pleasant one. Hence, a major task of the business teacher

---

[18]Kagan, Jerome, and Lang, Cynthia. *Psychology and Education.* New York: Harcourt Brace Jovanovich, 1978. pp. 202-302.
[19]Kuethe, *loc. cit.*

should be to devise ways to assist future workers to maximize their potential for job satisfaction, so that work will become a pleasant and rewarding experience.

There are several routes teachers can take to accomplish this goal. One recommended approach would call for the examination of research findings to identify those factors that tend to have an effect on job satisfaction. The knowledge gained should be used to determine how classroom instruction can be tailored to increase the probability for job success. While the research in this area is usually written within the context of motivation, it is pertinent for a discussion on attitudes; there is a relationship between attitudes and motivation.

The research of Herzberg and his associates led to the development of a theory of employee satisfaction and dissatisfaction, which is known as the motivation-hygiene theory. Based on the findings of the original study as well as the results of many follow-up studies, researchers have concluded that the following "motivators" serve to bring about job satisfaction: (1) achievement, (2) recognition, (3) the work itself, (4) responsibility, and (5) advancement.[20] To be more specific, positive job satisfaction exists when an individual believes that—

- the job provides an opportunity for achievement;
- recognition for a job well-done is present;
- positive feelings will develop from the conduct of the job and its tasks;
- he/she is important and job responsibility exists; and
- advancement potential is available.

Aware of these factors, teachers should use their ingenuity and creativity to formulate instructional procedures that will enhance positive attitudes toward work that will yield future job satisfaction. Although this challenge is difficult, a few suggestions are provided in the following sections.

Content domain. Teachers should review the literature and explain, describe, and discuss the research findings on job satisfaction. When students know what leads to positive and negative satisfaction in the world of work, they will be better able to respond in a more rational and intelligent manner. In addition to the direct lecture-discussion approach, teachers may develop participative techniques that will enhance attitudinal development. For example, opinion polls could be used that would allow students to express their feelings of satisfaction and dissatisfaction regarding relevant tasks or jobs. The tabulated results could be compared with existing job satisfaction research findings and used to stimulate class discussions. Other recommended activities include values clarification and behavior modification exercises, cases, problem-solving exercises, personality and interest inventories, self-analysis exercises, guest speakers, and films.

Experiential domain. A second approach to better prepare students to develop positive job satisfaction is to provide actual experiential oppor-

---

[20]Herzberg, Frederick; Mausner, Bernard; and Snyderman, Barbara B. *The Motivation To Work*. Second edition. New York: John Wiley and Sons, 1959.

11

tunities. When the educational process permits and reinforces feelings of achievement, recognition, and responsibility, a major step has been taken toward attaining the goals of the transfer learning principle.

Cooperative education programs lend themselves to this approach. If the work experience is carefully structured and supervised, it can be an excellent vehicle for maximizing job satisfaction. Through participating in actual work experiences, students are in a better position to compare and contrast positive and negative factors in their work. They are also in a position to identify how these factors contribute to satisfaction or dissatisfaction in their jobs. This feedback can be used as a basis for formulating classroom strategies designed to reinforce positive attitudes and to modify attitudes when necessary. Many of the activities cited in the previous section can be used for this purpose.

Affective domain. An analysis of the factors relating to job success shows the need for emphasizing interpersonal relations in the business education classes. The evidence has consistently shown that a major reason why individuals do not succeed on the job is their inability to get along with others.

Business student organizations, when properly structured, are well suited for fostering interpersonal skills. Specific objectives in the affective domain may often best be served by the extracurricular activities program, if it is planned and carried out to achieve these specific goals. Resultant student outcomes should be the development of positive attitudes, values, personality traits, ways of working with people, behavior, and commitment.

Teachers should devise additional strategies for developing interpersonal skills. Numerous classroom activities such as role playing, case problems, and simulations can be beneficial in this regard. Many professionally developed materials, exercises, and activities are available for classroom use. Some of these materials are the outgrowth of responses from various state departments of education, through funded projects, to the career education movement. One such funded Illinois project focused entirely upon occupational survival skills and contains a section with numerous activities that are designed to enhance interpersonal relations.[21] A classroom teachers handbook developed by NBEA through a grant from the U.S. Office of Career Education also contains a section of activities dealing with personal traits and human relationships.[22]

SUMMARY

Career education appears to be moving toward a status of permanence. Educators must come to grips with the realization that the movement continues to gain momentum, and it is indeed a viable trend that affects contemporary education in general, and business education in particular.

---

[21]Nelson, Robert E., project director. *Methods and Materials for Occupational Survival Skills.* Springfield: Illinois Office of Education, Department of Adult, Vocational, and Technical Education, 1977.

[22]Finch, Alton V., editor. *Career Education in Business Education: Classroom Teachers Handbook.* Reston, Va.: National Business Education Association, 1980.

There are three areas that are considered essential for the success of secondary career education programs.

Career education is a joint venture that calls for cooperation between teachers, counselors, administrators, parents, and the public. Business educators have an obligation to assist in bridging the gap between vocational and nonvocational education.

The success of the career education program also requires that cooperative participation exist between school personnel and individuals from business and industry. Business education teachers should assume the leadership in assuring that appropriate experiences will be provided for all business students.

The learning of attitudes is a vital component of the learning process. Attitudinal development has been a persistent problem for business teachers. There is a cumulative interaction between school experiences and individual differences in ability, attitudes, and motivation. There is also a cumulative interaction between attitudes and classroom performance. Negative attitudes lead to inferior performance, which results in additional frustration and the strengthening of negative attitudes. Yet, despite all of the complexities, business teachers must somehow guide learners to develop the types of attitudes that will help them to succeed in society in general and the work environment in particular.

CHAPTER 2

Impact of Technology on Communications And Interpersonal Relationships

SUSIE H. VANHUSS

University of South Carolina, Columbia

Of all the trends affecting the secondary business education curriculum, none has received greater attention than the current emphasis on the office of the future. The mind-boggling technological advances in word processing, micrographics, reprographics, data processing, and telecommunications have had and will continue to have a tremendous impact on communications in the office.

An explosion of paperwork has made the modern business office a communication center. The trend in management today is toward the information concept of management. The office is characterized as a decision-making center, and good decisions are based on adequate, usable, valid information. Simply stated, communication is the primary focus of today's office.

Despite the increasing importance of communications, evidence is mounting that many students preparing for business careers at both the secondary and collegiate levels have basic deficiencies in communication skills. The news media frequently reports that many high school students are reading at the sixth or seventh grade level. Scores on college entrance examinations have declined. Numerous surveys indicate that a major complaint of business executives is that their employees are deficient in basic skills such as spelling, punctuation, word usage, and vocabulary. These complaints are leveled at workers of all ranks ranging from clerical workers to stenographic to management-level employees. The remedy to correct the basic deficiencies has been popularized as the "Back to Basics" movement.

An in-depth study of the way communications are currently being handled and how they might be handled in the office of the future is prerequisite to developing strategies for preparing students to perform successfully in the modern business office. Educators must carefully appraise technological advances before designing curriculums to prepare students for office careers.

FORCES OF CHANGE

Numerous references are made to the revolutionary changes that will rapidly transform society from its current state of being inundated with paper to a paperless society. Micronet, an experimental office in Washington, D.C., is hailed as the first paperless office. Whether society will ever become a paperless society is purely speculative. One thing is certain, however; the change will be evolutionary not revolutionary.

Much of the technology of the office of the future has already been developed, but industry has not yet been able to implement it on a wide-scale basis. A Xerox Corporation film cites the Luddite factor as one of the major reasons why industry does not implement technology as rapidly as it is developed. The Luddites were nineteenth-century English workmen who destroyed labor-saving machinery because they feared the impact of these new machines on them and their jobs. There is a little of the Luddite factor in each individual—a natural resistance to change.

A number of forces of change are having a significant impact on the office. Technological change is making possible a systems approach to handling administrative support services. A number of subsystems will be discussed later in this chapter.

Another force of change is the unprecedented need for information and the manner in which that information is being handled. Data processing, word processing, and other office systems are being integrated. It is not difficult to envision a computer terminal becoming as popular as the typewriter in the office of the future. Hand-held calculators now perform essentially the same functions that early generation computers performed.

Changes are also being caused by the declining number of people available to handle information. Nationally, a tremendous shortage of secretaries exists. Labor experts predict the shortage will increase and become critical by 1985. The reasons for the extreme shortage are varied, but two reasons seem to be most prevalent—a history of low pay and the negative image of the secretary portrayed by the women's liberation movement. Because the secretarial profession is dominated by females, bright female students have been advised to avoid the profession and pursue a career in a male-dominated profession. Attempts to break down the stereotyped role and entice more males into the profession are rather slow in producing results. The greatest impact is being felt at the collegiate levels and has resulted in a significant decrease in enrollment in four-year secretarial and administrative support services programs. Secondary and two-year postsecondary secretarial programs have also been impacted by these societal changes.

The bright side of the problem is that secretarial salaries are increasing at a substantial rate. Graduates of collegiate secretarial programs now find that the salaries offered to them compete very favorably with teachers' salaries and with salaries of many other business administration majors. Secretarial graduates frequently can pick and choose among a number of lucrative job offers. Another bright spot is that a number of administrative and office management positions should emerge as a result of the shift towards a systems approach to administrative support services.

The impact of another force of change—the declining use and availability of paper—is already being felt. The declining use of paper is directly related to the declining supply of paper. Environmentalists are very concerned about the increased consumption of paper and its impact on the natural resources of this country. The shortage of paper is helping to speed up the integration of data processing with other office systems. One does not have to look at many pages of oversize computer printout with only a few lines of print per page to realize that the computer is one of the largest consumers and wasters of paper. By integrating micrographics, records management, word processing, telecommunication, and electronic printing, tremendous quantities of paper can be saved.

Tied in closely to the paper problem is the energy problem. The combined shortage and skyrocketing prices of petroleum and petroleum derivatives may significantly change the office of the future, since many petroleum derivatives are used heavily in office products.

OVERVIEW OF OFFICE SYSTEMS AND IMPACT ON COMMUNICATIONS

Word processing. Most people think of automatic typewriters when word processing is mentioned. The automatic typewriter is a key component of most word processing systems, but the hardware is only one aspect of the total system. It is interesting to trace the progression of the typewriter from the manual to the electric to the element typewriter to the self-correcting to the electronic to all levels of sophistication of automatic typewriters. With this progression comes a shift from a single function unit to a unit that is a component of a more complex system.

One of the most exciting concepts of the office of the future is part of a knowledge-acquisition probe being subjected to stringent productivity testing by Xerox Corporation. According to Reagan, the system, known as Project Alto, consists of four separate components or building blocks:

1. Work station
    Concept:
        Provides multiple functions for one user.
    Functions:
        Word processing
        Text composition
        Terminal emulation
        User to user communication
        File control
        Print/copy control
        Electronic mail
2. Server
    Concept:
        Provides a function to be shared among many users.
    Functions:
        Printing
        Filing
        Processing
        Communications
        Special input-output functions

3. Intra-office network

Concept:

Makes possible high speed communications among system elements via a passive medium coaxial cable.

4. Gateway

Concept:

Serves as an interface element between internal networks and between an internal network and foreign networks/devices.[1]

The integrated system just described is one example of word processing, telecommunications, data processing, records management, and printing combined at one work station and controlled by a basic typewriter keyboard and functions displayed in simple English commands. Other manufacturers have also indicated that they are developing multifunction products. Industry estimates indicate that the population of stand-alone, nondisplay word processing units will stabilize. The electronic typewriter will become more popular, especially in small offices and executive suites. The population of display systems and shared logic systems will increase significantly.[2]

The change in word processing technology will have a significant impact on schools which attempt hardware training. Schools are far less likely to be able to afford shared logic systems for classroom instruction. The most affordable units—stand-alone units—are predicted by industry to become relics of the earlier word processing days.

Significant questions for educators to ask include: (1) How do sophisticated systems affect the handling of communications? (2) What are the problems in communications experienced by users of word processing systems? (3) What knowledges and skills are prerequisite for employment in a company with a sophisticated system? (4) What strategies are appropriate to develop required knowledge and skills? (5) What types of personal skills, aptitudes, and attitudes must an individual have to adjust successfully to work in a sophisticated center?

Obviously, answers to these and many other questions will have to come from intensive research in the area. It would be beneficial at this point, however, to examine common observations relative to word processing. Typical requirements for employment in a word processing position appear to be: (1) good typewriting skill—at least 60 words per minute with a high degree of accuracy and (2) good communications skills. These observations are based on conversations with personnel and word processing managers and from extensive reading of classified advertisements in newspapers of various cities. Knowledge of hardware is generally not listed as a requirement.

Major problems cited are generally twofold: (1) the inability of word originators to dictate effectively, and (2) the inability of word processors to

---

[1]Reagan, Emmett. "The Office of the Future—Management of Information." Presentation at Graphic Communications Seminar, Xerox Corporation International Center for Training and Management Development, Leesburg, Virginia, October 10, 1979.

[2]*Information Processing and Tomorrow's Office.* Reprint from *Fortune,* October 8, 1979. p. 32. (Industry estimates by International Data Corporation.)

handle the English language. The problems generally are not technical problems. The equipment can handle repetitive work, forms, merging files from the computer, text editing, and a host of other functions, but the people involved at both the input and processing stage often have not developed the required communications skills.

A key issue that educators need to study carefully is the impact of word processing on shorthand. Is shorthand really a viable skill in today's office technology? Shorthand generally is not required for employment as a corresponding secretary in a word processing center. The Fortune Market Research Department surveyed top and middle management in major companies across the country to determine the ways in which executives dictate. The conclusion in the Fortune survey was, "Dictation directly to a secretary's shorthand remains the dominant mode. Sophisticated automated dictating systems have so far had little impact."[3]

The use of shorthand was also supported by a Dartnell Corporation survey conducted in cooperation with the National Secretaries Association, International. The Dartnell survey found that 39 percent of employers required shorthand for entry-level jobs with secretarial responsibilities, 65 percent required shorthand for middle-level secretaries, and 74 percent required shorthand for top-level secretaries.[4]

Another significant point to consider in determining whether shorthand is really a viable skill is that while verbatim transcription is the primary use of shorthand, it certainly is not the exclusive use of shorthand. Recording telephone messages, recording directions, and collecting data are all facilitated by the use of shorthand.

Perhaps the key point to be made is that regardless of whether secretaries operate from a word processing center or use shorthand and typewriting as communication tools, and regardless of whether word originators dictate to mechanical equipment or to a secretary, good communications skills are crucial. The implications of this for the business education curriculum will be discussed later in this chapter.

Reprographics. The impact of the copy machine is felt in a far greater number of offices than is the impact of word processing. Nearly every office has a copier of one sort or another.

Copiers range from single function units to components of large systems. A common question is the impact of copiers on the use of carbon paper. The cost of machine copies, particularly when hidden costs are analyzed, is higher than the cost of carbon copies. However, the quality of machine copies is significantly better than the quality of carbon copies. As long as this situation continues to exist, companies will make copies using both machines and carbon paper. The increasing need for judgment and decision-making ability, key factors in every office system including reprographics, has implications for the business education curriculum. The re-

---

[3]*Management Attitudes Toward Office Productivity and Equipment Suppliers.* Survey designed and conducted by Belknap Marketing Services for Fortune Market Research, February 1976. pp. 3, 36.

[4]Billmeier, Lillian E. "The Way We Are." *The Secretary* 37:6-8; June-July 1977.

duction in cost of xerographic equipment should decrease substantially the use of spirit and mimeographic duplicators.

Reprographics is also integrated into other office systems. One example of this integration is the ability of laser imaging printers to print from computer tape directly to regular size paper. In addition to saving tremendous quantities of computer printout paper, this system may revolutionize the management of forms. Historically, information has been added to pre-printed forms. Large supplies of forms were printed and stored for use. Instead, a master file of forms can be stored on computer tape, and the form can be printed at the same time the information to be included on the form is printed. Integrated office systems will certainly decrease the use of carbon paper.

Micrographics. Micrographics is becoming an integral part of records management in many companies. Initially, microforms were used primarily for the storage of seldom-used documents. Today, microforms are used extensively for frequently used documents. Retrieval speed is excellent, and in reference systems, the need for hard copy is reduced or eliminated.

Micrographics is also integrated into other office systems. Computer output on microfiche saves tremendous quantities of computer printout paper and is much faster and more efficient. Micrographics can also be a part of reprographics. Microfiche makes an excellent printing master and simplifies the distribution of documents.

Telecommunications. Telecommunications range from conventional telephone systems to the use of microwave bands and satellites for business communications. Document distribution, data distribution, and teleconferencing are key components of telecommunications. The movement toward a paperless society is based primarily on technology in telecommunications. Electronic mail has been around for many years but has only accounted for a minor share of the total mail. The integration of electronic mail into word processing and the technological advances in telecommunications seem to insure a substantial increase in the volume of mail transmitted electronically.

Electronic transmission of information may have a significant impact on the skills needed by all office workers including managers. A manager who does not possess keyboarding skill may be quite limited in accessing information. For example, in the experimental "paperless" office, all mail, telephone messages, and other communications are accessed through the use of a typewriter keyboard.

Information systems. The information system appears to be the overriding system which provides the framework for integrating all the traditional office support functions. The more the systems approach is used the greater will be the need for all office workers to be able to work with computer-based systems.

This brief overview of office systems is not meant to imply that all offices are rapidly converting to a systems approach based on advanced technology; it has been presented as a basis for discussing the implications of changing job skills in the business education curriculum. Perhaps the key point is that careers will be available for office workers which range from conventional, traditional office positions all the way to positions employing high-level technical skills in ultrasophisticated, automated office systems.

IMPLICATIONS OF CHANGING JOB SKILLS ON THE BUSINESS EDUCATION CURRICULUM

It is difficult to project the type of curriculum needed to prepare prospective employees for employment in a changing business world. Careful distinctions need to be made between the education responsibilities of schools and the training responsibilities of industry.

Schools have often been criticized for inadequately preparing students in basic skills. At the same time, demands are being made on schools to prepare students for employment in highly complex office systems utilizing highly sophisticated equipment. It is doubtful that schools can perform both of these roles effectively. If schools are to assume responsibility for high-quality education, they cannot be expected to divert time and resources to specialized training for industry. While schools can and must do a better job educating students, it is questionable whether they can or should assume the training role for industry.

Hershey makes the following observations in discussing employee training for equipment utilization:

> Although much of the most recently introduced hardware in both word processing and data processing requires only a few days of specific training, employers are likely to intensify their requests for new employees who have prior training on equipment. Part of this demand stems from the fact that few firms provide quality in-house training for new office employees. In some cases, vendors have played no small role in promoting the belief that secondary business educators should be responsible for designing programs—complete with the vendor's equipment, of course—to prepare job-ready graduates to fill equipment-laden office positions. Both the multitude of models on the market and rapid changes in equipment design make such programs costly and questionable. It seems essential that more and more firms must develop quality, in-house training programs for new office employees who need to operate sophisticated equipment.

> Conversely, private business schools and area vocational centers may opt to offer specialized programs. In other cases, secondary teachers may work mutually with business firms to provide "hands-on" machine experiences in the offices of the cooperating firms. However, it seems unlikely that many secondary business programs will be able to afford the costs of acquiring sophisticated and rapidly changing equipment for in-school training programs.[5]

What are the implications of the emerging office and what are the educational needs which schools must meet? Certainly, no definitive answer can be given to these questions, but several considerations can be suggested for inclusion in office education programs.

Keyboarding skills. The need for excellent typewriting skill has long been established. As typewriting equipment becomes more sophisticated

[5]Hershey, Gerald L. "Educational Implications of the Office of the Future." *Journal of Business Education* 55:67; November 1979.

and costly, it becomes increasingly evident that industry will not be willing to tie up costly equipment with technicians who have only marginal skills. In addition to traditional typewriting functions, the role of keyboarding skills in other office systems or subsystems must be considered. Three keyboards—the typewriter keyboard, the ten-key adding machine keyboard, and the touch-tone telephone keyboard—play important roles in computer-based information systems, records management, word processing, and telecommunications systems. The manager who expects to operate efficiently in the office of the future will, in all likelihood, have to develop good keyboarding skills.

Shorthand skills. Shorthand is a very viable skill for the secretary in the office of the future. The Fortune and Dartnell studies referred to earlier in the chapter confirm the continued use of shorthand in major companies across the country. The trend appears to be toward using *both* shorthand and recording devices.

While it is more likely that employees in centralized word processing centers will transcribe from mechanically recorded dictation, it is impossible to predict which students will be employed in word processing centers and which students will be employed in traditional positions. A student with good skills in both shorthand and transcription from recorded dictation is more employable than a student with only one of the skills.

According to both the Fortune and Dartnell surveys, top-level managers are more likely to use shorthand than lower-level managers. The secretary who wishes to advance to the top ranks might well find that shorthand is a required skill.

Communication skills. Of all the competencies needed for success in today's office, none ranks higher than the need for competencies in communication. A number of companies have analyzed the cost of the total graphic communications process. While the percentages might vary slightly from company to company, the following percentages from the American Optical Company seem to be typical of many companies:

Process	*Cost*
1. Origination	57 Percent
2. Copy preparation	6 Percent
3. Copy reproduction	3 Percent
4. Copy distribution	4 Percent
5. Recipient receives and understands communication	30 Percent[6]

It is important to note that the originator's time and the recipient's time account for 87 percent of the cost, whereas the physical processes account for only 13 percent of the total cost. The figures presented certainly indicate that managers need to develop good dictation skills as well as general communication skills.

Too often, emphasis is placed only on written communication skills.

---

[6]Myers, Edward. "Ideas in Action." Presentation at Graphic Communications Seminar, Xerox Corporation International Center for Training and Management Development, Leesburg, Virginia, October 10, 1979.

21

Although written communications are important, written communications constitute only a small portion of the total communications process. Rough estimates indicate that of the time spent communicating, approximately 45 percent is spent listening, 30 percent is spent speaking, 16 percent is spent reading, and 9 percent is spent writing. The business education curriculum must provide opportunities for students to develop competencies in listening, speaking, reading, and writing as well as opportunities to develop sensitivity in nonverbal communications.

LISTENING. Listening is a crucial skill because it affects not only technical job skills but also human relations skills. Every teacher in every subject at every level has both the responsibility and excellent opportunities to teach and reinforce listening skills. Once students have been taught how to listen, it is equally important that teaching techniques be used that motivate students to listen and that reward good listening skills.

SPEAKING. Oral communications are just as important as written communications. It is imperative that business English and business communications courses include an oral component. Emphasis can be given to developing skills in oral communications in every course.

READING. The common cry today is that students cannot read, and the standard answer seems to be to lower the level of readability of instructional materials. A number of issues are involved in the reading problem. How much confidence should teachers have in readability formulas? Even developers of readability formulas point out that they only give a rough estimate of a complex concept. Another issue concerns the level at which readability formulas are appropriate. Readability formulas developed primarily for elementary and middle schools (i.e., Dale/Chall) are often used to evaluate secondary and postsecondary materials. The reliability is questionable at advanced levels. In spite of these considerations, textbook adoption committees often use readability formulas as a key determining factor in the selection of instructional material.

Perhaps it might be more appropriate to raise the reading level of students rather than lower the reading level of instructional materials. Developing competence in reading is easier to write about than to accomplish, but a good starting place is with vocabulary. The vocabulary used in instructional materials for business classes should be realistic and comparable to the vocabulary used in modern offices.

NONVERBAL COMMUNICATION. The impact of nonverbal communication is significant. Students must develop an awareness of and sensitivity to this crucial area of communications. Nonverbal communication has received a great deal of attention because this area is a major component in assertiveness training. Although nonverbal communication and its role in assertiveness training are often associated with the women's movement, the area is far broader than this narrow interpretation. Both nonverbal communication and assertiveness training play a key role in organizational communications and in supervisory and management development. No one course has a monopoly on opportunities to teach students how to be more effective and more sensitive in nonverbal communication.

WRITTEN COMMUNICATIONS. Two different aspects are included in developing writing skills. One aspect is developing technical English skills, commonly referred to as basic skills. The other aspect is developing the ability to plan, organize, and write effective letters, memoranda, reports, and other types of business communications.

Numerous issues can be raised concerning the development of writing skills and who should be responsible for teaching them. Too often in the past, no one wanted to teach business English or business communications. In many schools a tremendous battle over communications courses is currently being waged between English departments and business departments. Declining student enrollments and the oversupply of teachers are the prime causes. The attitude of the teacher is more crucial than which department teaches the communications course. Regardless of who teaches the course, objectives and content should be clearly spelled out so that the communications course does not become a rehash of the old English course.

Three alternatives are commonly used for teaching communications at the secondary level: (1) communications units are integrated into existing courses; (2) a one-semester course is taught which usually emphasizes basic English skills applied to business writing; and (3) a full-year course is offered which usually covers three areas—basic English skills, written communications, and oral communications. Each alternative has merits, and modifications or combinations of the three alternatives can be used to meet the needs of students. The important point is that business teachers must provide opportunities for students to develop good communication skills.

Office procedures. Probably the most significant trends resulting from the office-of-the-future technology are the systems approach to administrative support functions and the emergence of the multifunction office work station. The merging of office systems will by necessity change office procedures. Students must understand concepts of performing work in an integrated office system. Concepts relating to the systems approach can be taught in separate courses dealing with specific office systems such as word processing, or they can be integrated into existing courses.

Emphasis on office productivity and work measurement will continue to increase. The business education curriculum must provide opportunities for students to develop an understanding of productivity and work measurement concepts. Even more important, students must be prepared to work in an office environment in which rigid quantitative and qualitative work standards are used. Rigid standards can create tremendous amounts of pressure, and students need to learn to work under such pressure.

Job specialization is another trend that might have an impact on the curriculum. The trend in industry is toward increased maximization of offices. Many positions in automated systems are highly specialized and repetitive.

Several research studies have indicated that job boredom and dissatisfaction can be a problem with specialized jobs in automated systems. More research needs to be done in this area. As a minimum, students need to be given an opportunity to analyze in depth various types of office positions, job requirements, performance standards, performance appraisals, financial rewards, and personal requirements. Depersonalization is often a result of automation.

Interpersonal skills. The discussion on technology and specialization does not imply that interpersonal skills are diminishing in importance. Good skills in interacting with other people will always be important.

SUMMARY

The positions available to graduates of office education programs will range from traditional positions to positions involving some concepts of automated systems to positions in ultrasophisticated integrated office systems.

The curriculum must provide opportunities for students to develop the following:

- high-level skill in typewriting
- good communications skills
- good transcription skills from both shorthand and recorded dictation
- an understanding of basic office procedures adaptable to both traditional offices and integrated office systems
- flexibility in adjusting to change
- a positive attitude
- good interpersonal skills
- the ability to make decisions.

The student who possesses these skills will be very employable in today's office as well as in the office of the future.

CHAPTER 3
Economic Practices

HOBART H. CONOVER
Albany Business College, Albany, New York

B. BERTHA WAKIN
State University of New York at Albany, Albany

In identifying the economic practices that may affect secondary business education curriculum in the coming decade, one must look at the climate and environment in which the development will take place. One cannot ignore the demographic factors since the composition of the population affects employment trends. Use of resources, particularly the use of energy resources in this decade, must also be taken into consideration as a very important element.

The coming generation of high school students will need training and education for several entirely different types of positions than those of the present time. Technological developments will almost insure that this will occur. For example: According to Mary E. Fenelon, CAM, assistant division manager with the Commerce Clearing House, Inc., New York, "Office workers will have to be trained in the use of more sophisticated equipment in the information/communications process. The office workers must learn to maintain the human touch and to let the customers know that they care, and that real people are working, not just machines."[1]

This generation will face reduced resource availability, specifically in the energy field. The nature and quality of life for this group will be considerably different from what they now know, because it will be necessary for many to change their lifestyles to accommodate these limited resources. Economic practices and decisions will also have an effect on the quality of life and lifestyles.

Business and industry will be faced with rapid technological developments and with the changing composition of the work force. Educators, particularly business educators, will be forced to update their knowledges and skills at a far quicker pace than they do now in order to help students to enter the world of work.

The first part of this chapter will deal with three economic aspects affecting secondary business education: the demographic characteristics that will have an effect on secondary education, the characteristics of the labor

---

[1] "Outlook: Appraising 1980 from a Manager's Perspective." *Modern Office Procedures* 24:45; January 1980.

force, and the social factors that will undoubtedly impact on secondary education. The rest of the chapter will deal with technological developments that will have an effect on secondary business education and will also include some comments about future trends.

POPULATION

There will be an uneven spread in the population of the United States between now and 1990. We have a "sandwich" generation; that is, we have a baby boom population sandwiched between two smaller generations. A smaller number of children were born during the 1930's and during the 1960's. In between, we have a larger population of the 1940's and the 1950's. The generation of young people born in the 1940's and 1950's will find that they will have a far more difficult time and fewer opportunities for reeducation, job advancements, or job changes. Their opportunities will be severely limited. Their expectations of a lifestyle similar to the affluence in which they grew up is not achievable.

Another facet of the so-called baby boom population is that there is a larger number of family formations. These family formations, or rather the mothers of these new households, are having fewer children. The population statistics will show fewer children per family but not necessarily fewer children in the total population.

This trend toward smaller families leads to some rather pressing problems in the housing field. Smaller families do not need large older houses. They are too big and costly to maintain for new young families. Many young families will also have problems securing the necessary financing for a home.

Currently, we are seeing a trend toward more people moving back to the inner city. This is especially true in areas where money was available for urban renewal. It is predicted that more people will be living in or near big cities in the next 20 years.

Another apparent dislocation in the population is the number or increase in number of women now in the labor force. This number is predicted to increase in the next decade.

With a growing older population, a higher level of output for medical care services will be required. Personal consumption expenditures will increase between now and 1990. They will represent the largest growth component of the Gross National Product. In 1952, personal consumption expenditures were 58.6 percent of the GNP; by 1990, PCE will be about 67.7 percent of the GNP. It is predicted that consumers will buy more durable goods. If the prediction proves to be right, there are many implications for the industries specializing in consumable goods.

Business will continue to invest in more energy-efficient, environmentally safe equipment, and government's share of GNP will decline somewhat Foreign trade is expected to be in balance by 1990.

As far as the energy situation is concerned, everyone needs to be aware of the problems. Each sector of the economy is affected by the sources of energy available. In the 1980's it is assumed that coal and electricity will be more readily available than other sources of energy and that their prices will rise less rapidly than the prices of natural gas and oil. Supplies of natural gas are projected to decline over the next decade except for a brief time in 1982 when Alaskan natural gas should become available. However, some inroads will need to be made in the production of synthetic fuels. Energy costs will continue to command a large share of the consumers' dollars.

LABOR FORCE

The projections of the number of people available in the labor force between 1980 and 1990 can be predicted fairly accurately, since the persons who will be 16 years old in 1990 are already six years old and can be counted with relative accuracy.

The labor force population will be heavily weighted with people aged 25-44 and with those over 64. The group between the ages of 16-24 will actually drop. Those in the age group from 45 to 64 and those under 16 will probably maintain their present levels.

The type of employment most likely to be open to this coming generation will be in the service industry, since the predictions are that the service sector of the economy will comprise over 22 percent of the total jobs available. According to the information from the Bureau of Labor Statistics, there will be an increase in the number of office and sales positions in the 1980-1990 decade.

The service-producing industries are those in education, health care, trade, repairs, maintenance, government, transportation, banking, and insurance. Of interest to business educators is the statistic that the demand for secretaries will be three times the demand for other clerical workers, according to the current edition of the *Occupational Outlook Handbook*.

In 1985, approximately 104.3 million people will be in the civilian labor force (barring any dislocation or major catastrophe). This is an increase over 1976 of about 19 percent. There is a large percentage of increase in women workers and a decrease in the percentage of male workers. The following graph illustrates predictions about the changes that will occur in the labor force between 1977 and 1990. Men will make up the largest group of workers, but their participation in the labor force will represent a slight drop from 77.7 percent to 76.4 percent. For teenagers, there will be a slight increase from 61 percent to 64.8 percent. This is in line with the prediction of the percentage of the population this group represents.

For women, the increase will be from 48.4 percent to 57.1 percent. This trend started in the early 1970's and seems to be a continuing trend for the foreseeable future.

The black population as a percentage of the labor force will increase from 11.6 percent to 13.1 percent. Persons aged 25-54 will expand from 61 percent of the labor force to 70 percent by 1990. There will be some decline in older members of the labor force.

The labor force growth will slow down in the 1980's because the working age population will be expanding more slowly than in the 1970's. The youth labor force will decline, reflecting the decline in the birth rate of the 1960's and the early 1970's. Concomitant with this development should be a significant increase in the proportion of the work force aged 25-54.

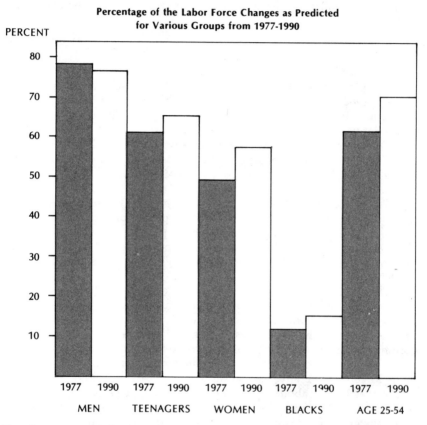

Percentage of the Labor Force Changes as Predicted for Various Groups from 1977-1990

These figures were extrapolated from the U.S. Department of Labor, Bureau of Labor Statistics, Bulletin 2030, 1979, *Employment Projections for the 1980's*.

The composition of the labor force has implications for the current secondary school generation. As will be discussed later in the chapter, the burgeoning technology will influence the amount and type of education that will be required for those who plan to enter the labor force. There will be many new and different types of jobs.

According to the Census Bureau, school enrollments from elementary school through college are likely to remain relatively stable between now and the year 2000. At the present time, children under the age of 15 number about 53 million. By 1990, they will number about 58.1 million, and by the year 2000, they will number about 58.6 million. The age group 15-29 presently numbers about 58.6 million. In 1990, that group will number about 54.9 million, and by the year 2000, the number will be about 55.4 million. Although there are a few dips in the age groups, they seem to level off by the year 2000. One must keep in mind that these are predictions that do not take into account any major catastrophes that may occur.

With these figures as a basis, one could say that there will not be a need to provide new schools. Therefore, over the next 20 years we should be able to improve the quality of education. There will probably be a surplus of professionally trained persons. It would seem that the population of the coming generations between now and the year 2000 will be better educated than the generation of the 1970's.

Twentieth century technology has both created and eliminated hundreds of thousands of jobs. The dislocations, however, are unevenly spread. This is also true of school age populations. While some areas of the country will have declining populations, others, particularly those in the South and Southwest, will experience some growth.

SOCIAL FACTORS

The present generation of secondary school students will face in the future a shortened time in which the major adult role of "parent" is performed, and a much longer "empty-nest" period after the last child leaves home.

Improved health habits, better care, and more available facilities result in a longer lived population. The number of people over 65 in the overall population will increase significantly. This group of people, with more leisure time, will travel more and participate in many types of activities often classed as hobbies. They will require more in the way of health care. This increase in the life span of people should alert educators to the fact that other skills should be taught, those that help individuals to use all the talents they have and to develop avocational interests in addition to those necessary to earn a living.

Another statistic that has social implications is that the number of women in the older age group will outnumber the men. On the average, women still have a longer life span than men. This may change somewhat as the number of women in the work force increases.

The "sandwich" population will face other types of challenges. There will be stronger competition for upper-level jobs. They will be overqualified for the available jobs. This may lead to dissatisfaction with lower-level jobs and to more people with mental health problems. It is also predicted that there will be more white-collar crimes.

TECHNOLOGY

During the next decade Americans will have at their disposal an array of new electronic marvels to assist them at work and in the home. Word and text processors that compose, edit, and distribute business communications electronically will become commonplace in business offices. And electronic mail systems, designed to transmit communications throughout the world, will replace a large part of today's "hard copy" production. The microcomputer will soon be as common as today's typewriter and will provide immediate access to data and information at distant points throughout the country, if not the world. Personal computers in the home and multiple television sets, some with wall-size screens, will provide families endless data, news of ongoing world events, and entertainment. Home computers will monitor home heating, lighting, and cooling systems in an effort to conserve energy and reduce energy costs. Video-cassette recorders and video-disc movies will lessen the desire to travel outside the home for entertainment.

Many shopping, banking, and consumer services will be provided through automated and self-service systems—some operated directly from the home. And to simplify the task further, electronic funds-transfer systems will replace much of the cash, credit card, and checking services which we currently rely on so heavily for payment.

Trends point to tremendous acceleration in the use of measuring devices, computers, and automated medical-records systems in the health services that will greatly enhance the quality of medical diagnosis. This improved diagnosis will unquestionably bring pressures for more extensive medical care, care facilities, and government services. The demand for improved health care and health personnel will, in turn, encourage the use of automated devices that can be used by medical-technical personnel for performing many of the tasks now restricted only to the fully licensed physician. Videophones, cable television for medical conferences, and extensive use of the computer for medical case histories and medical prescriptions are likely to be commonplace by 1990.

Improved diagnosis and medical care will allow an unprecedented number of persons to enjoy life and to live longer than ever before. Despite efforts to retard population growth, by the year 2000, the world will likely have to accommodate at least two billion more persons than at the present time.

The expansion of modern industrial technology has increased the annual energy consumption of nations throughout the world a hundredfold. The resultant energy crisis has thus provided the oil-producing countries with a noose not only to effect political bargaining but also to bring about the realignment of international economic systems. Many nations are now using scarce raw materials as bargaining tools for their industrial needs. A vast number of metals, including gold, copper, lead, platinum, tin, and zinc, are likely to be exhausted in the near future. Although technology may find substitutes for some of these scarce natural resources, future industrial growth may be sorely impeded.

RESOURCE LIMITATIONS

The rich industrial countries of the world as well as the less affluent agrarian nations are keenly aware today of the need to conserve resources.

Between 1973 and 1979, oil alone imported into the United States increased from an average of 6.3 million barrels a day to more than 8.1 million barrels. Experts also hasten to point out that domestic oil and gas production have continued to decline faster than coal and nuclear power supplies—and conservation—have increased. Conservation is now advocated as a kind of ultimate solution to the energy and natural resource problems of many nations.

Gains from energy efficiency have already proved highly rewarding. It is reported that in the United States we have derived more energy from efficiency improvements than from any form of supply—including imports. Gains in efficiency also seem to be accelerating.

As the cost of petroleum has risen, Americans have become increasingly aware of the plight caused by energy limitations. Slowing the growth of energy demands will continue to be imperative in the years ahead regardless of the supply options that may be developed. Without question, conservation must be accompanied by the continued search for means of transition from fossil fuels to sustainable energy sources.

Energy shortages will certainly affect education as heating and transportation costs continue to escalate. School building design may be affected and efforts initiated to change the "spreading building complex" typical of today's educational plants. Even curriculum offerings may be curtailed in an effort to shorten the school day and to reduce heating costs.

Transportation must also be weaned from its heavy dependence on petroleum. Mass transportation and alternatives to automobile travel must be sought. Proximity to jobs and schools is also likely to become a family consideration in future home planning.

After what has been an extended period of affluence and self-indulgence, the American family and business may undergo something of a Spartan-like pride in coping with many sacrifices. Eventually emphasis may shift from stoicism to ingenuity as new conservation methods and techniques are able to accommodate multiple shortages.

Americans may never again enjoy the luxury of a society where so much is taken for granted. Changes in philosophy and concern for finite resources must continue to become more evident. Shifts will also be necessary in the approach to product design and production on the part of business. Ways must be found to make goods more durable and to serve multiple uses. Reconditioning should replace the "throw-away" philosophy through the practice of replacing parts or perhaps whole segments of products.

Recycling must also be extended beyond present concepts as a means for conserving scarce raw materials. Voluntary restrictions are needed to help reduce the daily consumption of scarce resources.

New energy sources and substitutes will, of necessity, continue to be a major objective of business and government. But even with new discoveries and technical breakthroughs, cost may cause the conservation and recycling ethic to prevail.

Space colonization may be man's great hope for coping with not only the world's population but with its energy and materials problems. Space colonization may become a phenomenon as powerful as the environmental movement. Ultimate survival would seem to suggest that the nations of the world plan the best utilization of their combined natural resources. But increased emphasis on nationalism continues the transformation of this earth into an environment seemingly hostile to man.

PRODUCTION, INVESTMENT, AND EMPLOYMENT

America is still outproducing and outconsuming all other industrial economies in the world. But during the past decade, deep and continuing trouble has become evident in our country's rate of production. The amount of production, per person, has caused the United States to slip from first to seventh place in per capita production among the countries of the world. This slippage is the result of many factors to be sure, but it must be considered a major concern of American business in the decade ahead.

The use of investment incentives to encourage business to replace antiquated plants and equipment is one approach to increased production. Capital spending must also be encouraged by new tax policies which release investment capital for plant and equipment modernization. Furthermore, environmental programs and other governmental restrictions on business should be scheduled so as to reduce their "drag" on the economy. Tax and investment incentives must also be used to encourage business to commit capital to new projects designed to reduce risks and production costs.

The incentive to invest in a business venture is eroded when interest rates on savings certificates, treasury notes, and money market funds are equal to or sometimes greater than the rate of return on a business investment. Major innovation and research have also tended to be slowed because of the increased costs and the need of investors for instant gratification.

Work in the future must provide a greater source of accomplishment and sense of importance if it is to provide the job satisfaction which today's worker seeks. As the education of most individuals continues to increase, young workers are becoming increasingly critical of their jobs. Rewards other than money are considered important. The young worker, in particular, is likely to change jobs willingly and often in search of increased job satisfaction. When young workers feel their work to be uninteresting and unchallenging, they do not hesitate to move elsewhere.

Rising expectations of workers in the United States and in the less developed nations of the world will stimulate the demand for consumer goods of many varieties. The worldwide explosion of radio and television communication is causing peoples throughout the world to become painfully aware of differences in lifestyles and living standards—especially between the poor and rich nations. They then press for technological benefits that will help to narrow the gap. Restlessness and public dissatisfaction are likely to grow as evidences of inequities and injustices become more apparent. Exposure to better standards of living can be expected to stimulate the increased demand for everything from improved plumbing and cooking facilities to better housing and means of recreation.

The 1980's will undoubtedly also see a continued increase in the price of most consumer goods and services. This may be aggravated further by severe labor shortages in certain occupations and social factors which tend to keep the rate of population growth down. Clerical workers will constitute both the largest and fastest growing occupational group through the 80's. Growth of employment opportunities in the service industries will accelerate rapidly; however, employment opportunities in the goods-producing industries will remain relatively constant.

The widening demand for consumer goods and services will only increase the problem of investment capital. The public sector can also expect to compete with private business for capital through increased taxes and government borrowing.

If outdated plants and manufacturing equipment in the United States are allowed to continue, technological advancements of many other progressive countries will soon surpass the United States by leaps and bounds. Decreasing returns on investment capital and government policy which is often hostile to private business tend only to further dampen business' incentive to expand.

THE FUTURE OF OUR CITIES

The rate of out-migration from many of our older cities has started to slow down, but the decline will probably continue for some time in the future. As one result of this out-migration, the racial-ethnic composition of many inner cities has undergone major changes. The future of many cities will be dependent upon their ability to hold their white and middle-class black populations.

The new lifestyle choices of older couples whose children have grown, of retirees and senior citizens, and of young newlywed and unwed couples could also have an important influence on city populations and city renewal. Many two- and one-person households are already involved in "gentrification"—the movement of well-to-do persons into poor working-class neighborhoods of our cities.

The failure of incomes to keep pace with living costs may cause average-income Americans to also become less mobile. This will not only hold people in our cities but will result in the rehabilitation of housing in "chic" inner-city neighborhoods.

The revival of our cities will be dependent upon the ability to reduce crime, improve schools, and clean up decaying neighborhoods. During the 15-year period from 1960 to 1975, the rates of both violent and property crime rose steadily and dramatically in many areas of the United States. Criminal behavior in all its forms constitutes a pervasive problem in America —particularly in many of our larger cities.

For decades our cities have provided wider choices for leisure time and cultural pursuits than are available in most suburbs. Cities must continue to encourage this advantage and to actively promote activities directed to the many cultural pursuits.

SCHOOL CURRICULUMS AND EDUCATIONAL SUPPORT

The specter of declining enrollments in some areas of the country and enrollment increases in other areas will haunt American education for the foreseeable future. During the 1980's many school districts will be hard pressed to hold their share of state and local revenues. Inner-city secondary schools and entire sections of the Northeast and Midwest will probably find their enrollment declines exacerbated by the movement of families to the South or suburbs. Most colleges and universities will also face these enrollment hazards. Not until the 1990's will total school enrollments begin to reach the level attained in the seventies.

The hope of many educational institutions lies in their ability to provide programs appropriate to the needs of part-time students and adults. Another facet of educational planning relates to the tendency of more and more women to enter the work force and to remain in employment longer. This trend will undoubtedly create demands for changes in school curriculums and for increased school-centered services. The tendency of women to defer marriage will also result in their desire for more career preparation.

The single-parent family is another demographic trend likely to affect educational services. Furthermore, in areas of the country where immigration from foreign countries is heavy, special demands will be placed upon the schools to provide content and remedial services to meet the special needs.

The combination of factors identified would seem to encourage schools at all levels to include increased opportunities for students to develop personal business skills and consumer capabilities so that they may use their earnings and discretionary income to its full potential.

PROBLEMS OF YOUTH

It is not unusual for adults to be critical of the shortcomings of youth. But many of the envisioned "problems" are in reality attributable to the gap between the accepted values and behavior of youth and that of adult society. Attitudes of youth toward work and job responsibility often fall within this category. However, employers consistently point to the indifference of young workers toward acceptable job performance—of the inability to distinguish between satisfactory and unsatisfactory work standards, of the near-cynical attitude toward job responsibility, and of the lack of self-motivation and self-discipline. Classroom teachers, on the other hand, are more apt to see in youth their indifference to the pursuit of excellence in school work, lack of respect toward teachers and parents, and lack of concern for rules and regulations. Cynicism and lack of respect for social institutions and customs are cited as criticisms.

Youth problems seen as especially alarming today relate to promiscuity and crime, use of alcohol and drugs, and the breakdown of personal morality. Today's youth are undoubtedly victims of weakness or breakdowns in many of our most revered institutions: the family, the church, and the government. Peer-group pressures, lack of self-sustaining forms of recreation, and limited employment opportunities are directly related to these larger social ills. Other attitudes attributable to youth are the resultant carry-over of trends which plague the larger society—the "throw-away syndrome," the addiction to waste, and the need for instant gratification. Similarly, lack of social responsibility, dependence on society, and lack of respect for law and government are not peculiar to youth.

Equally pervasive throughout today's society is the lack of fiscal common sense—the ability to manage effectively one's personal resources. Affluence, wanton use of credit, and debt addiction hold little stigma for most youth or adults.

The problems attributable to youth must therefore be considered in the light of the larger society and of personal and social tendencies which have accumulated over a long time. Rather than wring their hands, adults must seek to modify their own actions and to provide opportunities for youth to participate in the solution of both their own and the larger societal problems.

SUGGESTIONS FOR CURRICULUM MODIFICATION AND EMPHASIS

As we have examined many of the trends existent in today's society, a great many new responsibilities seem once again to be placed upon our schools. Curriculum modifications and/or changes in emphasis relating to economic education are encouraged to take into consideration the following personal and societal needs:

- The curriculum must emphasize planetary citizenship and the need for the nations of the world to strive for a better balance between world resources and human aspirations.

- The curriculum must emphasize the obligation of every individual to serve society through work.

- Opportunities for service to the school, to the community, and to social institutions should help youth to develop a better sense of responsibility and of the duties associated with all forms of opportunity.

- The curriculum must provide youth with early opportunities for more active and constructive participation in adult action groups and other democratic institutions so as to develop their participation skills, their ability to diagnose cause and effect relationships, their powers of persuasiveness, and the power of orderly group processes.

- The curriculum must afford increased opportunities for problem analysis, the diagnosis of complex relationships, and the rational solution of group problems.

- The curriculum should encourage teachers and students to plan together and for greater self-fulfillment through self-directed learning experiences.

- Preparation for work and life should be envisioned as an ongoing process involving serial or recurring job preparation as well as the search for more rewarding uses of leisure time.

- The curriculum must emphasize the dignity and self-worth of all individuals as well as their unique contributions to the greater society.

- Increased opportunities must be provided for youth to assess careers and leisure from the standpoint of personal satisfactions and the need for astute management of one's personal resources.

- The curriculum must emphasize the effects of accelerated changes caused by the rapid technological development and the need for advanced planning and the consideration of alternative futures.

SUGGESTED READINGS

Bureau of Labor Statistics. *Employment Projections for the 1980's*. Bulletin 2030. Washington, D.C.: U.S. Department of Labor, 1979.

Bureau of Labor Statistics. *Occupational Outlook Handbook*. 1978-1979 Edition. Bulletin 1955. Washington, D.C.: U.S. Department of Labor, 1978.

Cornish, Edward (editor). *1999— The World of Tomorrow*. Selections from The Futurist: A Journal of Forecasts, Trends, and Ideas about the Future. Washington, D.C.: World Future Society, 1978.

Shane, Harold G. *Curriculum Change Toward the 21st Century*. Washington, D.C.: National Education Association, 1977.

U.S. Department of Commerce, Bureau of Census. *Social Indicators, 1976*. Selected Data on Social Conditions and Trends in the United States. Washington, D.C.: Government Printing Office, December 1977.

CHAPTER 4

Accounting and Data Processing

JAMES SMILEY

Morehead State University, Morehead, Kentucky

Many business educators believe that a sound strategy for teaching accounting and data processing on the high school level is to effect a true integration of the two programs. However, many problems have prevented this from happening—equipment costs, limited instruction time, the hesitancy of many accounting teachers to approach the subject of data processing, and the requirement of an associate degree for entry into many of the data processing jobs. While the eighties may not be the decade when this integration of accounting and data processing will take place, more progress in this direction hopefully will occur.

UPDATING COURSE CONTENT

Accounting and data processing are important components of the high school business curriculum, with accounting being the more predominate of the two. Recent enrollment data shows that accounting continues to be one of the more popular programs in the business curriculum with significant increases in the number of students taking both first-year and advanced accounting courses. These increases are in contrast to the relatively stable and small enrollment in data processing and to the overall declining enrollment reported for business education in general. Thus recognizing that a large majority of business students are likely to learn about data processing through the study of accounting, this chapter focuses on the need to update the accounting program with an emphasis on modern methods of processing business data.

When anticipating the changes of the 1980's, educators need to remind themselves that the future of education theory and practice is not a decade away or even a year from now. Rather, the future of teaching is only as far away as the next class discussion, demonstration problem, or simulation. In the same sense, the future of accounting will not be a specific point in time that will usher in a great transformation of teaching techniques and student accomplishments, but rather it will be grounded in the history of accounting pedagogy as well as in the currently accepted accounting practices and procedures. Accounting instruction also will continue to be influenced by other factors such as the increasing application of electronic technology and by the necessity for people working in businesses and other organizations to have varying levels of competency in accounting—the language of business. Therefore, a discussion of the trends affecting the evolution of high school accounting can conveniently begin with a reflection on the major issues in the past as well as an assessment of the current status of the program in the business education curriculum. Through such a reflective and assessment process should come ideas for updating the content of the first-year and advanced accounting courses.

High school accounting is a multifaceted program. It is a program that is popular with students in both rural and urban areas and in comprehensive high schools and vocational centers. Accounting is a program that may be taught as a requirement for an entry-level vocational program, as a general education elective stressing the personal uses of accounting, or as preparation for the study of business or related areas at a two- or four-year postsecondary institution. Finally, accounting may be taught as a component in integrated vocational block programs or in separate classes of varying lengths.

As a result of being a program accommodating such diverse groups and purposes, accounting has naturally been surrounded by controversies. Among the controversies have been debates over whether the first-year program should be devoted to job skills with the second-year program devoted to theoretical applications, whether high school accounting contributes to student achievement in accounting programs on the postsecondary level, whether to allow students to use hand-held calculators on examinations, and whether the title of the course should be accounting or bookkeeping. However, the most crucial controversy continues to be focused on what should constitute the content of high school accounting.

On one side of the debate over content are business educators who claim that high school accounting should be taught with an overwhelming emphasis on specialized procedures performed by entry-level employees. This position entails the teaching of routine procedures such as journalizing and posting and the occasional preparation of a trial balance. Stating that high school graduates do not prepare financial statements or become involved with the latter steps of the accounting cycle, the contention is made that high school programs should not go beyond the trial balance step in developing job competencies. Other topics in such a course might emphasize banking procedures, payroll procedures, and accounts receivable and payable.

Another side of the controversy over content is the argument that the analysis of data should be taught along with the specialized procedures associated with the steps of the accounting cycle. Proponents of this position claim that the entire accounting cycle should be taught so that students will learn to view the individual accounting operations as comprising a single system for processing data. These business educators also stress that teaching the entire accounting cycle results in students learning to trace the flow of work through the office as well as the importance of working with others in related jobs. Furthermore, the argument is made that students who begin their careers as bookkeepers or accounting clerks performing specialized tasks are not likely to remain in these positions but will advance to more responsible jobs as a result of gaining work experience and/or more education. Essentially then, this second view holds that accounting programs need to teach problem solving as the basis of business decision making in regard to clusters of jobs. Such an approach will enhance students' adjustment to work situations and improve their mobility once they have entered the labor market.

Teachers accepting this second view are likely to regard accounting as having both specific and broad objectives. Specific objectives may be expressed as performance goals related to actual jobs and presented as students progress through accounting topics. The broad objectives refer to the students served by high school accounting. These students may be classified into three groups—specific vocational, general vocational, and general education. Such broad objectives are useful in planning and organizing accounting programs. The specific vocation objective refers to those students who want to work as accounting clerks, bookkeepers, or paraprofessionals in CPA offices upon graduation from high school. The general vocational objective refers to all other business education students—probably the majority in first-year accounting—who plan to enter the labor market in other areas such as secretary, bank teller, cashier, receptionist, or computer programmer. Finally, the general education objective refers to students who take accounting in order to learn about businesses as economic entities and to understand the basic principles of management and organization. This last group may be nonvocational students who take accounting as preparation for a two- or four-year program in business, agribusiness, prelaw, or other areas where a basic understanding of accounting is necessary. Students in all three groups may be further motivated to study accounting for its personal-use value. With the advent of the home computer, accounting topics take on new meanings in regard to family budgeting, depreciation of a house or automobile used partly for business purposes, or keeping records for a family-owned franchise.

Need for flexibility. Regardless of the perspective held in reference to accounting content, a large degree of flexibility should be built into any philosophy of accounting in order to accommodate students with different abilities, career aspirations, and motivation levels. An example of this flexibility is evident in many of the curriculum guides developed by advisory committees composed of high school teachers, teacher educators, curriculum specialists, and consultants from businesses. For instance, the New York syllabus recommends that first-year accounting be divided into four modules: (1) the accounting cycle for a service business, (2) the accounting cycle for a merchandising business, (3) multibookkeeping system (payroll clerk, office cashier, accounts receivable clerk, and accounts payable clerk), and (4) simulation of an accounting system for a merchandising business.[1] The advisory committee for this syllabus recommended that all the steps of the accounting cycle be included in the course content but at

---

[1]University of the State of New York. State Education Department. Bureau of Occupational Education Curriculum Development. *Bookkeeping and Accounting 1 & 2 Syllabus.* Albany, N.Y.: 1977. pp. 13-52.

different levels of competency. The recommended competency levels progress from the acquaintanceship level on to the practical-use level, the proficiency level, and finally the job proficiency level.

Upon examination of this curriculum guide, teachers will note that selected topics such as the subsystems in module three—payroll, accounts receivable, accounts payable, cashier—are recommended to be taught at the job proficiency level in the first-year course. On the other hand, many of the remaining topics were recommended to be taught at the practical-use level and at the proficiency level. Several topics, especially in modules 1 and 2, that are associated with the latter steps of the accounting cycle, are recommended to be taught only at the acquaintanceship level and not in terms of developing immediate vocational competencies.

By building flexibility into instructional strategies through the recognition of competency levels, students can be evaluated on their understanding of the various steps of the accounting cycle in relation to the competency expected for a specific module. This approach makes it possible to teach the entire accounting cycle during the first-year course along with the specialized procedures required for entry-level employment. By varying the level of competency expected with each step of the accounting cycle, teachers can emphasize the development of job skills as well as an understanding of the accounting cycle as a flow of data from the point of origination—creation of source documents—to the point of use—interpretation of financial statements and management reports for decision making.

The advanced accounting course is recommended by the New York syllabus as the place to develop more of the job competencies needed for entry-level positions. In other words, advanced accounting provides a means for fine-tuning the vocational skills needed for employment and in developing greater job proficiency with the later stages of the accounting cycle. The advanced accounting course may be divided into several sections including: (1) a review of basic accounting principles and procedures, (2) notes and special merchandising procedures, (3) completing the accounting cycle, (4) data processing, (5) business ownership and management, (6) internal control—departmental operations, voucher system, budgeting, and (7) simulations, review, and career information.[2]

Another recommendation included in the syllabus is that advanced accounting is for students who may eventually assume responsibilities beyond the journals of original entry. Advanced accounting is also for students planning to study accounting on the postsecondary level and for those who hope to be a manager or to operate their own business.[3] The advisory committee and consultants who helped develop the New York syllabus concluded that high school graduates should be prepared for more than specific jobs. The consultants in particular believe that employees are more valuable when they understand the entire accounting system and the effect of their jobs on the tasks performed by other employees.[4]

---

[2]Ibid., pp. 57-94.

[3]Ibid., p. iv.

[4]Ibid.

In Tennessee, the state department of education commissioned the development of a curriculum guide for office careers for the junior high through community college levels. The development of this curriculum guide recognized the need to view business education as a continuous process and to articulate programs at each level. In developing this guide, tasks required for jobs in five clusters were identified through research and matched with the minimum levels of competency needed for each of the jobs. The five job clusters were secretarial-steno, clerical-machine operator, bookkeeping-accounting, supervising-management, and data processing. The basic tasks identified for the specific jobs in the five clusters are listed in Table 1. The numbers to the right of each task refer to the minimum level of competency needed by an accounting clerk in order to satisfy all requirements for employment. The degree of job competency increases from Level 1 to Level 5.[5]

Each job in the five clusters is defined in terms of the level of competency needed in each basic task for entry-level employment. An example of how these levels of competency were matched with selected jobs is shown in Table 2 using the financial recordkeeping task.

TABLE 1. Accounting Clerk

Basic Job Tasks	Level of Competency
Clerical	2
Dictating and Transcribing	0
Editorial	2
Filing	1
Financial and Recordkeeping	5
Math Skills	4
Mailing	1
Miscellaneous	0
Office Machines	2
Securing Data	2
Telephoning and Communicating	2
Typing Skills	1
Working with People	2

TABLE 2. Financial and Recordkeeping Task

Job	Level of Competency				
Accounting Clerk	1	2	3	4	⑤
Assistant Computer Operator	1	2	3	④	5
Bookkeeper	1	2	3	④	5
Cashier	1	2	③	4	5
Computer Programmer	1	2	3	④	5
Executive Secretary	1	2	3	④	5
General Office Clerk	1	2	③	4	5
Teller	1	2	③	4	5

Table 2 illustrates that a number of jobs require a knowledge of accounting, but at different levels of competency. It also illustrates that

[5]Tennessee Department of Education. Division of Vocational-Technical Education. *Education for Office Careers.* Nashville: Vocational Curriculum Laboratory, 1971-72.

FIGURE I. Competency Levels*

TOPICS	Accounting I Modules			Accounting II Modules	
	1	2	3	4	5
	Services Business	Merchandising Business	Special Applications	Managerial Uses	Financial Uses
1. Journalizing (General Journal)	P	E	J	J	J
2. Posting to General Journal	P	E	J	J	J
3. Trial Balance	P	E	J	J	J
4. Worksheet	A	E	J	J	J
5. Income Statement	A	E		J	J
6. Balance Sheet	A	E		J	J
7. Statement of Changes in Financial Position					J
8. Banking	J		J	J	J
9. Payroll	J		J	J	J
10. Subsystems: (Journalizing and Posting)					
Cash Payments		J		J**	
Cash Receipts		J		J	
Sales/Accounts Receivable		J		J	
Purchases/Accounts Payable		J		J	
11. Adjusting Entries	A	P		E	E
12. Closing Entries	A	P		E	E
13. Ruling Accounts (not necessary when using Balance Ledger Account Forms)	A				
14. Postclosing Trial Balance	A	P		J	J
15. Reversing Entries					P

Vertical column annotations:
- Column 1: Career/Accounting Concepts/Data Processing Methods; Project and/or Practice Set for Service Business
- Column 2: Careers/Accounting System and Data Processing; Project and/or Practice Set for Merchandising Business
- Column 3: Career Information; Simulation or Electronic Data Processing Unit
- Column 4: Job Process and Careers; Project and/or Practice Set for Manufacturing Business
- Column 5: Project and/or Practice Set for Corporation

1. A = Acquaintanceship level: The student will not be called upon to demonstrate the skill.

2. P = Practical-use level: The student is able to perform the task.

3. E = Proficiency level: The student is able to perform the task with considerable proficiency.

4. J = Job proficiency level: The student should be able to accept entry-level employment.

*Adapted from New York Syllabus
**Departmental Journals/Ledgers

instructional strategies designed for accounting must be flexible in terms of accommodating the career objectives of different students.

The Tennessee guide also contains job descriptions that are correlated with D.O.T. and U.S.O.E. job requirements. For instance, the description of the duties of an accounting clerk is as follows:

Accounting Clerk

D.O.T. 219.488   U.S.O.E. 14.0303

The accounting clerk's duties vary widely. A great many firms require their accounting clerks to perform paraprofessional duties supporting the accountant in organizing, designing, and controlling financial data. All accounting clerks perform a variety of routine calculating, posting, and typing duties to support accounting. The accounting clerk posts transactions, totals accounts, computes and records interest charges, refunds, cost of goods, and similar transactions. The accounting clerk may type vouchers, invoices, accounting statements, and payrolls. The greater the responsibility given to the accounting clerk, the more paraprofessional this position becomes.[6]

Designing programs. Accounting teachers looking at resources such as these two curriculum guides would probably draw ideas from each in developing a program for their own students. A possible result of such efforts may be a broad outline of topics for inclusion in the accounting program matched with expected levels of competency. Such an outline may be similar to the one shown in Figure I.

The topics listed in Figure I include the steps of the accounting cycle as they relate to competency levels to be developed in a two-year accounting program. However, the topics are not intended to represent a complete list for a high school program. While the accounting program depicted in Figure I is divided into five modules, other modules may be developed to meet the needs of specific students. More time may also be alloted for developing greater depth with the modules in high schools offering up to three years of accounting instruction.

The broken lines in the illustration identify the need to allow time for special activities including the integration of data processing methods, completing practice sets, and conducting an accounting simulation involving job rotations. The letters (A, P, E, J) indicate the level of competency expected for the topic in the corresponding module. Of course these competency levels may vary with employer expectations in different areas of the country.

Examples of electronic applications to the processing of data, i.e., preparation of sales slips via the electronic cash register, should be included in the study of accounting as early as possible. Along these same lines, the basic steps of the data processing cycle should also be presented as they relate to the steps of the accounting cycle. An example of how the two cycles can be integrated is to present students with a flowchart matching the steps of the accounting and data processing cycles.

---

[6]*Ibid.*

DATA PROCESSING CYCLE[7]

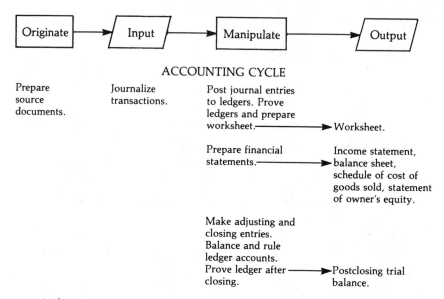

ACCOUNTING CYCLE

Prepare source documents.	Journalize transactions.	Post journal entries to ledgers. Prove ledgers and prepare worksheet. ────────►	Worksheet.
		Prepare financial statements. ────────►	Income statement, balance sheet, schedule of cost of goods sold, statement of owner's equity.
		Make adjusting and closing entries. Balance and rule ledger accounts. Prove ledger after ────► closing.	Postclosing trial balance.

A discussion of the two cycles should include an explanation of the steps of the data processing cycle along with examples of input devices, output devices, and the components of the central processor—the unit that performs the data processing operation in electronic accounting systems. From here, the discussion can be further expanded to include the application of basic data processing operations to specific accounting procedures. An illustration of the data processing cycle and operations in relation to payroll procedures is shown in Figure II.

The unit on electronic data processing in Module 3 (Figure I) may be developed around hands-on experiences with a computer terminal, or it may be designed for teaching without the use of expensive equipment. Either way the students should learn that the computer performs the same operations that they can do themselves, but at a much faster and more efficient rate. Students should also learn that the computer can do no more than it is programmed to do and that the accuracy of the output depends on the accuracy of the input. Topics that may be included in the electronic data processing unit include: components of a computer system, programming a computer, overview of computer languages, and applications of electronic data processing to operations such as accounts receivable, inventory control, and payroll.

UNDERLYING CONCERNS

While updating the high school accounting program may begin with a topical outline built around broad objectives, accounting teachers are likely

---

[7]Weaver, David H., and others. *Accounting 10/12.* Third edition. N.Y.: Gregg/McGraw-Hill Book Co., 1977. p. 438.

FIGURE II. Data Processing/Payroll Accounting[8]

DATA PROCESSING CYCLE	ACCOUNTING ACTIVITY-PAYROLL	DATA PROCESSING OPERATION
Origination	Receives from time clerk time cards on which number of regular and overtime hours worked have been computed.	Communication
Input	Arranges time cards by employee number.	Sorting
	Checks accuracy of hours worked.	Computing
	Multiplies hours worked by pay rate to determine earnings. Writes amounts on time cards.	Computing Recording
Manipulation	Enters employee numbers and names in payroll register.	Recording
	Codes and enters marital status and number of exemptions from employee earnings records in payroll register.	Classifying and Recording
	Enters data about hours and earnings from time cards in payroll register.	Recording
	Determines and enters income tax, FICA tax, other deductions, and total deductions in payroll register.	Computing and Recording
	Subtracts total deductions from gross earnings and enters net pay for each employee in payroll register.	Computing and Recording
	Transfers data from payroll register to employee earnings records.	Recording
	Computes and enters year-to-date earnings on employee earnings records.	Computing and Recording
Output	Files updated employee earnings records.	Storing
	Sends payroll register totals to accounting clerk as basis for journalizing the payroll and issuing the checks.	Summarizing and Communicating

---

[8]*Ibid.*, p. 451.

to have several underlying concerns that they want to accomplish in addition to developing basic job competencies. Such concerns will influence the development and implementation of specific instructional strategies. A review of business education literature suggests that the things that are of great concern to accounting teachers also coincide with the trends that are likely to influence the evolution of high school accounting through the 1980's and on into the 1990's. Several of these concerns (goals) are discussed in the remaining pages of this chapter.

Communications network. Let's begin this part of the discussion with the concern that teachers have in presenting accounting as part of a communications network. Early in the first accounting course, students learn that accounting is defined as the language of business. This is a simple definition, but it is also one that has important overtones in terms of what and how to teach. As a language, accounting is a means of communicating information to a number of users of financial and managerial reports. These users may be classified as being either internal or external to the business.

Internal users include department managers, vice presidents, controllers of large firms, or the owner of a small business. For example, department managers in a merchandising business need accurate, concise information that will allow them to evaluate the production of each employee, the sales level for the department, and the status of the inventory in the department. Such information is "communicated" through the accounting system—often electronically with computers, word processing, and telecommunication devices.

External users of accounting data include investors, unions, government agencies, creditors, and the general public. An example of information needs of a creditor might be the balance sheet showing assets, liabilities, and the owner's equity. Provided with a balance sheet, the creditors can subtract current liabilities from current assets and determine working capital—the accounting resources available to run the business beyond what is required to pay current obligations. The creditors may also divide current assets by current liabilities and determine the working capital ratio. Assuming assets are $150,000 and current liabilities are $75,000, the ratio of assets to liabilities is 2:1. In other words, the creditors learn that there are two dollars in current assets for each dollar that must be paid out for current liabilities. With this information, the creditors can check with sources such as Dun and Bradstreet and see how this business compares with others in the same industry.

Investors represent another external group that makes use of financial statements. Individuals owning common stock in a business can divide net income by the number of shares of common stock outstanding and determine earnings per share. A high earnings per share may reflect a higher return on an investment.

Therefore, as part of a communications network, accounting is involved in providing information for decision making. In turn, the method used to provide such information may be viewed as a system for processing data through the accounting cycle. Thus the accounting system of any business may be approached by looking at the equipment, forms, procedures, and people needed to process accounting data.

Equipment. Much of the equipment used to process data through the accounting system involves the basic skill of keyboarding. Some of the keyboard-type equipment that will be used in accounting work during the eighties are the electronic desk calculator, electronic typewriter, keypunch, CRT terminal, electronic cash register, and hand-held calculators. Still other types of electronic equipment incorporating a keyboard are word processing units which may be used to prepare financial reports and customer statements.

The electronic desk calculator has been described as the work horse of the business world.[9] Specifically, Charles Lecht, president of Advanced Computer Techniques Corporation, describes the hand-held programmable calculator as having the same power as the IBM 650 computer of 1954. The IBM 650 cost $200,000 and weighed seven tons; the hand-held calculator costs $300 and weighs less than a pound.[10] These and other electronic devices increase the ability to process data and to provide information about more aspects of any size business. This increased volume of information will put more emphasis on accounting as an information system staffed by individuals who can prepare data for processing, format data for particular users, verify increasing numbers of reports, and highlight the significant points in reports. In looking at accounting in the 1980's, the president of the American Institute of Certified Public Accountants identified the information explosion brought about by electronic devices and by satellite communications systems as one of the major forces influencing the profession.[11] This resulting information explosion in accounting will probably change even more the requirement for employment from an emphasis on routine skills to a concern for information verification and analysis.

Forms. Accounting in the eighties will continue to require business forms of one kind or another. However, the amount and variety of paper forms used will be altered by the spread of electronic processing to more of the accounting routines. Concepts such as the paperless office, electronic mail, and electronic funds transfer (EFT) will have a growing effect on the accounting system of a business. Instead of having rows of file cabinets stuffed with invoices, more businesses are expected to store accounting information on microfiche filed in small trays, on diskettes, or on some other form that requires considerably less space. For instance, a one-inch stack of microfiche may contain as much information as recorded on 14,000, 8½ x 11 inch pages.[12] Furthermore, financial reports are already being sent to regional and district offices by telecommunication devices in lieu of duplicating numerous copies of the reports, addressing and stuffing

---

[9]Gottheimer, Debra. "More Power to the Calculator." *Administrative Management* 39:42; July 1978.

[10]Frotman, Alan. "Choosing the Right Computer System: An AICPA Conference Weighs the Options." *Journal of Accountancy* 148:48; July 1979.

[11]Olson, Wallace E. "The Accounting Profession in the 1980's." *Journal of Accountancy* 148:54; July 1979.

[12]"Some Advantages of Microfilm Systems." *Administrative Management* 39:38; May 1978.

envelopes, and transmitting the reports via the postal service. Still another technique for storing data is COM—Computer Output Microfilm. With this technique, businesses are able to store computer-processed data directly onto microfilm.

Banking is also going electronic. In addition to placing electronic tellers at shopping centers and other convenient locations, banks are using microfilm (and readers) to keep up with information about deposits and savings accounts. Some banks are also using CRT units for checking customer balances; others are participating in arrangements involving electronic funds transfer (EFT). In other words, while money and checks probably will not disappear, many of the large routine cash payments may be replaced with EFT procedures. EFT represents a more efficient, economical, and convenient procedure for transferring funds than the present system of using cash and checks. Xerox, for instance, pays about 40,000 salaried employees through a national system of electronic payments. With this system the employees receive a nonnegotiable statement informing them that their checking accounts have been increased automatically by the amount of their net salary for that pay period. Checks are not issued to the employees.[13]

The implication of the increasing use of electronic equipment in processing accounting data and in reducing the volume of paper is important in keeping high school programs current. More and more accounting clerks and others involved in processing data will need to understand the procedures these electronic devices are performing. Thus teachers will need to reinforce the basic understanding that electronic data processing equipment and word processing units simply represent a faster, more efficient way of processing data through the routine procedures of the accounting system. In reference to jobs, it is vital that students understand that the output from electronic devices must be verified for accuracy and in terms of the relevance to the need for the information. In summary, a good way to teach students the importance of verifying reports electronically produced is to teach them the importance of accuracy as they process data through the accounting cycle using the manual method of recording and processing. Journals and reports prepared electronically must be as accurate and complete as those prepared manually.

Procedures. In teaching accounting procedures, students should be taught to avoid locking into one way of performing routine tasks. Since accounting is an art, and since procedures are often adapted to data processing methods, it is impossible to assume that there is only one way to complete a given assignment.

Accounting procedures may change with time to reflect the current social and economic conditions. Procedures also change as a result of a different interpretation of acceptable accounting practices. An example of procedures that have changed are those involved in closing accounts. At one time the usual procedure for closing accounts was to: (A) close the revenue account to the income summary account, (B) close the expense/cost accounts to the income summary account, (C) close the income sum-

---

[13]Kaplan, Sheldon D. "Moving Money with Today's Technology." *Administrative Management* 40:58; September 1979.

mary account to the drawing account, and finally, (D) close the drawing account to the owner's capital account. This procedure is diagrammed below.

The current practice, however, is to close the income summary account directly to the capital account. The drawing account is then closed to the capital account as a separate closing entry. Note the change in the procedure as illustrated below.

The reason for the change in the closing procedure is because of the business entity concept. As one of the basic accounting postulates, this concept dictates that personal transactions should be kept separate from business transactions. Thus closing the revenue and expense accounts into the drawing account results in a mixing of the net result of business transactions and personal withdrawals—a violation of the concept. Therefore, the procedures for closing the accounts were changed.

Agencies that bring about changes in accounting procedures include the Financial Accounting Standards Board (FASB), Securities Exchange Commission, and Internal Revenue Service. Of these agencies, the Financial Accounting Standards Board will exert the greatest influence on future accounting practice and procedures. As a subunit of the American Institute of Certified Public Accountants, FASB will have a significant impact on what constitutes acceptable accounting procedures.

Associated with procedures are definitions of terms which also change with time. Two such terms are depreciation and capital. At one time depreciation referred to the decline in the value of plant assets resulting from its use. However, inflation brought about a change in this definition. Many assets, instead of decreasing in value, actually increase in market value as time passes. This means that depreciation no longer can be defined as a decrease in value. Therefore, depreciation was redefined as follows: depreciation is an allocation of the cost of an asset to those accounting periods that will benefit from its use. In learning the importance of depreciation, students will also need to understand that the book value of a plant asset is not the same as its market value.

At times the accounting equation has been stated in a number of ways: Property = Financial Interests, Assets = Liabilities + Proprietorship, and Assets = Liabilities + Capital. However, the preferred form of the equation is Assets = Liabilities + Owner's Equity. Owner's equity is a category of accounts as are liabilities and assets. Cash is a specific asset; accounts payable is a specific liability; the capital account is a specific owner's equity account. Other owner's equity accounts are the temporary accounts—revenue, costs, and expenses. Proprietorship or capital should not be used as a category of accounts in the accounting equation.

People. The fourth component of an accounting system is the most important—the people who make the system work. As students learn to process accounting data and to interpret the significance of accounting operations in the life of an organization, they will be interested in learning about the people who actually perform the activities in the world of work. Students will be motivated to learn about the office of the 1980's and the impact of electronic devices on the processing of both numbers and words. The increased application of microcomputers and micrographics will shift entry-level job requirements even more in the direction of requiring skills in the preparation, editing, and verification of management and financial reports. Job titles are likely to change as well—the secretary will become an administrative assistant, the stenographer will become the communications specialist, and keypunchers will become data-entry specialists. In turn, terms such as accounting paraprofessional, accounting technician, and financial information specialist may become more popular in describing jobs now referred to as bookkeeper. (At the professional level the accountant is becoming known as the money specialist or the scorekeeper of business activities.)

Smith described the jobs in the office of the future in the following manner:

> The personnel in the office of the future will be different in several aspects. For one, we will find more men. Two reasons for this are the effectiveness of affirmative action and the increasingly technical nature of office jobs, making them

more attractive to males. More people will be employed on a part-time basis than have been in the past. Office employees will tend to be well educated and astute, and may grow restless if work does not challenge them. They will not be satisfied with "routine office work."[14]

Accounting will be at home in the office of the 1980's. With electronic devices doing routine tasks, accounting employees will have more time to devote to more challenging activities.

Other concerns. Other aspects of teaching accounting as an information system are the ease of incorporating principles of internal control, using flowcharts to teach procedures and work flow, and organizing accounting topics around each subsystem—cash receipts, cash payments, sales, and purchases. In reference to internal control, the objective is the protection of assets from fraud or misuse (including electronic fraud) and the assurance that all accounting procedures are performed accurately, completely, and on time. While aimed primarily at protecting the assets, internal control procedures also serve to protect the honesty of the employees.

Flowcharts can help students learn the flow of work through the accounting system by outlining the route a source document takes as it is processed from one work station to another. Such flowcharts can also be used to illustrate the importance of human relations and the kinds of communications that take place between employees and people outside the business. Flowcharts can also help students visualize seemingly complicated procedures as a series of simple, related tasks. One word of caution in flow-charting—while flowcharts can help students comprehend job relationships and work flow, flowcharting as a skill should not be taught in high school accounting.

Finally, the systems approach encourages a natural sequencing of topics and concepts in the accounting program. For instance, a unit on the sales subsystem will include topics such as controls of sales on credit, the sales journal, accounts receivable ledger, sales taxes, and sales returns and allowances. Furthermore, as students progress through these topics, specific jobs such as order clerk (D.O.T. 249.368), shipping clerk (D.O.T. 222.387), and accounts receivable clerk (D.O.T. 219.488) can be discussed in reference to the accounting procedure being studied. Other class activities can be devoted to understanding accounting concepts through the analysis of realistic management cases. Management cases help students sharpen their problem-solving skills by evaluating alternative solutions to business problems rather than looking for the one right answer. In these situations, the student is taught to exercise judgement in making the best choice from a set of alternatives.

CONCLUSION

Updating the high school accounting program must be a continuous process if the course content is going to keep pace with changing accounting practices and new technologies associated with trends toward the

---

[14]Smith, Harold T. "Office of the Future: Part Three." *Management World* 6:27; July 1977.

paperless office and the office of the future. Accounting programs in the 1980's need to emphasize the analysis and flow of data as well as the uses of financial and managerial information.

Instructional strategies must be developed around job competencies and yet be flexible enough to accommodate any student who wishes to learn about the language of business. Such strategies (as well as the role of teachers) must be adaptable to competency-based, individualized programs as well as to small and large-group programs. High school accounting also needs to be articulated with accounting taught at the two- and four-year financial and managerial information.

As electronic data processing spreads to smaller businesses, concern must be directed to interpreting the impact of such technology on actual jobs. Electronic data processing has not reduced the number of people working in the accounting area; however, it has affected the responsibilities assigned to accounting positions. Electronic technology makes it possible to have more information about all financial aspects of a business. This increase in financial information requires employees who can both prepare and interpret data. Thus the transition of high school programs from the how's of bookkeeping to the why's of accounting should continue through the 1980's.

CHAPTER 5

Business Administration and Entrepreneurship

DEAN CLAYTON
University of Arkansas, Fayetteville

PHYLLIS J. JOHNSON
Huntsville High School, Huntsville, Arkansas

Business administration and entrepreneurship courses have been offered under varied course titles since their inclusion into the secondary school curriculum around the 1900's. Presently, courses related to business administration and entrepreneurship most often incorporate the terms principles or management, or both, in the titles. The major purpose of business principles/management at its inception in the secondary school curriculum was to prepare students to enter small businesses, usually family-owned, after graduation.

The offerings in business administration and entrepreneurship were primarily senior level, usually twelfth grade, and have remained most often taught on this level in secondary schools. In past decades, very little time has been allocated in the business education secondary school curriculum to train young people in business administration and entrepreneurship. Interestingly, the objectives have changed during the past few years with an apparent renewal of the "small business ownership aspect" or what is commonly referred to as "entrepreneurship."

Because of an increased number of students in secondary schools entering postsecondary education either in mid-management or business administration, the offering of content in business administration and entrepreneurship is serving as a preparatory course. In addition, the offering is becoming more and more preparatory in nature, with an increasing number of secondary school students entering directly into small family-related businesses and management-training programs in larger nonfamily-related firms.

Although it is doubtful that few secondary school graduates move directly into positions demanding a great amount of managerial responsibility, many graduates will find themselves employed where promotion to a supervisory position is likely in a short period. The preparation of students to handle such first-line supervisory managerial responsibilities appears to add further impetus for course offerings in business administration and entrepreneurship on the secondary school level.

With the advent of the *economic education movement* especially during the sixties and the *free enterprise movement* during the seventies, interest has been further kindled in business administration and entrepreneurship for the secondary school student. Because of business administration's and entrepreneurship's close relationship to these movements and a large amount of governmental funding in the late seventies to incorporate business ownership and management concepts into the curriculum at various levels of education, the eighties may foster the *entrepreneurship movement* with a new surge toward small business ownership education.

The movement appears especially apropos when it is reported by the Small Business Administration that about 19 out of every 20 firms in the United States are considered small businesses. In addition, approximately five-hundred thousand new businesses are started every year, but according to Dun and Bradstreet, one-third of these new businesses fail within the first three years—many within the first year.

The purposes of this chapter are mainly twofold: (a) describe ongoing curriculum models and materials related directly to business administration and entrepreneurship on the secondary school level; and (b) describe emerging trends in the world of business which may have direct implications for content in business administration and entrepreneurship on the secondary school level. Hopefully, the curriculum models and materials which are briefly described will assist business education teachers in secondary schools to utilize and refine, when practicable, these models and materials in light of the emerging trends in business which are apparently becoming a reality in the eighties.

CURRICULUM MODELS AND MATERIALS

Commercial publishers, state departments of education, colleges of education and business, curriculum consortiums and laboratories, recipients of governmental and private grants, and private and public profit/ nonprofit organizations are some of the major sources for curriculum models and materials related to business administration and entrepreneurship. The following are some of the curriculum models and materials which might be used in beginning, augmenting, and/or maintaining successful programs on the secondary school level.

Junior Achievement. A model program related directly to business administration and entrepreneurship on the secondary school level is Junior Achievement. For over 60 years, Junior Achievement has been providing American secondary school students a broad and flexible background of business experience. Well over two-hundred thousand students enroll in Junior Achievement programs each year. The program has been winning the endorsement of a wide range of leaders in business, government, and education.

Basically, the Junior Achievement program involves the formation, operation, and liquidation of "minicompanies" by students. Students involved in the program have direct contact with volunteer advisers from local business organizations. In addition to a coordinated program on the local level, students who are successful entrepreneurs may also win substantial prizes in regional or national contests. Over 80 secondary school districts grant some type of credit for students participating in the program.

Computerized businesss decision game. A cooperative arrangement with the Department of Business Administration at the University of Arkansas—Monticello, the Arkansas Power and Light Company, and secondary school business teachers is providing students in Arkansas with an opportunity to compete with other secondary school students in a computerized business decision game. Students in participating schools form teams that are organized as a corporation which produces a certain product (the product changes each year). Approximately one thousand students have participated in the game in less than a decade. The primary objective of the computerized game is to reinforce the concept of management by objectives. Evaluation of a team's performance is determined by its selection of objectives and its ability to accomplish them.

Teams are organized into competitive firms with input (decisions) placed in the computer weekly. The procedure is repeated each week for eight weeks with weekly feedback. The eight weeks simulates business operations for two years. After the eight weeks, each team's rate of return is determined and a biennial report to stockholders is prepared. This written report and an oral explanation are presented to a panel of business personnel in establishing the final winners.

The state supervisor of business education in Arkansas, in an article in the November 1977 issue of *Business Education Forum*, invited other business teachers to join in the use of the computerized business game as a method of promoting a better understanding of the American free enterprise system. The game should be especially appropriate for students involved in business administration and entrepreneurship education on the secondary school level.

Business ownership exploration. Although business administration and entrepreneurship have generally been assigned to the upper grades in secondary schools for preparatory purposes, there is a trend to introduce business ownership and management earlier for prevocational or exploratory purposes. For example, the National Business Education Association received a U.S. Office of Education grant in 1972 to develop a course of study to acquaint seventh through ninth grade students with business ownership and management as a possible career choice.

The materials which were developed provided information relating to (a) the advantages and disadvantages of business ownership, (b) the reasons why business ownership might or might not fit into students' future career decisions, and (c) an awareness of the educational areas in which competence must be attained in order to become an owner of a business. Curriculum materials developed and made available to teachers for field testing included (1) four sound filmstrips, (2) an annotated bibliography, and (3) a teachers guide. Business education teachers made extensive use of this material in exploratory business and related classes on lower grade levels in secondary schools during the pilot project, but it is not yet available for classroom purchase.

Preparation for small business ownership. A corollary to *business ownership exploration* was developed in 1974 by the Athena Corporation of Bethesda, Maryland, through a U.S. Office of Education grant. Instructional modules were developed along with several simulation games to accompany the materials, which were on the tenth through twelfth grade level. The modules were mainly preparatory in nature, but did serve as exploratory for those students who had not been exposed to previous information relating to small business ownership and management. The technical aspects of owning and operating a business were not emphasized; conversely, one of the major purposes of the project was to develop materials that emphasized the humanistic aspects of owning and managing a business.

Other curriculum models and materials. Additional governmental funding in the late seventies made business administration and entrepreneurship curriculum models and materials available on a large scale. These funded projects gave added impetus to schools for incorporating business ownership and management into the curriculum. Although a large volume of the materials developed was for postsecondary and adult levels, the usage of the materials was not necessarily limited to these levels. For instance, a major curriculum undertaking funded by a U.S. Office of Education grant entitled "A Model for Vocational Education Program Development in Entrepreneurship," which was aimed at the postsecondary and adult levels, was discovered to be highly successful when used with appropriate teaching strategies on the secondary school level.

"Project Awareness" had its inception on the national level in the late seventies through the secondary school student organization Future Business Leaders of America. Since its beginning, almost two-hundred thousand secondary school students have participated in the project annually. One of the major purposes of the project is to place these students in contact with business in order for them to become more aware of businesses' problems and challenges. Students participate "in school" and "out of school" with projects related to the private enterprise sector of our economy. State, regional, and national awards are given annually for schools fostering the most outstanding programs in "Project Awareness." Additionally, a publication entitled *Guide to Integrating FBLA into the Curriculum* provides several cocurricular projects in which decision making, fund raising, and competition are included for business administration and entrepreneurship education.

Business Education Forum began a "Forum Feature" during the mid-seventies devoted exclusively to business ownership in which curriculum models and materials have been shared with its readers. For instance, Junior Executive Training (JET) was described as a statewide reimbursed course offering in selected schools on the secondary school level. Potential entrepreneurs focus upon the managerial process, considering the functions of planning, organizing, staffing, and directing, as related to the activities and responsibilities of the supervisor or administrator. A business education teacher desiring to enrich the offerings in business administration and entrepreneurship on the secondary school level should review the articles in the "Forum Feature" related to business ownership to gain further insight into programs such as JET.

Probably one of the best sources for materials dealing with small business ownership is the Small Business Administration. Numerous topics related to business ownership are provided in the Small Business Administration's publications. Curriculum materials which are excellent course supplements may be secured from any district office of the Small Business Administration. In addition, the Small Business Administration will assist secondary school business teachers in developing special programs and course offerings in business administration and enterpreneurship.

EMERGING TRENDS IN BUSINESS

Business teachers must not only be well grounded in basic principles of management but must also sense and accept the challenge to continually search for those emerging changes which students must cope with in the future. Some of the more obvious trends in business which are projected for the eighties involve governmental laws and regulations, communications, marketing shifts, and world competition. The necessity for sound course content as the basis for classroom instruction is, of course, of paramount importance. For this reason, this section's forecast is intended to assist teachers in being alert to those changes which may have a significant effect on business and consequently a significant effect on the content included in business administration and entrepreneurship offerings on the secondary school level. Business educators must be flexible and willing to incorporate new methods and ideas in their classes as, or before, these changes occur in the business world.

Governmental laws and regulations. Government, which has permeated so many aspects of American life during the last decade, will gradually loosen its grip as the American people regain their confidence and turn back toward the values that shaped our country—individual responsibility and personal freedom. The emphasis in the economy will once again be organized around the free enterprise system. The shift, though almost imperceptible, away from demands for government help, government protection, and ultimately, government interference has already begun.

Pressure from business, most especially small business, will produce a dramatic decrease in many regulations that hamper smooth, efficient business operations while doing little to protect the average citizen. Several bills have been introduced in Congress to lessen the impact of federal regulations on small business. For example, a bill was considered by the Senate Labor and Human Resources Committee that would exempt any business employing ten or fewer people from Occupational Safety and Health Administration (OSHA) regulations. The Federal Trade Commission has offered for consideration a proposal that would reduce the paperwork necessary for small businesses wishing to merge with other firms. In another development, if the administration's position prevails, the railroad industry would be deregulated by 1984.

Fiscal aid from Washington during the eighties for business will lie primarily in the areas of amended tax rates and credits. The credits will be aimed, for the most part, at improving and increasing productivity. In fact, improving productivity has become a popular cause in Congress and will continue to be the key to much legislation during the first part of the decade. Some of the options that have been introduced to assist business are an additional accelerated depreciation for property purchased by small business for $25,000 or less, a loss carry forward for new firms for ten years instead of the present seven, and the creation of federal research and development funds for small, innovative firms. Cognizant entrepreneurs will keep abreast of the changes and use them wisely to their advantage.

Two other areas that will reflect change with respect to business and governmental regulation are consumer protection and environmental protection. The public will still expect and want a certain amount of protection, but government will find new and less costly ways to safeguard the consumer. For example, product liability insurance may be offered to companies that presently have a difficult time securing or affording it. The customer, as well as the manufacturer, would be covered under this process. An underlying concern of business during the eighties will be the push by environmentalists for more stringent governmental controls. However, higher energy costs may bring about a general reduction in environmental programs.

Although there may be a decrease in the overwhelming number of laws churned out by government, business will still need competent, knowledgeable managers to effectively grapple with the laws, rules, forms, and regulations that will continue to concern business. Ignorance of these statutes will not be excused (penalties can be very great), and business educators must stress the importance of keeping informed of new developments in all these areas.

International competition and markets. Mutual interdependence exists today between our nation and the developed countries of the world, but the eighties will see a dramatic increase in trade with Eastern Europe, Asia, and those countries just beginning to develop world trade. The United States will become more dependent than ever on export markets and on foreign sources for raw materials. Economic stability and growth during the decade will be largely influenced by both our access to and the success of these new markets.

One forecast from Chase Econometric Associates points toward a slowing of economic growth in developing countries due primarily to the energy crunch, thus reducing these markets for United States goods. However, most studies indicate strong gains in economic indicators of these countries, but warn of the increased competition with our industries at home. Possibly the foreign market generating the most excitement as the decade begins is that of China. According to a survey conducted by the Gallup Organization for the Economic Policy Center of the Chamber of

Commerce of the United States, over 55 percent of the respondents confirmed that their companies have been investigating the possibility of selling products or services to China. Many of them were near reaching an accord on trade agreements.

Keen competition will be reflected in slower growth for some of our industries, most particularly in the textile and steel industries. More and more foreign-based assembly plants will be built by large industries, and this will force the producers of components in the United States to become more innovative and productive. The growth of multinationals will continue as businesses look for easier and cheaper ways to control all aspects of production and distribution.

Students of the eighties will be stepping into a worldwide marketplace, which will require an expanded knowledge of their foreign associates' laws and policies. Perhaps the most important attribute our students can learn is an appreciation for and an acceptance of these countries' customs. A seminar held at the University of Arkansas recently featured an internationally recognized speaker who emphasized the need for students interested in moving into the multinational field to become proficient in at least two languages, because "informed businesspersons in the years ahead will recognize that English can no longer be considered the *only* language of business in the world."

Reductions in tariffs and the lowering of trade barriers throughout the world could avoid too much self-protectionism, and if there is one certainty with respect to the future and trade it is this—isolationism is out! While the United States will find itself challenged directly in some markets, such as automobiles, the potential for a more open and equitable trading period exists. Small businesses will find the world marketplace open to them as well, but they will have to develop expertise in understanding the international market. One problem may well be that of locating and reaching these markets while keeping the price of goods competitive. The solution for the small businessperson may be to form centralized distributing centers through which their goods could be handled more efficiently.

Communications. If there seems to have been a revolution in communications during the seventies, the eighties will be known as the "miracle era" in this field. Orbiting satellites will lead to dramatic diversifications in communications between nations. Transforming conventional communication systems at home and at the office will be a telephone network incorporating the light wave system. Such a network is already in operation in Chicago and has proven to be quite efficient. These systems are designed around hair-thin threads of glass that carry laser signals of light. While these fibers can handle many more signals than a comparable strand of wire, they need only one-fourth as much energy to move information from one point to another. Not only do these systems carry voices and transmit written data, but video facsimiles will be flashed on monitors found in communication centers.

Communications in business will undergo a dramatic change. Most office workers will face an ever increasing battery of electronic devices.

Many manual tasks of today will be replaced by automated methods such as word-text processors that will compose, edit, and distribute business information electronically. Even small businesses will be able to afford these new and exciting machines because of the revolution brought about by the digital circuit. At the beginning of the seventies, for example, a single chip of silicon could "remember" 16 pieces of information, but by 1985 over 250,000 pieces of information will be found on a chip. The major bottleneck for small businesses in the use of automation will be the nonstandardized aspects of their ventures. Businesses, particularly small ones, survive by being different, but the cost effectiveness of electronic equipment will exceed the drawbacks.

The sophisticated knowledge and specialization required for these machines will not replace the basic skills necessary for effective communication. The student should learn that, regardless of the method used, the purpose of communication is to produce a message that has clarity and meaning. Often writers in business fall into the trap of using polysyllabic words to indicate their education, and overuse of certain vague words—*finalize*, for example—is very common in business usage. The adequately prepared businessperson of the eighties must have strong, solid communication skills.

Word processing system centers will become functional on an even larger scale, and small businesses will become attached to systems that serve many different companies. These centers will handle billing, correspondence, contracts, and invoicing. The work will be done more quickly and efficiently a few miles away for small businesses.

Communication between management and the employee should broaden as the humanistic trend begun during the seventies continues. Management will solicit the opinions of their workers by placing them on decision-making committees and boards. Courses in human relations at the secondary school level should expand tremendously with case studies becoming a commonly used method of talented teachers. Minicourses in techniques for effective listening and empathetic sensitivity training will be offered to business administrators as well as to personnel managers. Field work for students in small businesses will be made possible through grants from the Small Business Administration.

Certainly the decade ahead promises to open up new vistas in all areas of communication. The teacher at the secondary school level will be laying the foundation upon which the students will build their future. Business teachers will find that these years demand excellence and up-to-date knowledge in all aspects of communication in order for students to succeed in the changing and demanding business environment.

Market shifts. What do business administrators and entrepreneurs have to look forward to with respect to markets for their products during the coming years? Will the consuming public make dramatic shifts in their demands of products and services? How much effect will the energy shortage have on business markets? What do forecasters predict for the labor market's composition during the decade? Business administrators and classroom teachers should be aware of the changes that will influence these markets.

Most economists agree that one trend—inflation—is here to stay. How much inflation is a matter of debate, but people have already learned to live with it and will accommodate it in the future. Inflation has already brought about a change in spending patterns as people expect more for their money and will be more prudent in their purchases in the future. Discount stores should continue to see a growth in shoppers.

Smaller homes and apartments will place a premium on space, necessitating home appliances that are capable of performing more than one operation, thus eliminating the need for many appliances. Furniture of the eighties will become even more multifunctional as the trend toward houses with rooms that have many uses becomes greater. One "innovation" may see the return of the closet bed.

Energy consumption will be monitored by home computers, and appliances will be designed to conserve energy. While there will be a large increase in the number of households, many of these will be of the single-only variety, creating the need for food and other packaged articles in smaller sizes. The teenagers of today may find themselves still living under their parent's roofs five years from now because of the high cost and limited availability of housing.

One addition to the home of the future may be the entertainment room, because increased affluence will permit people to invest in more elaborate television and stereo equipment. Programming on television should be as varied as the world itself because of the communication satellites and the new technology. Through the use of this technology people will have greater choice in the programs they watch, and eventually they may be shopping, banking, and doing research from their entertainment rooms.

A greater percentage of the average American's pay will be spent on leisure activities. Vacation time will find people seeking out vacation spots that offer all ages a variety of activities, and because of the cost of energy, these one-stop resorts will furnish the transportation as part of a package deal.

Although recreation vehicles will still be popular, smaller, more economical models will be manufactured. If the seventies could be called the jogger's decade, the eighties may be known as the bicycle era. Bikes will boom everywhere, and the choices offered for sale will be wide and wild— from fancy three-wheel models with shopping baskets for the energy-conscious shopper to leaner, racier versions for the racing enthusiast as well as sporty, vividly painted models for the youth bicycle clubs that will become popular.

As America's taste buds become more sophisticated, another pastime that will grow in popularity will be eating out in theme-oriented restaurants featuring gourmet foods. There can be little doubt that one of the growth industries of the eighties will be that of leisure.

Health needs will cause an expansion in all phases of the health industry as the proportion of older people in America increases. From nursing homes to drugs to eyeglasses and hearing aids, the nation will feel the impact of the burgeoning "young old" age groups of folks over 65 years of age. Bionics will truly come of age during these years with limb transplants becoming commonplace and donor banks for organs located in complex medical centers. Week-long retreats at health and exercise spas—formerly the exclusive rite of the rich—will become affordable for the middle class. Local farmer markets offering a variety of naturally grown foods will become more prevalent in parking lots and around city squares as the search for health and vitality becomes a permanent feature of American life.

Where will these markets be found? Certainly the migration to the Sunbelt will continue unabated. Retirement communities will boom, and small towns will become the "in" place to be. The move to the country—40 acres and some cattle—will slow as land prices continue to soar, and more people will be forced to move within easy commuting distance of their work. Even shopping centers located well outside of city centers may feel the pinch as the local stores within walking or bicycling distance win back their share of the customers. Shuttle service between shopping areas and cluster housing will become popular with the merchants and their customers. The small business will have the advantage in terms of being able to move closer to the customer's marketing area.

Knowing which markets to enter and where to find them will be of ever-increasing importance. Even though small businesses will face fierce competition from new business and the international market, they will continue to be the backbone of our economic system. The combination of personal satisfaction and challenge of being one's own boss will outweigh the risks involved. Innovation will be the key to small businesses' growth and survival during this period. Hopefully the government will provide the incentive for the creation of new products and ideas through small business loans, tax credits, and reduction of unnecessary paperwork.

What about the labor pool that will be furnishing business with its employees during the decade? The U.S. Department of Labor's Bureau of Labor Statistics has estimated that the labor force will expand by 15 percent with the largest influx coming from the ranks of women. Work will become an increasingly more significant part of women's lives as inflation and desire for a more expensive lifestyle force them into the marketplace. Women will probably constitute nearly one half of the work force by 1989. Educators must exercise greater care in the advice and encouragement given to women students in order that they may better prepare for careers. Women must not be trained for jobs that are stereotyped or on the verge of being eliminated. Underachievement and dissatisfaction with a job can lead to disillusionment and further division between men and women.

More oldsters will refuse to take early retirement in the face of longer life expectancies, inflation, and legislation favoring extended age requirement for retirement. Many of them will want part-time work leading to more job sharing and "flextime" work schedules. Energy costs may force employers of large industries to turn to the four-day work week in greater numbers. Some employers may follow the lead of a large Midwestern retailer who began free busing for the company's home-office employees at the beginning of 1980.

Employees will have a brighter, better educated market from which to pick their employees, but ambitious workers will not be satisfied with dull, routine-type work. The belief that a job should be gratifying has already become part of the average worker's expectations. An increase in fringe benefits will most likely be among the workers' demands. Unions will hope to benefit during this period by increasing their ranks. However, by the end of the decade relations between employees and employers should have improved because of the opportunity given to employees to participate in the decisions of management.

CONCLUSION

Curriculum models and materials. The seventies reflected an exciting decade for the development of curriculum models in business administration and entrepreneurship. Changes in the curriculum were more evolutionary, then revolutionary. Instructional strategies for greater learning have been refined with an increase in student-involved activities. Junior Achievement is a striking example. In addition, cocurricular activities of other student organizations in business education have fostered the free enterprise system and assisted in paving the way into the eighties as possibly a decade of the *entrepreneurship movement*. Consequently, being a manager of a family-owned or other type of business enterprise will continue to gain momentum in the eighties.

Greater emphasis will be placed on business administration and entrepreneurship with both exploratory and preparatory purposes. Curriculum models which have been extensively funded during the seventies should be utilized, when practicable, in order that the "wheel will not need to be reinvented." Furthermore, computerized business games and other innovative instructional practices need to be publicized and shared with business education teachers.

Junior Executive Training (JET) should become a recognized vocationally reimbursed offering on the secondary school level throughout the United States. This will provide a greater impetus for business administration and entrepreneurship education. Hopefully, a better balance will then exist between the skill-building offerings and the offerings commonly referred to as basic business with business administration and entrepreneurship content.

Emerging trends. Even though there will be an acceleration in the pace of change in the marketplace during the decade ahead, one element will not change—that is the need for trained and educated people who have the skills and initiative necessary to carry on the business of America. Business, government, and industry will be dependent on the students of the eighties to step in and carry our country's private enterprise system to new success and prosperity. The important role of education in preparing those administrators and entrepreneurs cannot be underrated.

The need exists for an expansion of course offerings, as well as a general upgrading in content in present courses. In-depth skill development must become the backbone of classroom instruction. However, the fact that the formulation of effective, intelligent decisions has been and will continue to be a major function of the successful businessperson must not be forgotten by the education community. Students must be given an opportunity to analyze, summarize, and synthesize in order to be prepared for the problems confronting the world in which they will find themselves.

It will be the task of the classroom instructor to provide the opportunity to cultivate these analytical skills. Business education stands at the crossroads as the eighties begin. Will we assume our responsibilities to the students, businesses, and government to educate for the future? The answer is dependent on each of us.

SUGGESTED READINGS

Allison, Ann. "Integrating Student Organizations into Basic Business." *The Balance Sheet* 60:153-55; December 1978 — January 1979.

Anderson, Carrel M. "Will Schools Educate People for Global Understanding and Responsibility?" *Phi Delta Kappan* 61:110-11; October 1979.

Anderson, George W. "Preparing Secondary Teachers To Teach Business Management." *Business Education Forum* 29:27-28; April 1975.

Arkansas State Department of Education, Division of Adult, Technical, and Vocational Education. *A Model for Vocational Education Program Development in Entrepreneurship.* Project No. G007603753. U.S. Office of Education Grant. Little Rock: Arkansas State Department of Education, 1977.

Balsley, Irol W. "What New Office Technology and Government Regulations Mean to Business Education." *Business Education Forum* 34:56; November 1979.

Bottoms, Gene. "Addressing National Concerns Through Vocational Education." *Business Education World* 60:27; September-October 1979.

Butler, Tommie; Henry, Mavis; and Musick, Joseph A. "A Secondary School Adventure in the Free Enterprise System." *Business Education Forum* 32:20-23; November 1977.

Byrnside, O. J., Jr. "Business Ownership and Management Curriculum Development Project." *Business Education Forum* 27:3-6; February 1973.

Carlock, LaNeta L. "Accept No Substitute for Excellence." *Business Education Forum* 34:16-17; December 1979.

Clayton, Dean, and Ruby, Ralph, Jr. "Stress Managerial Skills in High School Business Program." *Business Education Forum* 32:29-30; January 1978.

Crickmer, Barry. "Profits Are for Everybody." *Nation's Business* 67:27-30; October 1979.

Daughtrey, Anne Scott. *Methods of Basic Business and Economic Education.* Cincinnati: South-Western Publishing Co., 1974. p. 473.

Dierks, Caroll J. "An Approach for Integrating Vocational Student Activities into the Business Education Curriculum." *The Balance Sheet* 60:12-14, 43, September 1978.

Friedman, Milton. "Will Freedom Prevail?" *Newsweek*, November 19, 1979. p. 142.

Gratz, J. E., and Gratz, Elizabeth. "Beyond the Basics: Other Communication Levels." *Business Education Forum* 34:37-39; October 1979.

Guide to Integrating FBLA into the Curriculum. Washington D.C.: FBLA-PBL, Inc., 1978.

Huffman, Harry. "Business Educators and Basic Skills." *Journal of Business Education* 54:198-99; February 1979.

Jones, Joey, and Jolley, Freddie Sue. "Potential Entrepreneurs Learn Managerial Skills." *Business Education Forum* 33:30-31; April 1979.

McNamara, Robert S. "Will We Face Up to the New Balance of Wealth?" *Newsweek*, November 19, 1979. p. 144.

Maxwell, Richard. "Junior Achievement: Career Education Since 1919." *Business Education Forum* 30:22-24; April 1976.

National Business Education Association. *Business Ownership and Management, Final Report.* Project No. V257012. U.S. Office of Education Grant. Reston, Va.: the Association, 1975.

Nelson, Robert E., and Bober, Gerald F. "Small Business Ownership: A Neglected Career Option." *Business Education World* 57:22-23, 30; March-April 1977.

"Outlook." *Nation's Business* 67:20; December 1979.

"Project Awareness Uppers!" *Tomorrow's Business Leader* 11:8-9; Fall 1979.

Shane, Harold G. "Forecast for the 80's." *Today's Education* 68:62-63; April-May 1979.

"Small Business Keeps America Working." *Nation's Business* 67:50-54; June 1979.

Stinson, Marilyn L. "Women in the 70's; Have Opportunities Really Changed?" *Journal of Business Education* 54:75-76; November 1979.

VanHook, Barry L. "Business Management in the High School Curriculum." *Business Education Forum* 32:15-17; March 1978.

U. S. News and World Report, October 15, 1979.

Walden, Jim. "Entrepreneurship: It Takes More Than a Dream." *Business Education Forum* 33:27-29; April 1979.

"Its a Small, Smaller World." *Women in Business* 31:6-7; October-November 1979.

Part II
DETERMINING CURRICULUM NEEDS IN SECONDARY BUSINESS EDUCATION

CHAPTER 6

Role of the Local District Administration and Teaching Staff in Implementing Change

EARL BOWICK

Larimer County Schools, Fort Collins, Colorado

This chapter will examine the process of curriculum change and the role of school personnel who are directly involved in providing responsible leadership for such change. In addition, the chapter will review (1) the personal qualities essential for success in these leadership roles, (2) the responsibility of the classroom teacher to continuously update course content, (3) the impact of in-service activities on curriculum change, and (4) the impetus of new teaching and learning systems.

DETERMINING CURRICULUM NEEDS

The rate of evolution and development in the field of business education has created myriad problems that relate to determining curriculum needs and then translating those needs into curriculum materials that aid instruction at the secondary level in business education. One procedure for determining curriculum needs in secondary business education is to explore a perceived need. This perceived need could be enunciated by educators, parents, students, employers, or employees.

Feasibility study. A feasibility study must be conducted to determine if, in fact, there is a need for a curriculum development activity in a given area. During this study, a brief annotated bibliography could be developed that would identify existing curriculum materials; and based on this information, a determination could be made on whether to continue the activity or to terminate it at this point. If the feasibility study indicates that further curriculum development should take place, efforts should be continued to further define the desired outcomes.

Priority list. Armed with this information, a priority list can be developed and presented to the decision makers in the district. They must be given the opportunity to identify the priorities in conjunction with the goals and aspirations of the school district and/or the particular high school. These goals and aspirations statements usually have been developed by the school board, district administrators, teachers, and parents.

Occupational analysis. It is recommended that an occupational analysis and training need survey be completed before any other curriculum development activities begin for a new vocational course or unit offering. Is there a high demand for the occupation as indicated by the number of new positions that are available in the community, the region, or the nation for persons with this particular training? Is training not available at the present time? Such an occupational analysis and need survey might show, for example, that curriculum development for word processing is the number one priority.

Performance objectives. Next, performance objectives must be prepared. Once prepared, the listing should be made available to state and local supervisory personnel for use in determining the direction curriculum development activities will take. This is a sensitive area, and the business teachers must take a major role in preparing performance objectives since they directly impact on their instructional strategies and programs.

Other considerations. In making curriculum decisions, other areas to consider are: What are the legal requirements for increasing standards and other changes? Has there been any major equipment change that would affect instruction? Another consideration is the social impact of the curriculum change. The changing values and meaning of work in the human experience, changes in the structure and composition of the work force, problems associated with school and community dropouts, barriers between school and community, the information deficits that ill-prepare the student for career decisions, and the special needs of by-passed populations will all have to be considered if a particular curriculum decision is implemented.

Curriculum developers must address the fact that each person has his/her own worth, uniqueness, and separateness. Will the instructional program be evaluated? Will the curriculum decision provide alternative experiences and an environment that will allow the student to maintain a sense of dignity and self-worth in the occupation in which he/she has trained for employment? These questions must be addressed and answered before curriculum changes are made.

CURRICULUM ORGANIZATION

Administrators at all levels must consider the organizational pattern of the curriculum so that particular attention will be given to individual success. Students must progress from simple to complex learning activities for the curriculum to be successful. The curriculum developer's personal beliefs about the individual in education, beliefs about society and economics, and philosophic attitudes about business education are three factors that will have an effect on the curriculum development efforts.

A major element of curriculum organization involves the principles of learning. For example: (1) Students learn best when they are ready to learn. Therefore, will the curriculum efforts impact a student population which has the mental and physical maturation to perform the functions that revision and change call for? (2) Will the instructional activities allow the student adequate drill and time so that he/she can actually incorporate both what is taught and what is practiced? Will there be a measurable change in behavior due to the instructional effort? (3) Are the classroom atmosphere and the equipment adequate to make the instructional effort satisfactory so that the student will truly absorb the concepts? Based on the absorption factor, can the student retain the material for either further training or direct entry into the world of work? (4) Is the curriculum change based on a previous successful learning experience of the student? It is necessary for students to feel comfortable and to progress from relatively easy learning activities to the more complex.

STAFF ROLES IN CURRICULUM DEVELOPMENT

In most local educational agencies, the school board is the policy setting group. This is fairly traditional in that school boards have been identified by state legislatures as the official and legal voice for any educational activities in a school district. Since membership on a school board is usually elective and each person who sits on a school board does so in a part-time capacity, school boards have chosen to appoint a full-time administrator charged with effective operation of each school district, and that person has been identified as the superintendent of schools. The superintendent reports to and is held directly accountable by the school board for educational activities in the district. The school board is the legal entity that has final say in the goals, mission, and total educational effort in the school district. Therefore, the superintendent must be completely informed on any curriculum change that may be proposed in the district.

The superintendent is faced with an almost overwhelming explosion of knowledge and activities that directly relate to the effective operation of the school enterprise. When the local district's size and budgetary resources permit, the chief administrator surrounds himself/herself with assistant superintendents and directors of secondary education to whom the specific activities of special education, vocational education, finance, and transportation, to name a few, can be delegated. The superintendent must be an educator, an organizer, a philosopher, and a magician.

Suggested model. The following chart is a suggested model that can be used in implementing curriculum change.

REVIEW COMMITTEE. Proceeding from a felt need articulated by a classroom teacher, a proposal for curriculum change can be taken to the immediate supervisor and thence to the director of secondary education, the assistant superintendent, and eventually the superintendent. At the completion of this activity, the administrative go-ahead for determining curriculum changes having been given, a review committee (and this may be a standing committee or it may be an appointed ad-hoc committee) will analyze the request for a curriculum change. The review committee might consist of an assistant superintendent, a building principal, the assistant superintendent or director of secondary education, and at least one teacher, one student, and an advisory committee member.

An analysis of the request for a curriculum change is conducted by the review committee. If approval is immediately given, curriculum development or modification could begin. Should the approval request be denied, curriculum development or modification will usually be terminated. If approval to further develop the idea is given, appropriate developmental activity will begin. Developmental activities will usually include preparing the rationale and objectives used to determine the curriculum need, the procedures for evaluations that must be considered, and the operational feasibility of the suggested changes.

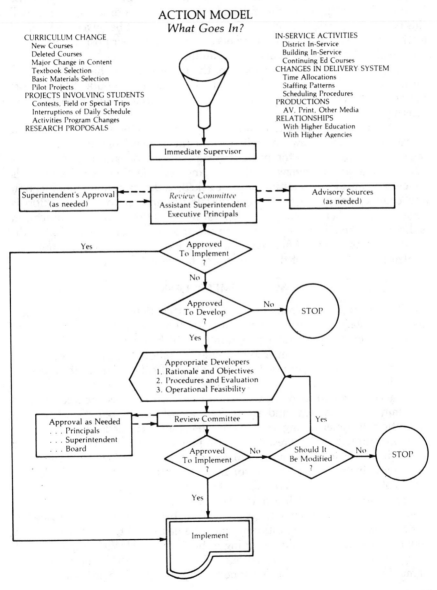

ACTION MODEL
What Goes In?

CURRICULUM CHANGE
  New Courses
  Deleted Courses
  Major Change in Content
  Textbook Selection
  Basic Materials Selection
  Pilot Projects
PROJECTS INVOLVING STUDENTS
  Contests, Field or Special Trips
  Interruptions of Daily Schedule
  Activities Program Changes
RESEARCH PROPOSALS

IN-SERVICE ACTIVITIES
  District In-Service
  Building In-Service
  Continuing Ed Courses
CHANGES IN DELIVERY SYSTEM
  Time Allocations
  Staffing Patterns
  Scheduling Procedures
PRODUCTIONS
  AV, Print, Other Media
RELATIONSHIPS
  With Higher Education
  With Higher Agencies

Immediate Supervisor

Superintendent's Approval (as needed)

Review Committee Assistant Superintendent Executive Principals

Advisory Sources (as needed)

Approved To Implement ?

Yes

No

Approved To Develop ?

No → STOP

Yes

Appropriate Developers
1. Rationale and Objectives
2. Procedures and Evaluation
3. Operational Feasibility

Approval as Needed
  . . . Principals
  . . . Superintendent
  . . . Board

Review Committee

Approved To Implement ?

No → Should It Be Modified ?

Yes

No → STOP

Yes

Implement

RATIONALE AND OBJECTIVES. These considerations and questions must be answered: What are the resons for this curriculum determination being made at this specific time? What are the objectives? What are the outcomes that will accrue because of this curriculum determination? Will it improve the overall program? How will it fit into the total school offering? How will it justify and satisfy the district goals and objectives as determined by the board of education?

PROCEDURES AND EVALUATIONS. What are the procedures that will be followed in implementing this curriculum change or modification? How will this particular curriculum change be evaluated? Will it be by a standardized test? Will it be by a criterion-referenced test? What other positive outcomes will result because of this curriculum modification?

OPERATIONAL FEASIBILITY. What are the fiscal impacts that will be made by this curriculum determination? Is there an adequate budget to support the change? What funding sources will be required to maintain the new offering?

At this point, the curriculum developers will return the completed document to the review committee, and the review committee will then relay that document to the principal, superintendent, and board for their final consideration, review, and acceptance or rejection. After approvals have been gained, the question must be asked: Is the curriculum modification and change ready to be implemented? If the answer to that question is negative, the other recourse is to suggest modification. And if modification is the route, then it will be returned to the appropriate developers for modification. If the answer is positive, that it is approved to implement, then the implementation phase of the curriculum change will begin.

MANAGEMENT TASKS

The management tasks connected with curriculum development are many and varied. These tasks deal with the personal and institutional philosophy of the educational program for which curriculum is being developed. They can be determined by a review of school board philosophy and policies, particularly those statements that specifically relate to the business education offerings.

Tactical and strategic goals. Another facet that must be addressed is determining the tactical and strategic goals of the school district or the institution in determining curriculum development needs. Usually these goals are omitted, and the result may be a patchwork approach to curriculum development. Another area that must be considered is: What are the specific objectives, institutional and personal, and what are the quantifiable end results of the change? This borders not so much on curriculum development but program accountability and also the issue of expenditures for value received by patrons of school districts . . . cost benefit, if you will. In viewing institutional objectives, questioning must be narrowed to what, when, and how much: What curriculum is going to be developed? What impact is that going to have? What segment is that going to deal with? What is the time frame? When is it going to be developed? When is it going to be implemented?

Another factor to consider is allocation of resources—materials, dollars, teacher time, administrator time, and certainly try-out time.

Accountability. When considering accountability in curriculum development, one must address the four concepts of input, content, process, and product. The input of ideas, philosophies, viewpoints, and resources available for curriculum development is vital. What will the content of the change be—the end product? What will that do in terms of job placement, human relations skills, dollars earned, and individual student self-satisfaction for having participated in this course? What will it do to stimulate the cognitive activities that will allow the student to be a better citizen in our society?

Cost benefit. Another aspect of curriculum management would be a systematic comparison of the benefits and costs of alternative objectives in establishing priorities for goal achievement. Cost benefit analysis is necessary to ensure that our effort is going to return a product that is worth the dollars put into it. This is particularly important now in American education because of the dollar crunch in terms of inflation and a shrinking work force. Allocation of resources is a management task that must be scrutinized with intensity as well, since allocation of resources must ask the question: Is this the best and most efficient way to accomplish our goal, which is employment of our business education graduate, or is there another way that could accomplish the goal in a shorter time with better results? Ongoing program evaluation both formative and summative must be continuous, and the final results must answer positively the question: Were the desired outcomes achieved?

Student benefit. Lost in the maze of flowcharts, systems analysis, job and task analysis, is the student. The idea seems lost that education must be of service to the student. A major leadership task in curriculum development to keep in mind is the question: What must the student be able to accomplish, to say, to think, or to perform at the completion of the program? To accomplish this, curriculum development activities must be effectively planned, organized, and controlled. Throughout this developmental, organizational, and demonstrative phase, documentation of progress must be made. Where were the pitfalls? What was accomplished? One effective way to do this is to maintain a systems approach so that it is possible to retrace the steps and determine what led to that particular insight or that particular outcome which has proven to be most satisfying and rewarding for both teacher and student.

Keeping current. An area that business educators seems to be reluctant to explore and to take advantage of is the incorporation of the latest tools of the trade—for example, the use of the minicomputer in teaching bookkeeping and accounting functions. Some of the basic concepts may have to be taught in the traditional manner, but lesson plans that have been developed over the past 20 years, traditional teaching techniques, the use of wall charts and the like are not necessarily the way to accomplish the goal of giving the student attitudes, skills, and knowledge necessary to get and to hold an entry-level job in a bookkeeping or an accounting enterprise. Many recent surveys indicate that well over 90 percent of the businesses in communities are indeed using some form of computer for bookkeeping activity whether it is financial bookkeeping or recordkeeping or inventory control.

Another tool that is not used enough in business education is data processing terminals. More and more, small, medium, and large businesses are connected to computers through a CRT terminal network located in their businesses. The electric typewriter, word processing equipment, and related processes are also underutilized. Business educators continue to teach content and courses that are comfortable to them and not necessarily representative of what is needed by business, industry, and the student. Business community needs can only be found out through input from advisory committee members, cooperative training station sponsors, and periodic surveys of what is actually happening in the town, the city, and the region. This is a mandate in business education—remain current.

Rapid changes are occurring in business, thanks to microprocessors and computers. A serious problem in curriculum development is getting teachers back into business to update their skills and at the same time allowing them to receive credit on the salary schedule. One of the most effective ways to bring about far-reaching changes in the business curriculum is to get instructors into the world of work for short retraining periods.

Leadership characteristics. Leaders must possess the ability to transmit a feeling that each individual is contributing toward the attainment of a goal. A recent study indicated that one of the major sources of teacher dissatisfaction is their feeling that they are being treated as an insignificant part of the whole. Teachers are the most important facet of the educational enterprise, and they need to be encouraged and rewarded. Leaders must demonstrate confidence in their teachers and reinforce the feeling that they are important. Certainly adequate technical preparation which fosters teacher self-confidence is necessary. Curriculum changes and high teacher morale are both needed if students are to gain the necessary skills, knowledge, and attitudes for employment.

Role of the classroom teacher. After the direction and thrust of the curriculum have been determined, the vital element that will keep that program functioning and moving forward successfully is the willingness of the classroom teacher to continuously update course content. This is a difficult task, but it is very important, and it is one that is usually overlooked after the curriculum updating, modification, or improvement has taken place. There are several approaches the teacher can use to update course content. Among the most effective ways are returning to the business world for more occupational experience, enrolling in new campus offerings, participating in in-service activities, mastering new teaching and learning systems, and utilizing input from advisory committees.

RETURN TO THE BUSINESS WORLD. In most states business education programs require teacher work experience in a related field before final certification is granted. Periodic returns to the business world would be the best way for teachers to acquire data for updating course content. This would take a strong commitment by the teacher to return during the summer and work as a secretary, a data processor, or office manager; nevertheless, this is the most effective way that a teacher can grow and keep course content current. However, the need for returning to school and earning a master's or doctoral degree could hinder that effort. Usually little or no credit is awarded for work experiences by a teacher, either on the salary scale or toward obtaining an advanced degree.

An effective way to resolve this problem and encourage teachers to acquire work experience might be through the development of teacher cooperative training agreements with business and industry. Business personnel and teachers could jointly commit themselves to six, eight, or ten weeks of planned work experience. The teacher could develop a research paper about the work encountered and be awarded college or university credit for the learning experiences. A college or university could apply that credit toward a degree, and the teacher would also gain steps on the district salary schedule.

Another plan to encourage teacher work experience programs might be through the effective use of sabbatical leaves. The sabbaticals could be nine weeks, a semester, or possibly one year in length. Such a plan would allow the teacher to return to the business world with pay being provided by the school district and the employer. This could be done through an agreement which would assure, among other things, that the information gleaned by the instructor would be used to update or modify course content.

RETURN TO THE COLLEGE CAMPUS. In order to continuously upgrade course content, the teacher might also return to the college campus for additional course work in business education. Perhaps this is the least painful way for the teacher to update course content and at the same time be rewarded through transcripted college credit which would allow movement on a salary schedule and progress toward an advanced degree. However, unless graduate course work is strongly laced with internships and visits to businesses, this route may be one of the least effective. This is due in part to weaknesses within the collegiate system. Professors may or may not be current with what is actually happening in the field of business education. The edict to "publish or perish" and the concern over shrinking enrollments create quivers in the hearts of deans and department heads and force professors into other activities that may or may not be directly related to keeping current in the field.

Another weakness is that even with a college professor who is strongly motivated toward keeping abreast of the field and providing graduate students with practical hands-on experiences, budget constraints may limit the expenditures for equipment and professional cooperative coordination time, which is so necessary for a strong internship program. Another limiting factor would be the inability of the professor to participate in work experience programs to update his/her skills. Colleges and universities are locked into a numbers game with state legislatures for operating funds. The baby boom is over, and teaching jobs at all levels are not as plentiful as they once were. Campuses and secondary schools that once were full are now empty. Faced with budget cuts a la Proposition 13 in California, professional accountability is being carefully scrutinized. Returning to the college campus may be one of the least effective ways to upgrade course content, but again that depends entirely on the campus, the enthusiasm and zest of the professor, and certainly on the budget.

IN-SERVICE ACTIVITIES. In-service activities are popular. They satisfy the mandate that teachers participate in new learning experiences, but unless these experiences are carefully planned and evaluated, they can be ineffective. In order to be effective, in-service activities must deal with the teachers' specific problems. The in-service activity could follow this format. (1) Teachers would determine the specific needs they have in upgrading themselves, and this information would be forwarded to the in-service activity presenter. (2) The in-service activity would be a hands-on kind of effort, resulting in a product that the teacher could take back to the classroom for use. (3) The in-service activity would be evaluated on a predetermined scale by the administrator, the teacher, and the presenter. (4) The presenter would eventually visit all of the in-serviced teachers and help them with specifics in their classrooms.

NEW TEACHING AND LEARNING SYSTEMS. There seem to be as many new teaching systems on the market as there are new innovations in the business area. New teaching systems imply the utilization of the most up-to-date hardware and software that the school district can afford. This is an expensive proposition, but it is necessary if the school district's commitment is to provide the skills, knowledge, and attitudes that a student needs. By implication, then, the requirement is that teachers be able to take the new innovations, be they a minicomputer or total word processing system, and apply their expertise as professionals in implementing and transforming the unknown to the known via learning activities that are based on sound educational principles. In secondary business education, the day should be long gone where classrooms contain manual typewriters and key-driven calculators, but they aren't. The old saw will be used that the fundamentals can be taught on these. Bunk! Why must teaching the fundamentals be separated from using equipment that is as close to the current state of the art as can be bought?

Vocational directors, deans, department heads, and teachers must push administrators to help secure the needed current hardware and software so that the students leaving the secondary business education program have had training for entry-level employment on the most current equipment available. This may involve going out into business world for which educators are providing trained workers and securing industry's help in curriculum development and state-of-the-art equipment for training. It seems that most business education teachers are reluctant to approach businesses in this manner. But again, when educators solicit business personnel for help, whether it is for curriculum materials, equipment, or a training station, one needs to have a plan of action, with the benefits spelled out very clearly, and then a definite statement of "asking for assistance" must be made to whomever is approached. School districts ideally should purchase and use state-of-the-art equipment in the classroom. If this is not possible, the next best instructional technique would be to teach about these current pieces of equipment, to place the student in a cooperative education situation, and to develop a training plan for using the equipment. Again, this has both budgetary and personnel implications.

SIMULATION. Another teaching method would be to simulate the work environment in the classroom. The simulation would be only as strong as the materials that were developed and the hardware that was available for the teacher to accomplish the goals and objectives that have been established for the student. Simulation is most effective when followed by cooperative education experiences.

SUMMARY

In an article in the October 1979 issue of *Educational Leadership*, the journal of the Association for Supervision and Curriculum Development, Gilbert A. Austin makes five interesting statements about education in America today. They are: (1) Contrary to popular belief, we cannot teach everyone from every background because family background is important to the point of being critical for achievement of the student in the school setting. (2) The relationship of family background to achievement does not diminish over years of schooling. Even though the student enters the school system at an early age, it may not be possible to impact that student because the relationship between family background to achievement won't change as the child progresses through the school years. (3) Variations in school facilities, curriculum, and staff have little effect on achievement independent of family background. (4) School factors that have the greatest influence independent of family background are the teacher's characteristics—not the facilities, not the curriculum. (5) Attitudes such as sense of control of the environment or a belief in the responsiveness of the environment were found to be highly related to achievement independent of family background.

We can include in our educational system the most modern equipment facilities and a curriculum that is based on sound educational psychology (including such factors as how students learn, how teachers teach, and the need for trained personnel in industry and business), but the ultimate result is still dependent on the raw material available—the student. Impact on the student can be accomplished, but it must be recognized that teachers are faced with almost insurmountable obstacles in learning to deal with the problems both conscious and unconscious that each student brings to the classroom. A constant that doesn't seem to be affected by curriculum, teaching methods, or multimedia presentations is a dedicated teacher working in a warm supportive atmosphere with a student who is ready and willing to learn.

CHAPTER 7

Involving Advisory Committees To Update Subject Matter Content

LOIS HLAVAC

Pittsburgh Public Schools, Pittsburgh, Pennsylvania

In the study of literature, the quotation "No man is an island, entire of itself" is worthy of remembrance. The same analogy can be applied to the development of general curriculum in the public school system as well as to the specific subject matter content in secondary business education. News magazine headlines exclaiming, "Give Us Better Schools!" and newspaper articles pertaining to the "growing crisis" in our schools document the shortcomings of today's educational programs and the desire of the public to become involved, with the hopeful expectation of improvement of education.

If business education and all vocational education programs are to be beneficial, they must be an integral part of the community in which they exist and must reflect the daily occupational life of that community. To accomplish this goal, close cooperation between the school and business, labor, and the industrial community is essential. One of the most effective formal means of providing this type of linkage is the vocational education advisory council or committee.

What is an advisory council? An advisory council or committee on vocational education is a group of individuals, mainly from outside the field of education, who because of their specific knowledge and expertise associated with the world of work, have been organized to advise educators on vocational education programs so the needs of the community and its individuals are realistically served. Advisory council members are not paid for their services and function only in an advisory capacity; they advise, suggest, and assist educators, but never do they establish, administer, or direct policy.

NEED TO INVOLVE ADVISORY GROUPS

Although the extent and quality of curriculum planning in a school system depends largely on the competence and efforts of administrators and teachers, this group of persons cannot be expected to collectively contain the knowledge that is necessary to constantly update the business education curriculum, or any other vocational curriculum, in this dynamic technological society where the office is the scene of the most dramatic changes ever being made in administrative and support services for our industrial society. The most organized and systematic means of determining the curriculum needs is through the operation of appropriate advisory committees.

Long before federal legislation mandated vocational advisory committees, professional educators were cognizant of the need to include input from other groups in the development of curriculum, that most important function and responsibility of the school system. Although the local boards of education have the overall policy-making and advisory functions, in specialized areas, such as vocational education, these boards delegate the day-to-day operations to the paid professional staff of educators (administrators and faculty) while reserving the advisory function. Therefore, business educators have had advisory committee input in the form of suggestions from the officially elected board of education for many years. There are instances of specialized programs, such as medical office assistant, being offered in a comprehensive high school because of the expressed interest and advice of medical members of the board of education. This is only one isolated example of subject matter content changes being instituted via elected boards.

LEGISLATIVE MANDATE

Vocational advisory councils at all three levels, national, state, and local, are mandated by federal legislation. The logical growth in this development of more systematized advisory groups proceeded from the appointment of the President's Panel of Consultants on Vocational Education in 1961 through the mandate for local advisory groups in 1976.

National advisory groups. Many different, loosely organized, and often self-appointed, national groups were responsible for presenting to the Congress recommendations which shaped the most important piece of vocational education legislation passed in recent years, the Vocational Education Act of 1963. The President's Panel of Consultants on Vocational Education was appointed by President John F. Kennedy in 1961, and its subsequent study provided a framework for the Vocational Education Act of 1963. This act stipulated that an Advisory Council on Vocational Education be assembled periodically to review the nation's programs of vocational education and report its findings and recommendations.

The first such council was appointed November 22, 1966, and transmitted its report a year later to the then Secretary of Health, Education, and Welfare, John W. Gardner. Recommendations of this body were incorporated in the Vocational Amendments of 1968, which then called for the creating of a National Advisory Council on Vocational Education on an ongoing basis and not just subject to call, and for the establishment of state councils.

The law requires that this 21-member national council meet at least four times a year and advise the U.S. Commissioner of Education concerning the administration and effectiveness of the vocational education programs that are mandated by the legislation. Due to changes in the administration in Washington and other factors, this national council has often fallen below its 21-member requirement and has not been consistently effective.

The national council established the framework for the implementation of state councils for vocational education. At this time most of the impetus for advisory committee functions relating to broad vocational issues emanates from the state advisory groups. The type of advice which has a real and immediate effect on updating the content of the subject matter in business education comes from the participation of the membership of the local advisory groups, specifically the program advisory committees.

State advisory councils. Formation of state advisory councils was provided for by the Vocational Education Amendments of 1968. In order to receive funds under the act, each state is required to establish a committee to perform the following functions:

1. Advise the state board on the development of policy matters arising in the administration of the state plan;

2. Evaluate programs, services, and activities; and,

3. Submit to the Commissioner of Education and the National Advisory Council an annual report on the effectiveness of vocational education, with recommendations for such changes which may be warranted.

The role of the state advisory council was further defined in the Vocational Education Amendments of 1972.

These councils are permitted to use federal funds to hire staff and conduct needed studies. At least once a year, the state council must hold a meeting or a series of meetings in various geographic areas of the state, during which the general public is given an opportunity to express its views on vocational education. In order for business educators to be influential in respect to the legislation being derived from these councils, it is important for them to attend and make presentations at the public hearings and to study the councils reports. In 1978, the Pennsylvania State Advisory Council published *Public Meetings Summary of November 16, 1978* and a lengthy *Ninth Annual Report, 1978.* A very important component of these annual reports from state advisory councils is the section on Evaluation and Recommendations. The exact address of each state advisory council, usually located in the state capital, can be obtained from the state department of education.

One example of the impact on the direction of business education which the recommendations from the state advisory councils may have is shown in the following two recommendations which were made in 1978 by the Pennsylvania State Advisory Council on Vocational Education. In relation to the role of vocational educators, including business education, in the education of the handicapped, the Pennsylvania Council made these two recommendations:

Recommendation 5. VOCATIONAL EDUCATION FOR THE HANDI-CAPPED. The Advisory Council recommends to the State Board of Education that it direct the Department of Education to fully implement PL 94-482 (the Vocational Education Amendments of 1976) and PL 94-142 (the Education for All Handicapped Children Act of 1975). The Advisory Council further recommends that such implementation be coordinated with the activities of the Bureau of Vocational Rehabilitation of the Pennsylvania Department of Labor and Industry.

In the narrative preceding the recommendation, the Council stated their belief that many handicapped students who could benefit from vocational experiences were denied opportunities due to limitations on space, faculty, and other resources, hence their recommendation.

Preliminary to Recommendation 6, the Council reported that it was aware of instances where Individualized Education Programs (IEP's) had been written incorporating a vocational education component without the involvement of the appropriate vocational director or a designee. Therefore:

Recommendation 6. The Advisory Council recommends to the State Board of Education that it require the representation of vocational directors or designees in the preparation of Individualized Education Programs (IEP) when vocational education is under consideration as a potential part of the IEP for the handicapped student.

The updating of both the content and the methods of delivery of the instructional program in secondary education to accommodate the mainstreaming of disadvantaged and handicapped students is a great challenge. Part IV of this yearbook, "Changing Secondary Business Education Content To Meet Special Needs," includes more complete coverage of this topic. The composition of many advisory committees and councils is such that there is adequate representation of members who are concerned with meeting the needs of special students, and their recommendations must have an impact on the updating of subject matter content and program offerings in business education.

Local advisory councils. Public Law 94-482, the Vocational Education Amendments of 1976, mandates the establishment of local advisory councils for each local educational agency or postsecondary institution receiving federal funds for vocational education:

Each eligible recipient receiving assistance under this Act to operate vocational education programs shall establish a local advisory council to provide such agency with advice on current job needs and on the relevancy of courses being offered by such agency in meeting such needs. Such local advisory councils shall be composed of members of the general public, especially of representatives of business, industry, and labor; and such local advisory councils may be established for program areas, school, communities, or regions, whichever the recipient determines best to meet the needs of that recipient.

It is noteworthy that the Amendments of 1976 specified that a local overall advisory council *shall* be established, but stated that councils for program areas, such as business education, *may* be established. Whether or not the overall general advisory council for vocational education is deemed to be adequate, or if individual program advisory committees are established, is left up to the discretion of the state. Many state vocational education departments have mandated local districts to have both a general overall council and specific program councils.

Regulation 6.23 of the Pennsylvania State Code mandates:

For each vocational education program, curriculum, or group of related curriculums, (with the exception of the Useful Home Economics Program), a lay advisory committee shall be formed to advise the program staff of appropriate educational objectives, instructional content, and levels of achievement. The lay advisory committee shall be composed of executives and non-executive personnel and homemakers.

Standard 339.13 of this code states that a lay advisory committee shall include vocational education students and recent graduates of the curriculum and shall meet at least twice each year.

A variety of names is given to the local council which relates to a specific career area or vocational program. For example, the Board of Cooperative Educational Services in Rockland County, New York, refers to these groups as *consultant committees* and has written a handbook for the operation of the committees. Historically, in the trade and industrial education division of vocational education, these specialized committees were referred to as craft committees. That nomenclature is still appropriate for committees serving carpentry or bricklaying, but a more descriptive and appropriate name is needed for these committees which service business and office education at the local district. There appears to be much usage of the term *lay advisory committee,* but *career* or *program committee* might be more appropriate titles as they are more descriptive.

Advisory board of regional vocational schools. In many states the greatest changes in program development in vocational education, including the more sophisticated and costly programs in business education, are taking place at the regional vocational school. In Pennsylvania, these schools are referred to as AVTS (area vocational-technical schools) schools. The Pennsylvania regulation (6.22) for the establishment of the advisory group for an area school states:

> The general advisory committee is composed of representatives from management, the ranks of employees including organized labor, and community education.
>
> A professional advisory council, composed of the chief school administrator from each participating school district, shall be included in the organization of each area vocational-technical school and shall advise the area vocational-technical board and the administration concerning the educational program, operational details, and policies of the school.

The primary function of the council is to advise the area vocational-technical board and the director of vocational education on matters concerning the educational program, operational details, and policies of the school. This council could be very influential in the recommendation for new programs such as word processing at the secondary level, which if located regionally, might become economically feasible. Therefore, the background and experience of the various board members is crucial to the input of advice that is relevant to business education. Since the primary role of these area schools has been to offer programs in the trade and industrial area of vocational education, there is often a scarcity or lack of members on the board who can make appropriate recommendations for new and emerging career programs in business and office education. The members usually change each three years, on a staggered basis, so it is possible to rectify this situation if business educators show the interest.

COMPOSITION OF ADVISORY COUNCILS

The decisions regarding the number of members and the various experiential backgrounds of the membership are largely influenced by the type of council which is being formed and its specific function. For example, many states recommend that the local overall vocational education advisory council consist of from 12 to 15 members. The lay advisory committee for a specific program may consist of as few as from six to 10 members if they are chosen carefully.

An advisory council, because it is composed of concerned representatives of business, industry, labor and other public sectors, is very aware of what is happening in the community—what skills are marketable and where they can be marketed. Successful councils are fingers on the pulse of the working community and can provide the vital link between the school and the world of work. They can help maintain and improve vocational education programs so they are realistic and related to the needs of their geographic region. With the aid of advisory councils, business education programs can be designed to ensure that a graduate can go out on the job with a good chance of success. It is essential to have the advisory group composed of members who can collectively offer this type of input.

Business education lay advisory committee. Of all the various committees that serve vocational students and educators at the national and state level, the one which has the most impact on actual curricular changes and program improvement is the local committee formed specifically to work with the business education program. In some large school systems where there are many different skill-centered programs falling under the umbrella of business, separate committees are established for job families or clusters. For example, there may exist a committee for accounting/data processing and another for office occupations. When new programs, such as word processing, are being considered, a separate advisory committee may be established. A necessary ingredient for the establishment of any funded vocational program is a needs assessment, and the advisory committee can be very helpful in this and many other functions.

Qualifications for membership. In order to ensure the best possible representation, guidelines have been developed for the organization of the advisory committee. The Vocational Education Amendments of 1976 state that each advisory council shall have at least one representative of business, industry, and labor. Council membership should also represent a cross section in terms of sex, race, age, occupation, socioeconomic status, geographical location, and other locally appropriate factors. In accordance with federal legislation, representation should include women, minorities, and the handicapped. A balance of big business and smaller industry also deserves consideration. In order to meet all of the criteria listed by the Amendments, it is apparent that a large committee or council is required. This probably accounts for the trend toward one large overall vocational advisory committee serving an entire city, regional vocational school, or other consortium.

It is not always possible to meet all of these mandates in the smaller program or lay advisory committees. The most common directive issued by state departments of business education is to include personnel from numerous types of business—large, small, service and manufacturing. It is also important to include students and recent graduates on the advisory committee.

In its 1969 publication, *The Advisory Committee and Vocational Education,* the American Vocational Association suggests that at least three essential points be weighed when qualifications of individual members are considered. They are (1) experience and enthusiasm, (2) character, and (3) available time.

In its publication 10 years later, the Florida State Advisory Council on Vocational Education suggests five criteria. In addition to the three AVA criteria, they add (1) an interest in vocational education with demonstrated leadership ability and (2) an awareness of the needs of the community and occupation represented.

It should also be noted that there are some factors which might disqualify persons from membership on an advisory committee. For example, persons having a vested financial interest in serving on the committee, such as representatives of equipment manufacturers and educational publishers, are generally excluded.

ROLE OF THE ADVISORY GROUP

A brief description of the role of a lay or program advisory committee is provided in the guidelines accompanying Standard 339.13 of the Pennsylvania School Code.

> The lay advisory committee serves in a more specific capacity than the general advisory committee. It concerns itself with planning and evaluating specific occupational curriculums. More specifically, the committee provides advice and counsel relative to such things as standards of work, adequacy of facility and equipment, course content, communications, and upgrading instruction.

One of the prerequisites for membership on an advisory committee is the availability of time to serve. Many articles point out functions which can be provided by an active and involved committee. The Senior Program Specialist for Business Education in Pennsylvania, in a recent position paper, enumerated 15 areas in which an advisory committee may offer advice and assistance:

1. Purchase of equipment, an automatic typewriter is an example
2. Rental of equipment, especially that used in data processing
3. Preparation and implementation of a follow-up study of recent business education graduates
4. Preparation and implementation of a survey of business offices
5. Designation of the types of business occupations for which training is needed
6. Recommendation of course content that should be offered and course content that might be revised, especially in word processing

7. Planning of field trips for students

8. Development of a list of speakers from business and the topics on which each is qualified to speak

9. Planning or operation of a cooperative work-experience program

10. Establishment of desirable standards of achievement for beginning office workers

11. Discussion and formulation of placement procedures, including the feasibility of the development and acceptance of proficiency cards and the production and dissemination of a directory that includes the personal data sheet of each business student

12. Planning a vocational business education program for adults who are preparing for a new or former occupation (adult preparatory)

13. Discussion of the role that the school might play in in-service training to update or upgrade currently employed business workers (adult supplementary)

14. Improvement of the business education department's public relations program

15. Providing assistance in Future Business Leaders of America projects and activities.

Recommendation of course content. Of these 15 areas of activity in which committees may participate, the one which is most significant for the purpose of this yearbook is No. 6: "Recommendation of course content that should be offered and course content that might be revised, especially in word processing." The Florida Council also recommends that committee members advise on the relevance and effectiveness of the vocational program in meeting job needs.

In order for an advisory committee to be of significant help in the updating of the curriculum, considerable time must be spent on "educating" its members as to the present program of studies. This process of familiarizing the advisory council with the present course offerings, the respective courses of study, the equipment found in each laboratory, and the overall sequencing of various courses within a specific occupational area, such as the secretarial program, requires many meetings and much study on the part of members. There is a serious problem in that so much time is used for this orientation function in the regular meetings that it often seems to dominate and leave insufficient time for suggestions flowing from the advisors. In preparing the agenda for meetings, the chairperson must make certain that sufficient time is earmarked for both functions, orientation and advice. In a situation where members are rotated on a staggered three-year cycle, this orientation of new members seems to go on forever. To alleviate this situation to some extent, a packet of materials should be presented to new members. This packet would include minutes of previous meetings, descriptive brochures, curriculum outlines, and courses of study for individual subjects. Without this effort to educate the members, the types of curriculum suggestions being generated will tend to be very general, such as "students should learn to be responsible," or "students should learn how to communicate effectively and how to do math!"

After receiving the proper orientation to the current offerings and objectives of business education, an advisory committee, well selected to be knowledgeable individually and collectively to the task at hand, will be able to offer valuable advice in these five general areas:

1. Establishing new priorities within the present course content
2. Adding new courses or programs to reflect new employment fields and to reflect the technological changes in today's offices
3. Identifying employment standards and production goals for office workers
4. Recommending new equipment for laboratories and helping in the decision to purge outdated equipment
5. Exploring the possibility of joint programs with other vocational and academic areas.

Establishing new priorities. In an article in the January 1976 issue of *Business Education Forum*, entitled, "Updating Business Education Programs," Harry Huffman listed 15 new concepts with examples of what some school districts were doing in these new areas of instruction. These new concepts and their applicability to a school district can be an interesting topic for consideration by advisers. In setting up the agenda for the local program advisory committee, members can be asked for specific suggestions as to such things as the extent micrographics, reprographics, or metrication should be included in the business education curriculum. Among other areas for discussion which can be taken from the current literature and research in the field is the use of simulations and case studies, for example, in stressing human relations in business. At a recent local advisory committee meeting in Pittsburgh, a member who is a word processing manager suggested that more emphasis be placed upon group assignments or methods of instruction, such as work-flow simulations, which encourage students to learn to work as a team, an attribute so essential to success in word processing centers. This adviser also suggested that teachers try to incorporate more situations in which stress, such as an almost impossible due date, is an essential element of the project. Advisers often tell us that educators build so much TLC (tender loving care) into instruction that it is difficult for recent graduates to adjust to the real-life, production-oriented situation of an office or business position.

The "Back to the Basics" emphasis presently being evidenced in educational literature is reflected by the comments of advisory committee members as to the need to sharpen up the computation and communication skills of our students. Some advisers are asking if listening as a communication tool is not being overlooked in our educational program. Several school districts have reported that their advisory committee members have urged more attention to the skill of proofreading.

Although advisory committees may not have members who are primarily interested in economic literacy, many do realize the importance of our students learning *about* business as well as *for* business. Members reflect the concerns of the general public about the education system and bring more to the group than just information related to specific marketable skills.

New courses or programs. The new program area in business education which is receiving the most attention at this time is word processing. Almost every convention and periodical contain some coverage of this topic and the debate on its incorporation into the curriculum at the secondary level. The growth of the International Word Processing Association in the United States has been phenomenal. There are chapters in most major cities, and the best way to obtain advice in regard to course content in this area is to have a knowledgeable member of this organization on your advisory committee. Although helpful information is available from equipment vendors about the highly sophisticated equipment and instructional and application packages, the most useful advice comes from employees of business, legal, medical, or governmental agencies which operate word processing centers. In some instances administrative managers of these centers are persons who have had a teacher education background, and this combination of expertise makes them an invaluable member of the advisory committee. A school district which is seriously considering the implementation of a word processing program, or any other specialized program, might wish to establish an ad hoc committee to assist in the feasibility study and needs assessment.

Some school districts, especially those located in large insurance centers, have established specialized programs relating to insurance careers. Project InVEST (Insurance Vocational Education Student Training) programs have been started in many secondary schools, often because one of the members of the advisory committee was a member of either of the two sponsoring organizations, the Independent Insurance Agents of America or the National Association of Insurance Women. Members have informed teachers of sources of materials, such as "Insurance Insights," a report to educators on property and liability insurance which is published by the Insurance Information Institute in New York City and is free to educators. The commercial publishers are now marketing insurance simulations, and advisory committee members can supplement these materials by providing actual insurance forms used by local insurance firms, sites for field trips, loan materials used in the insurance firms for in-house training purposes, guest speakers, and other activities which will help bridge the gap between the business world and the classroom.

If a separate advisory committee does not exist for accounting/data processing, members of the business advisory committee should have expertise in these areas. It is highly recommended that one adviser be a member of the Data Processing Management Association as that group can and will provide many of the same types of services as indicated previously for the Word Processing Association. These large national associations often have a member elected as the educational liaison, and that person is eager to be of service to local school districts.

New programs relating to entrepreneurship and business management are being added to the secondary curriculum. Several underlying forces are giving impetus to these new additions: the women's lib movement encouraging females to broaden their career horizons, the quest to attract more males into the traditionally female domain of business education, and the increased nationwide interest of young people for further education in business administration. Many of this later group are now interested in electing a few business courses at the secondary level to "try their wings" before pursuing postsecondary education or to prepare themselves for part-time employment while engaged in future academic study. It may require new course content and new course titles to attract these students. The creative abilities of advisory committee members can help in the packaging and marketing of these new courses.

While a formalized course in consumer education is mandated in some states, in others this area of instruction is a hodgepodge of partial coverage in social studies or in the elective areas of business education or home economics. Consumer groups, such as the American Council on Consumer Interests, are trying to make inroads in the secondary curriculum through their newsletter, "Consumer Education Forum," and through presentations to legislative groups responsible for school curriculums. The Joint Council on Economic Education is also hard at work trying to ensure that economic literacy is one of the goals of secondary education and that this objective is accomplished through the proper inclusion of economic concepts throughout all areas of the secondary curriculum. Again, the impact that these groups have on the curriculum of any school district can be influenced by their ability to become members of advisory committees and success in getting their message through to teachers, administrators, boards of education, and others who are ultimately responsible for what is or is not taught in the classroom.

Identifying employment standards. In 1977, a local advisory committee in Baltimore conducted an informal survey of the data processing job market in the metropolitan area. This type of study of specific job requirements and production standards helps in the development of competency sheets used to evaluate students during and at the completion of their vocational training. In the late sixties, 5,000 strokes per hour met employment needs, but advisory committee members from industry now state that double that speed is required for data entry clerks. These changing entry requirements affect business education programs, and the assistance of the advisory committee in collecting data to supplement governmental reports is vital to the operation of a successful program. The publications and minutes of one very active advisory committee indicate that they conduct a "Skill Needs Survey" annually for manufacturing firms and biannually for commercial and health services for projected employment requirements over the next one, three, and five years. To accomplish this task this advisory committee, which serves for all vocational programs for a regional technical school, established a special skill needs survey committee.

Recommendations for new equipment. On the basis of the study of data processing by the Baltimore Advisory Council, a new data-entry laboratory was established and the old unit-record equipment was phased out. In equipping an office machines laboratory educators are faced with such decisions as: What type of calculator, in addition to the electronic printing/display, should be continued? Isn't it time to discard the key-driven machines, even though some teachers still want to hold on to them? Does the programmable calculator have a place in the clerical lab, the accounting or data processing lab, or none of these? Advisory committees can help develop a long-range acquisition plan for equipment replacement which the administration must take into consideration in preparing long-range budgets.

With the dramatic changes being made in the word processing area, a logical plan would be to form an ad hoc committee to study this entire area. As educators we must then modify these suggestions keeping in mind such things as the transferability of training from one coding type of equipment like the memory typewriter to the newer cathode ray tube (CRT) sophisticated units. Can a one-line view unit, which is less than half the price of the full-page video screen, serve the in-school training needs of the community? What training responsibilities will equipment manufacturers and businesses have? Although vendors should be invited to make presentations to the ad hoc word processing committee, membership should not be open to vendors. The selection of members should represent a cross section of users in the employment area: legal firms, governmental offices, medical centers, and business offices with large and small installations. A member of the local chapter of the International Word Processing Association should be included in the membership.

The value and utilization of any advisory committee can vary widely, depending upon how much the administration and school board genuinely seek community involvement. As an example, the very active and productive advisory council for Erie County (PA) Technical School not only made the recommendation which led to the concept of a $3 million Regional Occupational Skill Center but also collected donations amounting to $700,000 from area firms. These contributions constituted the Erie County school district's share of construction costs. Thus the center was brought into fruition and a bond issue was avoided. It is rare that a school district will have this degree of support from their advisory committee. However, in those districts where support is lacking, the blame often lies with the school administration itself for not having the proper staffing to utilize the services of active advisory committees.

Joint programs with other vocational areas. Oftentimes the recommendations of advisory committee members of other programs include suggestions for course offerings or units of instruction which are business education in nature. One example is the outgrowth of the medical office program as a component of a health careers center. The technical expertise students need in medical terminology and knowledge of health systems is gained from the professional teacher who has a medical-related background. The business teacher thus feels more comfortable and willing to offer the related program of office skills and procedures. The onset of magnet schools, offering unique programs of such a quality to draw students from a large geographic area, is fostering more of this type of joint departmental effort. A high school for journalism would logically contain a component of notehand/typing, and although this may not be a new course offering, the areas of emphasis, grade level, and content of the course would be modified to meet the needs of the aspiring journalistic students.

There are many forces at work in the educational environment which can and will have an impact on the traditional offerings of business education. Business educators must be alert to the recommendations coming from any advisory committee which will have a potential influence on business programs.

ORGANIZING AND OPERATING AN ADVISORY COMMITTEE

Since state advisory councils for vocational education were mandated as early as 1968, they are now well established and have provided guidelines for the organization and operation of advisory councils within their areas. Information can best be obtained by writing to the state advisory council for publications such as these:

Florida: *Organizing and Maintaining Effective Vocational Advisory Committees*, 35 pages, 1979.

New York: *A Handbook for Members of Consultant Committees for Occupations*, 8 pages, 1979.

Pennsylvania: *How to: Approach, Develop, Vitalize, Improve, Structure, and Establish Local Advisory Councils on Vocational Education*, 33 pages, 1979.

In addition to the state advisory council publications, state supervisors of business education may also issue publications specifically for business educators. For example, a six-page position paper entitled "The Role of a Business Education Lay Committee" was issued by William Selden and James A. DiIorio in Harrisburg, Pennsylvania, in 1977. In establishing an advisory committee, the state regulations and standards must be adhered to in regard to membership and frequency of meetings. A general pattern appears to be the establishment of an overall advisory committee for vocational education which is then followed by the organization of various program committees. This latter committee, the one which will be the most influential in actually changing the curriculum in business education, is generally known as the lay or program advisory committee.

CONCLUSION

Advisory committees for vocational education have been mandated by federal legislation, and no local education agency can receive vocational funds without adhering to these regulations. The need for these committees is well documented and well founded, and advisory committees are unique in their ability to provide essential information for vocational education programs. A variety of names is attached to the smallest element in the advisory committee structure, the local program or lay advisory committee. This is a reflection of the ability to structure and tailor the function of committees to meet specific situations and needs.

All literature referring to the proper utilization of advisory committees points out clearly that they are *advisory* groups and that they can assume neither legislative nor administrative responsibility. When business educators send out the message "We need your help and advice," they are not indicating a weakness, but a desire to grow professionally in their ability to offer quality programs for their students. The business community is willing to be a partner in this challenging enterprise which needs the assistance of all segments of our society.

CHAPTER 8

Utilizing Local Surveys, Interviews, and Published Research Projects To Identify Desired Content Changes

MARY WITHEROW

St. Louis Public Schools, St. Louis, Missouri

Many periodicals today devote considerable space to articles about the office of the future, the equipment of the future, and the new personnel needs of the future. So it is only fitting that the secondary schools of this country be concerned about the curriculum needs of students being trained to take their places in the office of the future, using the equipment of the future and fulfilling the personnel needs of the future. With this thought in mind the usage of local surveys, interviews, and published research projects to identify desired content changes should be encouraged.

Surveys, interviews, and published research projects are three different entities, so they will be looked at separately. However, their use is often meshed, and this will also be observed in the example presented in this chapter. The needed steps in developing a concise, meaningful survey document for collecting information will be reviewed, and the summation process to bring about recommended changes will be examined. There will be an outline of some helpful techniques in preparing for and conducting a data-seeking interview, including some steps to follow in interpreting the data obtained to determine needed content changes. Finally, some major sources for obtaining business research projects will be recommended, with an emphasis placed on the type of research found desirable for use in determining local content changes.

A single chapter in a book cannot possibly indicate all the ways for utilizing local surveys, interviews, and published research projects to identify desired content changes. What is applicable to one area of the country may not be explicitly appropriate for another locale; instruments may need to be modified so that they will be applicable to the specific requirements of those using them. What is appropriate for a large urban city may not be identically usable for a rural setting. It is important to recognize there is a need for transfer employment training.

Surveys, interviews, and research need to be updated from time to time. Do not continue to base opinions indefinitely on one project, but keep projects simple enough they can be updated frequently. Once the survey and interview techniques have been tried, many uses will be found for them, such as for evaluation instruments, course content revision, and equipment purchases.

SURVEYS

Definition. Webster defines a survey as a critical examination to obtain certain information. The example which follows used a printed form to collect specific information about a current school situation.

Purpose. At the very outset, it should be noted that in order to be unquestionably reliable a survey form would have to be verified and the sampling validated. The results of a modest endeavor, however, will be revealing enough to surprise the user. The decision to conduct a survey indicates first of all that there is recognition of the need for some change. In the example described here, doubt presented itself as to the profitability of what was being taught. The desired results were not being produced. The survey undertaken to confirm this did bear out something previously apparent, but it might have brought to light something totally unsuspected.

Example. In the last few years there has been a deepening concern in St. Louis about the tardiness and absenteeism of students. They either do not show up for class or, when they do come, are invariably late—creating a show and interruption when they appear. This lack of promptness and attendance seemed to be an indication that the students were trying to say something about the irrelevance of what was being taught. Perhaps this reflection of disinterest was more than a teenage phase—perhaps they really didn't find the training relevant.

The survey itself was not the answer, but it did point the way for action and was a means of critically examining certain information. Actually a survey, an interview, and research were all used in the attempt to facilitate a change in attitude as reflected in the behavior of the students.

Procedures. There are certain steps to be followed in preparing for any survey:

1. Define the purpose. Be specific—many have a tendency to try to solve several problems rather than one specific issue, and the purpose becomes so splintered that it is hard to define the results.
2. Select the persons to conduct the survey.
   a. Find those interested in participating.
   b. Give them definite directions.
   c. Give them ample time to complete the survey.
3. Select the parties to be surveyed.
   a. Set a number to be contacted by survey.
   b. Select a random sampling.
   c. Recognize an acceptable percentage of responses.
4. Prepare the instrument to be used in making the survey.
   a. Make it concise.
   b. Make it definitive.
   c. Make it easy to complete.
   d. Make it easy to summarize.

In addition to the above procedural steps there are some additional warnings.

1. Do not wait until everything is perfect. Those who do will never get started.
2. Do select a survey with a purpose for which there are possible solutions.
3. Do complete the survey and get the summary available while people are still interested in the results. Then it will be easier to proceed to the action the survey is prompting.
4. Don't become discouraged if the results are different from those anticipated or hoped for. Give the results a chance to provide direction toward some changes.

The form used to obtain the enrollment and completion figures for an initial survey is shown in Figure I. It shows both enrollment and completion figures by school and course. Actually the form was two pages in length involving 11 schools and 24 subjects, but it was condensed so that it could appear on one page for this illustration. The department head in each school was required to furnish the information for a 5-year period.

Findings. This enrollment survey completed for the St. Louis area showed the following:

1. Enrollment in the entire department is decreasing as is secondary enrollment in general. Percentagewise the business department is holding its own with the overall school enrollment.
2. Specific subjects are in trouble because of low student involvement. Second-year shorthand (entitled secretarial practice) does not have large enough enrollment to justify offering the class.
3. Enrollment in advanced typing is 3.5 percent of the beginning typing enrollment.
4. All double-period course enrollments are declining. A few years ago double-period blocks were programmed to capacity.
5. Accounting enrollment is increasing.
6. New courses, like word processing and data concepts, are programmed to capacity.
7. The completion rate for vocational business education, which is a combination of beginning shorthand and advanced typing, is low compared to the beginning enrollment.
8. Office co-op (where the students attend school one-half day and work for a company the other half day) shows a steady increase in enrollment during the five-year period.

In fact, the findings were so unequivocal that one could restructure the curriculum offerings to a certain extent, without proceeding with the interview.

Recommendations. The following recommendations were among those made:

1. Recruitment activities should be increased to assure greater familiarity with the business curriculum among students, advisory groups, and other business organizations. The brochures and slide/tape presentations that were being used should be updated.

FIGURE I. Enrollment Completion in Business Education

School Year _____

SCHOOL	Bas Bus	Off Car Exp	Type 1	Type 3	Acct 1	Acct 3	Voc Bus Ed 1	Sec Prac 1	Off Mach	Off Co-op 1	Bus Law	Off Prac	Bus Com	Data Con-cepts 1	Data Con-cepts 3	Data Entry Dev.	Key Punch
BEAUMONT																	
CENTRAL																	
CLEVELAND																	
McKINLEY																	
NORTHWEST																	
etc.																	
	Trans Mach	Word Proc	Mach Sht	etc.													
TOTAL																	

2. Secretarial and office practice courses should be combined, as low enrollments in the present offerings do not justify their existence.

3. Emphasis should be placed on modifying the course content for advanced typing offerings to include more time on production drills, numerical exercises, simulated data-entry activities, etc., rather than a continuation or review of beginning typing content in the second-year courses.

4. Greater interaction should occur between students and the business world so that trainees can see workers in business offices, hear speakers from the employment section, view demonstrations of the latest equipment, and possibly be assigned to a company for a day or two to observe workers.

The survey form is very effective for internal evaluation; it is equally effective when mailed to parties outside of the school, for example to determine repair costs for various types of equipment.

INTERVIEWS

Definition. Webster defines interview as a meeting face to face, as for consultation; usually, a formal consultation. The following use of the interview gives another angle in the search for the answer to the original problem of student lack of interest as displayed by tardiness and absenteeism.

Purpose. To save time, a letter of introduction similar to the sample in Figure II was used. This letter was mailed to the selected companies prior to the interview. Their response assured that only interested companies were visited and actually speeded up the visits as a contact's name had been furnished.

FIGURE II. Letter of Introduction

Gentlemen:

I am a participant in a school program which is surveying jobs beginning workers perform in various types of companies, and I would like to talk to you about the training needed to fit these jobs.

The interview will provide information to be used in updating the current training program in secondary business education.

The companies taking part in this survey were selected at random—one source was the Chamber of Commerce Roster Issue. We hope you will be willing to participate and assure you that this is not a time-consuming interview.

Please let me know what time of day is most convenient and the name of the person I should contact.

Yours truly,

_____ School Personnel

Address _____

Phone No. _____

Techniques. The following are general techniques that may be applied to an interview:

1. Observe general impressions during the interview. Such items as working conditions or numbers of employees may be determined without specific questions.
2. Start the interview promptly.
3. Be businesslike and pleasant at all times.
4. Close the interview with appreciation for the interviewee's time.
5. Share the findings with those who have participated as interviewees or interviewers.
6. Implement the conclusions to modify curriculum content.

Format. Preparation of the format for the interview sheet is very important for the following reasons:

1. It will assure that the most helpful information is obtained without taking up a lot of unnecessary time from company personnel.
2. It will enable several interviewers to obtain similar information.
3. It will make the summary easier to prepare and evaluate.

Figure III gives an acceptable form for indicating the frequency of company response—often, sometimes, never. A numerical (1,2,3) response is equally appropriate. The interview form should not exceed three pages in length, and the interviewer should omit any question which the company employee hesitates to answer or which is felt not applicable to the company. The interviewer should complete the form (not the company representative), and additional comments may be jotted on the margin of the form.

Example. Interviews were conducted with personnel directors of local business firms to see what types of training were needed for beginning employment with their companies. In place of just using a mail survey form, a team of office co-op coordinators actually contacted companies and conducted the personal interviews.

Two hundred and nineteen companies were selected at random. These companies included various types, such as advertising, banking, business machine sales, breweries, brokerage, city government, construction, credit, food service, hotel and motel, insurance, law offices, manufacturing, publishing, radio and TV stations, real estate, retail, service organizations, state government, transportation, U.S. government, and wholesalers. These were selected at random from the local chamber of commerce directory.

Companies were selected to cover a range of sizes, based on the number of clerical employees. The six ranges used were 1-5, 6-10, 11-25, 26-50, 50-100, and over 100 clerical employees.

Employees considered worked from 40 hours per week to as little as 35 hours per week. The majority of employees were earning more than the minimum wage, and the working conditions were rated desirable or superior. Most companies had modern office equipment available for their employees.

These general items were noted as the interview progressed, either by observation or through the discussion with the personnel representative.

Some of the specific questions included in the St. Louis interview may be seen in Figure III.

FIGURE III. Interview Sheet on Hiring Standards for Beginning Office Workers

	Often	Some-times	Never
1. The following types of office jobs are available to high school graduates who have business education training.			
Typist	_____	_____	_____
File clerk	_____	_____	_____
Computer operator	_____	_____	_____
Word processing secretary	_____	_____	_____
Bookkeeper	_____	_____	_____
Other	_____	_____	_____
2. Skill tests are given for beginning jobs.	_____	_____	_____
3. Typing skill required:			
Below 40 wpm	_____	_____	_____
40-50 wpm	_____	_____	_____
50-60 wpm	_____	_____	_____
Above 60 wpm	_____	_____	_____
4. Familiarity with the following types of equipment is required.			
Computer	_____	_____	_____
Word processing equipment	_____	_____	_____
Typewriter	_____	_____	_____
Calculator	_____	_____	_____
Other	_____	_____	_____
5. The following employment procedure is used.			
Interview	_____	_____	_____
Letter of application	_____	_____	_____
Application blank	_____	_____	_____
Resumé	_____	_____	_____
6. Other	_____	_____	_____
	_____	_____	_____

Findings. The interview check sheet used in the St. Louis area showed the following:

1. Job titles are so varied that it would be advisable to explain the job duties involved for various assignments. This would also prove most advantageous in making curriculum content revision later.

2. There are more bookkeeping jobs for beginners than typing jobs. This was not true a few years ago, and it should be kept in mind that bookkeeping is

used in the broad sense to include payroll, credit, and even hospital admissions and dismissals.

3. The typing jobs are requiring more speed, and sophistication in the use of memory typewriters, word processing equipment, and even keyboard input for computers.

4. Companies are continuing to emphasize application knowledge rather than the operation of specific brands of equipment, because new equipment is being introduced almost daily in the business office.

5. Government rules and regulations are controlling employment applications. It is no longer permissible to ask age, sex, etc., on application blanks, and the information in employee files is controlled by the privacy act.

Recommendations. Now that the information from the survey is available and the interviews have been tabulated, how is the data compiled and the problem reconsidered? The problem as initially identified was: Does curriculum content play a part in student attendance and or tardiness? The following would indicate that this is so:

1. Students judge the compatibility of training offered and job requirements, and they do not like the incongruity of what they see. They are used to instant reactions, and when something doesn't coincide they rebel in the only two ways they know—by coming late or not at all.

2. Jobs are requiring advanced typing skill and not all students interested in clerical occupations are taking advanced courses, so the content of the beginning typing course should be modified to include more numerical and coded typing drills similar to computer input. More emphasis should be placed on timed output with interruptions, retyping of modified directions, etc. Emphasis should also be placed on recruiting students for advanced typing by previewing what is covered in the second year.

3. Company personnel indicated that beginning employees are being placed as computer operators, word processing operators, and microfilm file clerks. Employers are not so concerned about the operation of a specific piece of equipment as they are that student trainees are capable of proofreading data and making corrections before it is processed. Proofreading may be made from computer sheets or visual screens depending upon the hardware utilized by the business. Employers want students to know how to update computer storage.

4. Companies want students who will painstakingly read directions and sequence instructions.

5. Companies want students who can set priorities and work under pressure without blowing up.

6. Students need to learn computer terminology.

Many of the above suggestions can be incorporated into current course offerings once the staff is aware of the conclusions.

RESEARCH

Definition. Webster defines research as a careful search, or a critical study or investigation in seeking new knowledge, facts, or principles.

Examples. For this chapter, recommendations for research to be considered will be confined to those items which are readily available.

The Bureau of Labor Statistics provides the number of workers employed, the average job openings projected for each year for a span of years, and a summary of the prospects for employment throughout the 1980's for 250 jobs. This information is available in the Occupational Outlook Quarterly, obtainable from the Superintendent of Documents, Washington, D.C. This quarterly also provides summaries of the fastest growing jobs, jobs with the most openings, and projected change in employment by major occupational groups.

Business Education Forum, the official publication of the National Business Education Association, has many articles showing current research. For example, in the November 1979 issue there is an article reporting the results of a survey on the minimal competencies for graduation from high school. Much supportive data can be obtained from this magazine and others of this type.

The National Business Education Yearbook often is devoted in part to research projects or reports. For example, in Chapter 1 of the 1979 Yearbook, *Alternative Learning Styles in Business Education,* we find that research was conducted to show the movements that affected business education. Consulting past issues of this and similar yearbooks may provide the information sought.

One of the best sources for research for any purpose is the ERIC abstracts. Many states have a research coordinating unit in the department of education from which you can obtain abstracts from the computer files. The full text documents for the abstracts may even be obtained on microfiche upon request.

The libraries of colleges and universities have files of completed theses on the graduate level. These are often devoted to the very problem under consideration.

This list could continue indefinitely, but the main point is to be aware of some of the sources. The best advice is to keep a source list. If the information is needed, it is best to get current information anyway.

Findings. The training of students today must be for the job market of the 80's and beyond. There are openings for secondary students as tape librarians, unit record equipment operators, data entry operators, etc., so this career information must be included. Training must be in the format of the 80's, so include computing, coding, sorting, summarizing, recording, and communication in every class taught.

CHAPTER 9

Using Survey and Research Data To Reexamine Course Offerings and Update Content

CAROLL DIERKS and ELSIE DONNEL
University of Northern Colorado, Greeley

Do your curriculum and course content generally reflect recommendations based on research findings? What if you as a business educator reviewed the following conclusions:

> . . . a near total absence in the work of entry (bookkeeping) employees of: the preparation of financial statements; closing the books; posting from the general journal to the general ledger; . . . such activities are clear candidates for discarding from high school bookkeeping instruction.[1]

> Teachers . . . who are concerned with producing students who are skilled in shorthand transcription may not assume that good performance in prior educational or typing experiences will automatically lead to good transcription performance.[2]

Are you willing to make changes based on findings such as these? Will you reexamine the content of your traditional bookkeeping/accounting course? Will you include a pretranscription instructional segment in your shorthand course? Research findings can and should impact on your curriculum and course content.

Curriculum should reflect not only technological changes but also specific areas of student and community needs assessments, pertinent individual research, and research funded by governmental grants or agencies. A variety of tools and techniques can be used by educators to conduct the necessary local assessments and to apply the research findings in the identification of content changes.

Teachers have many sources available to them that describe current research findings. Frequently, a few hours of reading will disclose the data or research techniques the individual is seeking. Even though not all the desired information is there, perhaps the model or technique used can be applied to the local situation. Excellent models of research completed on curriculum, job skills, and task analyses are available. Many of these may be modified to fit the needs of any size community. One example is "A

---

[1]West, Leonard J. "Survey of Bookkeeping Job Activities in Relation to the High School Bookkeeping Curriculum." *Delta Pi Epsilon Journal* 27:31; November 1974.

[2]McLean, Gary N. "The Relationship Between Typewriting Performance and Shorthand Transcription Skills." *Delta Pi Epsilon Journal* 20:20-25; January 1978.

Questionnaire Evaluation of Your Business Education Program" prepared by Christine Stiegler.[3] She supplied guidelines for writing the questions as well as a model which can be adapted to any situation.

The multifaceted aspects of designing and conducting the research have been described in the preceding chapters. After the research is completed, the next step is to choose a model of curriculum development.

PLANNING THE CYCLE

In establishing a cycle for planning curriculum change and evaluation, business educators should consider the entire educational program. Planning for course or content updates in isolation from the total program in all probability will not meet learners' needs in the business education curriculum. Decisions made for changes in course offerings and content, based on departmental input on a continuous basis, will be more meaningful when based on research data. The process will reflect a rational and objective approach for meeting student, school, and business needs.

Departmental objectives. An important first step in organizing the planning cycle is the formation of long-range departmental objectives which include as a critical element an ongoing assessment plan to reexamine course offerings and content. To determine long-range departmental objectives, an internal (departmental) needs assessment is a must. An integral part of the long-range objectives should be the identification of priorities.

Answers to some of the following questions may help in providing direction for departmental objectives that pertain to course offerings and content:

1. How well do our graduates perform on the job (skills, knowledges, attitudes)?

2. How do the expected outcomes (standards) in our classes compare with employment needs?

3. Do we have the office equipment to prepare students for the jobs they will seek?

4. Are we achieving equity in male and female enrollment? Are changes needed in course title, stereotyped vocabulary, and content?

5. Are individual course objectives established and are they being met?

6. Are appropriate instructional and supplemental materials being used?

Departmental needs assessment. Who should be involved in conducting a departmental needs assessment? No plans, changes, or decisions should be made without the involvement of all teachers in the business education department. The teachers are the key! Certainly administrators, local business education supervisors, state business education supervisors, curriculum specialists, and business education advisory committee members can and should assist in reexamining course offerings and content

---

[3]Stiegler, Christine. "A Questionnaire Evaluation of Your Business Education Program." *Business Exchange* 1 and 2, April 1979. pp. 20-25.

utilizing the survey and research data available. However, the teacher is the pivotal point around which the change and updating will be made and will be successful.

The teachers of the department must be actively involved in the planning, implementation, and evaluation of course and curriculum modification. It is important that survey and research data be continuously shared with all teachers and all others involved with curriculum update so that their base of knowledge is equally current.

Data available. Business educators have a professional obligation to be knowledgeable about sources and kinds of data available for all subject areas.

The *Delta Pi Epsilon Journal* is a publication devoted primarily to research in business education. Techniques for conducting research as well as pertinent findings for all areas of business education are available. In addition to the *Delta Pi Epsilon Journal*, there are useful DPE service bulletins such as Leonard West's *Design and Conduct of Educational Surveys and Experiments* and Mildred Hillestad's *Research Process and Product*. These bulletins provide appropriate research procedures concerning kinds of surveys, experiments, techniques for gathering data, and finalizing the data.

Most business education periodicals publish research articles in each volume. The findings relate not only to theory, content, and techniques but also to summaries of studies and areas where additional research is needed. A good example is Judith J. Lambrecht's "Comparing Achievement Among Shorthand Systems: A Research Synthesis."[4] Also, excellent models of research completed on curriculum are available from various state departments of education. While most of these state agencies have greater human and financial resources to conduct more comprehensive studies, many of the basic techniques can be modified to fit the needs of the local schools. An outstanding example is Leonard West's study which compared bookkeeping curriculum and job activities in New York.[5] If high schools have followed his recommendations based upon this extensive study, content emphasis is considerably different from the content presented in the traditional texts.

Frequently students do not perform the kinds of activities on the job that are taught in the classroom. Our concern for the students covers many facets: first, students must be employable—they need to have employable skills, written and verbal communication ability, and the ability to work well with others.

Minimal competency skills have been identified by most state agencies; specifically, states such as Colorado have identified the most frequently needed content and skill competencies for the major areas of business education through statewide task analyses studies. Business people, the Colorado State Vocational Business and Office Advisory Committee,

---

[4]Lambrecht, Judith J. "Comparing Achievement Among Shorthand Systems: A Research Synthesis." *Journal of Business Education* 55:78-80; November 1979.

[5]West, *op. cit.*

teachers, and teacher educators assisted in the studies. This information was then used to develop minimal competencies for each occupational area. A program concept for business education was developed based upon these competencies. High schools within the state may then use this concept and these competencies as a guide, adding additional competencies as needed to modify course offerings for their particular local community.

Classification of research. Educational research falls into four categories: basic, applied, research and development, and action research. Classification of research design further identifies types of educational research. Those classifications are descriptive, casual, comparative, experimental, and correlation. Each type of the formal research can make a significant contribution to business education curriculum study. Individuals should select that kind of research that will best develop relevant course offerings to meet student and business needs, based on data gathered in local school district surveys. Remember—it is the versatile, flexible teacher who adapts research findings to make course and curriculum revisions.

EXAMINING THE COURSE OFFERINGS

Assuming content revision is necessary, how do business educators validate and implement those changes? Application of the discrepancy analysis model can be utilized to recommend content and/or course changes. Three steps are addressed in the discrepancy analysis model:

Step 1—Existing conditions (*what is*)

Step 2—Concerns analysis (*what should be*)

Step 3—Discrepancy analysis (identifying the differences between *what is and what should be*)

Determine existing conditions. Using the discrepancy analysis model, one collects the data related to the total business education program. Examples of the data can include identification of student performance levels, words per minute on straight-copy typewriting, transcription speed on office-style dictation, number of courses offered in a specific subject during the school year, enrollment figures, male and female ratio, and time allocations.

One must clearly determine the existing conditions in the course(s) to be reviewed. *What is* the status quo of these courses? Only factual data (hard data) should be collected in this step. Data should be gathered on existing conditions in those courses to be revised. For example, one should identify the amount of time spent on the major areas being taught based on the course outline. In addition, instructional strategies and materials should be examined.

Utilization of pertinent research can and should also be applied in Step 1. A recent study to determine the discrepancy existing between job tasks of the beginning accounting and bookkeeping worker and the content of the high school accounting and bookkeeping curriculum found that "the units of instruction taught in these courses may have little relationship to job tasks necessary for gainful employment in beginning accounting and bookkeeping occupations."[6]

Identify the concerns. The *concerns analysis* step provides information to the business education department to enable the instructors to examine *what should be*—that is, it is a process of defining the perceptions of parents, students, teachers, administrators, and businesspersons.

Concerns analysis allows parents, students, teachers, administrators, and businesspersons to express, negotiate, and rank their concerns for the education of youth. A proper concerns analysis allows different societal groups to function as an informal unit to provide local direction for education program development.[7]

For the specific purpose of reviewing and updating course content, the scope of the concerns analysis at this step is limited to the course offerings under study; however, the concerns analysis as a step in total curriculum review and revision within the discrepancy analysis model is an effective tool. For continual curriculum review and revision, a business education priority survey can be designed and utilized in a predetermined time line, e.g., three- to five-year cycle.

Types of concerns that may be identified in this step are—

1. Students need better typewriting skills.
2. Proofreading skills are weak.
3. There is a need for more qualified office workers.

Collect the data. Departmental plans should be made for the collection of data for the concerns analysis by the following:

1. Identification of a broad range of concerns through advisory committee meetings, departmental meetings, student and parent surveys
2. Determination of the scope of concerns analysis study as it is limited to specific courses
3. Development of data-gathering instruments
4. Collection of data from the various groups that should have input into the course content
5. Summarization of the results of the survey by the various groups
6. Assignment of weights to the various groups' input; e.g., businesspersons' opinions might be given twice the weight of teachers
7. Ranking the concerns based on the data.

Caution: concerns analysis does not distinguish between students' needs and the concerns of adults. Varying needs will be expressed by different groups, so those individuals planning curriculum changes need to be aware of the audiences being surveyed. The results from a concerns analysis study should be used only as a springboard into discrepancy analysis—the third step.[8]

[6]Reap, Margaret Casey. "Job Tasks of the Beginning Accounting and Bookkeeping Worker Compared with the Content of the Hich School Accounting and Bookkeeping Curriculum." *Delta Pi Epsilon Journal* 22:10-18; January 1980.

[7]Spooner, Kendrick, and Ryan, John. *Wyoming Center Education Planning Handbook*. Cheyenne: Wyoming Department of Education, 1977. pp. NA8-NA13.

[8]*Ibid.*

Identify the difference. The third step in reviewing course content is to identify the difference between the concerns (*what should be*) and the existing conditions (*what is*). This step examines the concerns of the various groups and compares the concerns with what is presently being taught in the courses reviewed. A discrepancy analysis simply uses what the various groups have as their standard (e.g., students must be able to type more accurately) to direct investigation into the students' performance (e.g., average number of errors on production letters = 5).

> If students are not performing at the level of expectations as shown in the concerns analysis, there is a discrepancy between what the various groups believe should exist and what in reality exists.[9]

A sample diagram, using typewriting as a hypothetical case, identifies data and concerns that may be collected.

FIGURE I

Sample Course and Content Review

Concerns Analysis (What Should Be)	Existing Conditions (What Is?)

Better typewriting skills
Proofreading skills needed
More accurate typists
Recent/newest office typewriters
Better communication skills
Need for qualified office workers
	Traditional method—no allowance
	  for individualized instruction
	Four semesters of typewriting
	Range of straight-copy speeds at
	  end of four semesters—50-90
	  wpm
	Range production-typing speeds
	  number of enrolled—25-40 gwpm

Discrepancy

What Is The Difference?

The typing skill developed in our classes is not producing qualified typists for employment.

In the hypothetical case, follow-up studies show that the students are not being hired in office positions by local businesses and that those being employed are not being promoted. As the differences (discrepancies) are documented, a need has been identified and a problem area has been defined. If a business education department has documented data that substantiates a need for course revision, the department has identified a problem. As described in Figure I, examples of the problem areas are production-typing speeds and proofreading skills. Action for planning and implementing changes follows defined departmental procedures. Teachers would now examine course content, course objectives, time allotments, and student performance levels. The rationale for course change as well as specific content implications can then be developed from this discrepancy analysis model.

---

[9]*Ibid.*

IMPLEMENTATION

After identifying the major differences between *what is* and *what should be*, the short-range and long-range goals and strategies should be planned. These goals should fit the departmental plans and time lines.

Use a time line. Time is a valuable and scarce resource—time for planning, time for collecting data, time for meetings, time to prepare the changes. A time schedule cannot be overlooked; one should design a realistic time frame that can help the various individuals working with curriculum change produce meaningful results.

Major strategies and activities should be clearly identified using a time line method. "The time line, an effective and long-range time-saving tool, provides a day-to-day reference as well as historical review of the department's activities and responsibilities."[10] Another effective technique in detailing activities and time lines in a framework is the Gantt schedule, showing in graphic form the activities which must be accomplished concurrently and linearly in relation to the total time available. (Samples may be found in most research resources.)

An overall model of departmental strategies should include goals, activities, responsibilities, and budget items for the entire department. The plans for the course or courses being examined must fit within the parameters established in the departmental strategies. (See Figure II.)

Use a budget. Financial resources become a second valuable tool in planning as well as implementing change.

1. What are the available funds that can be considered in preparing a budget?

2. Is money available so that research studies can be purchased for easy review by all members of the department?

3. Is money available to schedule in-service education to instruct teachers in utilizing the data to update course offerings?

4. Are funds available for compensation to teachers for the time and effort spent working on the improvement of course offerings? Or for scheduling special workshops for the same purpose? Or for released time for developmental activities for the teachers?

These kinds of questions must be addressed for each of the offerings scheduled for updating and revision.

As the department narrows its target for the curriculum update and course revision to specific content, a laundry list of objectives should be developed to include those regarding a time line as well as the other aspects of the tasks. For example, the following concerns may serve as a starting point:

1. A comparison of the rank order of items from *what is* and *what should be* should be used to analyze the amount of time used to teach that concept in the past and the amount of time needed to teach the concept in light of the newly recognized need. For instance, if the accuracy of proofreading has been a weakness and approximately six hours are devoted to teaching

---

[10]Wood, Merle W. "The Time Line: An Effective Tool for Planning and Management." *Business Education World* 59:25; September/October 1978.

FIGURE II. Departmental Strategies

GOALS	ACTIVITIES	RESPONSIBILITY	VARIABLES AFFECTING BUDGET
Set business education departmental long-range goals	1. Identify objectives 2. Conduct internal needs assessment 3. Set time lines 4. Set priorities and assign tasks	All business education department members	Number of teachers in the department Size of school

Be informed and knowledgeable about research studies	1. Prepare preplanning activities
	  a. Determine what the types of research are
	  b. Review the adaptability/ versatility of studies
	2. Review research studies
		Subject matter teachers	Geographic location of community
			
			Local school district tax base
			
			State and federal research dollars

Evaluate present offerings/content	1. Conduct discrepancy evaluation
	  a. Review course offerings and content (*what is*)
	  b. Conduct concerns analysis (*what should be*)
	  c. Prepare discrepancy analysis (*what is the difference*)
		Students, teachers, parents, administrators, businesspersons, BOE advisory committee	

Formulate new course and/or content recommendations	1. Specify changes 2. Synthesize feedback from all involved in curriculum update	All business education department members	
Implement changes	1. Obtain new materials 2. Utilize research results 3. Determine appropriate teaching strategies 4. Develop performance objectives and evaluate criteria 5. Request approval from administration	Business education department	
Evaluate	1. Plan 2. Schedule 3. Collect data 4. Analyze 5. Effect change	Various groups (graduates of program, advisory committee, other school personnel)	

proofreading throughout the four courses of typing, (a) examine the materials used for teaching the principles, (b) review current research studies related to proofreading skills, (c) examine the teaching techniques, and (d) adjust both the materials and techniques to better meet the recognized needs.

2. Consider the financial resources for the purchase of supplemental materials or the development of one's own. Has a sufficient amount been budgeted to achieve the desired goals?

3. Do the departmental strategies include built-in released time for teachers to make content modifications? Depending upon the scope of the changes, the teacher or teachers involved may need a lighter teaching assignment in order to accomplish the objectives.
4. Is there availability of support staff for typing, duplicating, or assisting with clerical details?
5. Has additional input been planned from other sources such as advisory committee members, other school personnel (if pertinent), businesspeople?
6. Have teaching strategies, methodologies been renewed? Do they need to be modified to permit better teaching/learning? For example, if teachers have always taught traditionally, have they developed the techniques/strategies of teaching on an individualized basis?
7. Has a follow-up plan been designed to determine if the proposed content update and revision will achieve the desired results in student performance?

A good illustration of how curriculum update can change the performance level students achieve is illustrated in the following example.

The teachers of Adams City High School in Commerce City, Colorado, decided to evaluate their typewriting program. Their concerns included the number of sections being offered, space, enrollment, staff, and typewriting skills. After listing the various alternatives and their advantages and disadvantages, the members of the department decided to develop an individualized program using the audiovisual tutorial (AVT) system.

After remodeling the space available and purchasing the AVT equipment, the faculty was able to increase the student capacity by approximately 70 percent, decrease the number of sections offered from 20 (traditional approach) to 12 (AVT), and increase enrollment by 72 percent. They had previously experienced a declining enrollment. Also, their records indicate a vast improvement in the students' timed-writing results after the implementation of the AVT individualized program.

The procedures they followed are similar to those described here. The discrepancy evaluation model helped the teachers identify changes, and research on student enrollment and performance provided continuous evaluation data.

Evaluating the application of the discrepancy model. Even though most business education departments have some form of periodic evaluation plan that is used to assist teachers in maintaining a viable program, a specific evaluation of the updated and revised courses should be developed and carried out during and following course revision.

An evaluation plan should be developed concurrently with the revision and updating procedures. (See Figure II.) The plan should take into consideration the kinds of activities that should be assessed, what kind of data is obtainable, and who will collect and analyze the findings and prepare the final report. The information obtained from the checkpoints along the way as well as the final report should be used as a basis for refining the course and making any other major changes that may be deemed necessary as a result of the findings. The procedures used will be dependent upon the purpose of the evaluation.

A basic evaluation plan will include several facets, such as the following:

1. Stating purposes and objectives for the evaluation
2. Identifying and clarifying process and product objectives
3. Specifying measurement instruments
4. Specifying procedures for data collection
5. Specifying procedures for analyzing the data
6. Specifying the format for reporting information
7. Determining sequence and time of evaluation activities.[11]

Even though an evaluation plan is finalized, there may still be changes because of unforeseen circumstances.

An acceptable approach is to use the same measuring instruments for a follow-up study with those students who completed the updated and revised course as was used to determine that the course needed to be changed. Other data collection considerations could be as follows:

1. Interviews—with employers, employees
2. End of the year student questionnaires
3. Review of course objectives/time line/test results
4. Performance tests/employability skills
5. Periodic progress reports on student achievement
6. Observation
7. Logs
8. Attitude scales.

If it is impossible to involve all students who completed the revised course in long-range follow-up evaluation plans, at least a random sample of students should be involved. Time, budget allocations, and human resources available influence the extent of the evaluation. Regardless of the approaches selected, those planning the evaluation need to be thorough in their planning and procedures.

The data gathered for the evaluation must be handled carefully. If data is not adequate, it is impossible to make sound decisions on the future changes for the course. An evaluation data matrix may be developed to insure adequate procedures. Those components are (1) objectives, (2) evaluation techniques, (3) criterion measures, (4) data collection dates, (5) person responsible, (6) data collection procedures, (7) data analysis, and (8) data reporting.

For a complete description of how to plan the evaluation, refer to the next chapter.

---

[11]Spooner, *op. cit.*, p. EP-1.

CONCLUSION

It is crucial that students develop employability skills and be capable of high productivity on the job. Involved, interested business educators who are alert to research findings, who are flexible in designing course assessments, and who are willing to make changes in course content based on research findings will find the discrepancy analysis model a valuable technique. Knowing *what is* (existing conditions) and *what should be* (concerns analysis) leads one to the *differences* (discrepancies) and clearly identifies the needed changes in course content for updating and revising current offerings.

PART III

IMPLEMENTING CONTENT CHANGES

CHAPTER 10

Developing Competency-Based Objectives And Evaluation Methods

CARL E. JORGENSEN
Virginia Department of Education, Richmond

B. JUNE SCHMIDT
Virginia Polytechnic Institute and State University, Blacksburg

In little more than a decade, the term "competency-based education" (CBE) has become a part of the vocabulary of the educational community. Competencies, performance objectives, criterion-referenced measures, and performance guides have come into widespread use as more than 38 states have mandated a minimum competencies program. While the use of competence to measure achievement is not new in education, an emphasis on accountability that began in the 1960's has put the spotlight on competency-based education.

The business education program has focused on specific skills in the secondary program, and through the years, standards in the skill areas have been listed in instructional guides and published instructional materials. However, the current emphasis requires individuals to examine the goals of an entire program and to state competencies for it.

THE MINIMUM COMPETENCY MOVEMENT

Although a number of states are involved in the minimum competency movement, little agreement exists as to what should be included as minimum competencies, who should determine them, or how the program of minimum competencies should be implemented. Some programs have been implemented at the state level with uniform standards for all students in a state, while other programs are developed at the local level to measure certain identified basics. For some states, part of the program to measure competency in the basics is administered from the state level and other competencies are determined and measured at the local level.

Although a lack of uniformity in implementation exists, support for the competency movement has come from all levels of the educational community. Predictions are that the competency movement will be the outstanding change in the educational program during this century.[1] However,

---

[1]Neill, Shirley Boes. *The Competency Movement, Problems and Solutions.* Sacramento: Education News Service for the American Association of School Administrators, 1978. p. 5.

no program can be successful without systematic implementation. The need for such an approach has been noted in many publications; significantly, the April 1979 issue of *The American School Board Journal* directed school board members to prepare for minimum competencies in their school districts.[2] Each locality need not reinvent the wheel; when a competency program is developed by the local school system, the system should pool resources and use competencies, objectives, and criterion-referenced measures which are already available if they are appropriate. Krajewski emphasizes that a good public information program is needed if a community is to support the move to minimum competencies. Most important to the success of any change in education is the involvement of teachers who have the ultimate responsibility for teaching students who will be tested on the minimum competencies.

Any program of minimum competencies should not be so broad that teachers feel that the preparation for the competencies is an overwhelming task or that many students feel it is not possible to achieve the competencies and thus lack the drive to achieve them. Raybin observed, ". . . the program of minimum essentials should be administered in enough depth so that motivated students with the capacity to learn can do so."[3]

As a result of the minimum competencies movement, the entire curriculum has been affected. Questions have been raised that must have answers. Answers to these questions will affect the competencies as they are incorporated in competency-based business education programs. To go beyond basic skills when preparing individuals for entry into the world of work is essential. McClung questions objectives developed for some competencies in an article about minimum competencies.[4] He comments, "Furthermore, tests that go beyond basic skills and attempt to measure the affective aspects of social responsibility, good citizenship, self-concept, and job preparedness are vulnerable not only because it is questionable that these 'skills' can be measured but also questionable whether they can be generally taught, given the current state of instructional and curricular research." To have the proper depth in business education programs, ways must be determined to measure competencies in the affective domain.

The public has been understandably concerned with the educational system. With a declining enrollment, costs per student are increasing at an accelerated pace. Also, test scores on the widely used Scholastic Aptitude Test have been declining for a number of years adding fuel to the public concern for the products of schools. Further, many news reports during the last decade have pointed to a lack of basic skills in reading and math by individuals who have received diplomas as high school graduates. All of these things have caused the public outcry for greater accountability.

With the implementation of minimum competencies programs, the real needs of students must be served and minimum standards must not become

[2]Krajewski, Robert. "Here's How To Prepare for the Rush Toward Minimum Competency." *American School Board Journal* 166:4, 39-40; April 1979.

[3]Raybin, Ron. "Minimum Essentials and Accountability." *Phi Delta Kappan* 60:374-75; January 1979.

[4]McClung, Merle Steven. "Are Competency Testing Programs Fair? Legal?" *Phi Delta Kappan* 59:398· February 1978.

maximum standards. Further care must be exercised that the educational program does not become so centered around the minimum competencies that more and more of educational time is assigned to meeting these standards while the needs of average, above-average, gifted, and other students may be ignored.[5] In working toward a total curriculum that is competency-based, business educators must identify their responsibilities. A challenge is presented in structuring the entire curriculum by the minimum competencies movement.

IMPROVING THE CURRICULUM

Since the 1950's, many attempts have been made to more accurately define the outcomes of the educational program. Many individuals have focused on the need to accurately state the intentions of the curriculum. The classification of educational goals and the evaluation of the attainment of those goals were addressed through the *Taxonomy of Educational Objectives*, edited by Benjamin S. Bloom. This taxonomy identified a classification system for various learning experiences and suggested appropriate evaluation methods.

With the passage of the Vocational Education Act in 1963 and the opportunity for business education to receive funding for occupational preparation programs, the timely publication, *Preparing Instructional Objectives*, by Robert F. Mager, became available. Mager, along with Kenneth M. Beach, Jr., prepared an additional publication that identified a system for *Developing Vocational Instruction*. Their work and the work of others have provided a solid foundation for the move to competency-based vocational education. As teachers have become competent in writing objectives, hundreds of objectives have been written for each educational program. Organizations have been established to organize and classify the objectives for teachers to use. One of these organizations is the Instructional Objectives Exchange (IOX) in Los Angeles. This organization has collected and published objectives for many areas of business education. While the intentions of those preparing and assembling objectives were good, the result has been a collection of so many objectives that they are unmanageable. Any system that cannot be managed by the teacher with some ease is doomed. The objectives have accordingly served as the basis for the development of curriculum materials. English describes the procedure as follows: "Curriculum development is most often characterized as a process in which a group of experts sequester themselves for a given time period to 'write' a curriculum. . . . it is then disseminated to administrators and teachers to be 'implemented.' "[6]

The development of enabling and terminal competencies for CBE has been characterized by more comprehensive statements that are manageable within the classroom setting. To adapt CBE within current school settings

---

[5]Bunda, Mary Anne. *Competency-Based Graduation Requirements: A Point of View.* TM Report 66. Princeton: ERIC Clearinghouse on Tests, Measurement and Evaluation, Educational Testing Service, 1978. pp. 9-12.

[6]English, Fenwick W. "Re-Tooling Curriculum Within On-Going School Systems." *Educational Technology* 19:7; May 1979.

frequently requires some compromise as to the CBE elements that will be implemented. Regardless of the structure, teacher involvement is a key to successful implementation since much of the current emphasis has been mandated by state legislatures and administrators. Teachers who are not involved with the implementation are expressing the feeling that CBE is being forced on them whether or not it is educationally sound.

One of the business education leaders in the move to CBE, Adele Schrag, has warned, ". . . (CBE) is in danger of being one of the most misinterpreted concepts in education today. . . . Competencies are simply indicators of successful performance in a given role. . . . Teachers are lulled into believing that checking off such tasks produces workers who are competent."[7] This concern is shared by many because the initial approach is frequently the development of competencies based on job analysis. These competencies usually do not take into consideration personal employability skills that are needed to be successful on the job or the development of work values which are important for employee motivation. Teachers frequently state that measurable competencies for this area cannot be prepared. While measurement of competencies in the affective domain is difficult, it is not impossible.

COMPETENCIES

Competency-based education programs serve as a means for providing accountability. They make possible defining the product of a program in terms that are specific and identify the skills end knowledges in which the program completer is competent. CBE, like career education, has gained wide acceptance wiithin a very short period of time. Individuals have been able to identify the worth of this approach which had its first application in teacher education and the military. The approach strengthens what was already being utilized in occupational preparation programs. Cilley, Elson, and Oliver discuss the CBE approach saying, "What is new is the insistence on the use of validated competencies, thoroughly systematic procedures for delivering instruction, and more objective student assessment devices."[8] They observe that this feature "constitutes a revolution in the presentation of vocational training."

Competencies are stated prior to instruction and the student knows what the basis for evaluation will be. Each student is thus held responsible for mastering the competencies. The basis for grading is attainment of competencies rather than measurement against other students. After determining that job openings exist in an occupation and that students are interested in the occupation, a task analysis is completed. This serves as the basis for developing objectives.

Developing competency-based objectives. From the job analysis it is possible to identify those tasks which are most difficult to learn and to develop accompanying objectives. Use is made of research studies that

[7]Schrag, Adele F. "A Message from a Leader in Business Education, CBE in Perspective." *Journal of Business Education* 54:246; March 1979.

[8]Cilley, Richard N.; Elson, Donald E.; and Oliver, J. Dale. *Competency-Based Vocational Education. Participant's Guide for In-Service Training.* Blacksburg: Virginia Polytechnic Institute and State University, 1977. p. 9.

identify tasks performed by office workers. From these studies role-relevant objectives are prepared. Advisory committees can, in turn, determine the appropriateness of objectives for a given community.

Personal employability skills and work values. In addition to reviewing task inventories to develop competency-based objectives, it is also important to identify personal employability skills and work values that should be included in the instructional program. Objectives with accompanying evaluation measures and/or performance guides are prepared for these.

Curriculum development. After the competency-based objectives for a program have been agreed upon, the curriculum is developed. This includes the sequencing of activities, the identification of instructional materials and simulation activities, development of learning modules where needed, and preparation of criterion-referenced measures.

EVALUATION

Because competencies are often stated in terms of minimum competencies or essential competencies, the criticism has been made that student success in a CBE program cannot be charted. Identifying individual differences to the prospective employer can be difficult. The typical model for CBE is one that provides for differences in learning time only. However in CBE, criterion-referenced tests are based upon the standards for entering an occupation or for successfully working with individuals in the occupation. Certain objectives may also be related to skills needed to function as a consumer and a citizen (areas for which business education also has responsibility). Since the criterion is stated in advance, no misunderstanding on the part of teacher and student on the evaluation exists. The system is usually a "pass" or "no pass" system.

Since the majority of business educators teach in school systems that require grades, since parents seem reluctant to accept anything less than evaluation based on a grading system, and since employers ask the school to differentiate prospective employees on some type of grading scale, attention must be given to some means of assigning grades.

One method of assigning grades that has been used by business teachers for years is providing for different levels of achievement within an objective. Business teachers have always based grades in skill areas on production ability. Those students with the higher rates of production receive the higher grades. These rates are determined in advance and when the criterion rates are based on business standards, CBE requirements have been met. All students are evaluated on the standard rather than on comparison with the progress made by other students.

A study of job analyses and the tasks performed by workers will show that some tasks are performed by beginning workers and others may not be performed until a worker has been on the job for some time. Competency-based objectives can be prepared for those tasks that every beginning worker in an occupational area must perform and additional ones prepared for tasks that may be performed by a beginning worker or a worker with some experience. For grading purposes, students may receive a passing grade if they accomplish those competency-based objectives that all beginning workers must be able to perform. Additional credit or a higher grade may be assigned for the completion of additional competency-based objectives. The number of additional competencies required for each grade can be prespecified.

Grading may also be based upon the satisfactory performance of the required competency-based objectives plus paper-and-pencil tests. These may test cognitive understandings from the learning activities. Grades on the paper-and-pencil tests constitute part of the grade and the completion of competency-based objectives the other part. In addition, some business teachers have developed a work attitude checklist which is completed periodically for each student. Work attitudes may be included as part of the grade of the student.[9]

Flexibility is a must as business teachers attempt to implement CBE and use criterion-referenced measures. Rather than being frustrated by an instructional system that has many restraints, the teacher should examine the ways in which the best of CBE may be incorporated into the existing educational setting.

A PLAN FOR CBE IMPLEMENTATION

Virginia, similar to other states, is committed to providing quality vocational programs. The legislated *Standards of Quality and Objectives for Public Schools in Virginia*, 1978-80, address this commitment in Goal 3. It states that ". . . each pupil, consistent with his or her abilities and educational needs (be aided) to qualify for further education or for employment." The Virginia Board of Education has interpreted this goal as requiring for high school graduation the attainment of a marketable skill for each student who plans to enter employment following high school. Based on this requirement, the Virginia Department of Education recommends three main ways to attain a marketable skill: (1) completion of the full sequence of courses in a competency-based occupational preparation program, (2) completion of a competency-based senior intensified occupational preparation program, and (3) completion of part of a competency-based occupational preparation program that enables the student to develop the competencies needed for a specific job as described in the *Dictionary of Occupational Titles*.

CBE standards. To assure the use of competency-based objectives and accompanying evaluation methods in every vocational offering, the Division of Vocational Education has adopted four standards:

- Role-relevant competencies that include standards are identified and stated.
- Competencies are specified to students prior to instruction.
- Criterion-referenced measures are used to measure achievement of competencies.
- A system exists for documenting the competencies achieved by each student.

Meeting the CBE standards. The Business Education Service is assisting teachers in meeting the standards in a variety of ways. Task force groups

---

[9]*Ibid.*, pp. 109-10.

composed of teachers, local supervisors, and teacher educators have been formed to identify competencies, develop criterion-referenced measures, and assess documentation systems. A major effort of the groups has been the preparation of competency-based course outlines for all business and office education offerings recommended by the Business Education Service. The outlines will provide teachers with suggested competencies appropriate for meeting the first standard.

IDENTIFICATION OF COMPETENCIES. Each course outline contains a course description, a listing of skill or learning areas, a topical outline, and enabling, terminal, and personal employability competencies. Content of the outlines is based on the following:

1. Vocational-Technical Education Consortium of States (V-TECS) catalogs of performance objectives, criterion-referenced measures, and performance guides when available for an occupational area along with computer printouts for the catalogs listing tasks performed by beginning workers

2. Teacher input as to what is required of students for initial employment and as to what can reasonably be expected of students

3. Content previously recommended by the Business Education Service as appropriate for each course

4. Current instructional materials available for business and office education offerings.

The 12 skill areas identified for the secretarial, stenographic, typewriting, and related occupations course outlines along with an example of a terminal competency in each area are provided in the following table.

Skill Area	Terminal Competency Example
	CAN THE STUDENT:
Calculating Machines	Operate ten-key calculating equipment at a minimum rate and with an error tolerance acceptable for employment?
Communication Skills	Compose and typewrite in mailable form appropriate business correspondence for three given situations?
Financial Records	Accurately compute five net pay amounts including calculation of gross earnings and deductions?
Mail Processing	Correctly open, stamp, sort, and route ten routine pieces of incoming mail?
Maintenance and Care of Office Equipment	Clean typewriter keys or elements and remove dust, change ribbon, and make machine adjustments?
Office Experience	Acceptably synthesize previously learned knowledges, skills, and attitudes to complete the task of a given position in a model office?
Records Management	Accurately file 25 documents alphabetically?
Reprographics	Justify the most appropriate method of duplication—stencil, photocopy, or offset—for ten case situations?
Shorthand and Transcription	Prepare two typewritten transcripts of material from office-style dictation in mailable form?

116

Typewriting	Typewrite from handwritten or edited rough-draft copy three mailable average-length business letters with special features and appropriate copies?
Word Processing	Transcribe from recorded media three average-length business letters in mailable form?
Personal Employability Skills and Knowledge	Identify skills and personal traits and match them with available job opportunities?

The terminal competencies are stated at levels considered minimum for advancement to the next course or for job entry. For a double-period occupational preparation offering, 60 to 70 terminal competencies are listed. Even though performance levels for each competency are stated at minimum, teachers may find that students do not achieve all of the competencies. Accordingly, a decision will be required as to what constitutes acceptable performance. Achievement of 80 percent of the total competencies in an occupational preparation program seems a logical requirement and should provide a marketable skill. This means that an individual student will be required to achieve 80 percent of the competencies at the 100 percent level of performance.

Teachers are encouraged to strive to have students achieve more than 80 percent of the competencies and to have them achieve at levels of performance that exceed those stated in the competencies. This procedure will allow for teacher flexibility in meeting individual needs and in the assignment of grades. Many CBE advocates emphasize that achievement of competencies must be on a pass-fail basis—either a competency is achieved or it is not—and all competencies will be achieved if enough time is allowed. This concept cannot be implemented in a large-scale move to CBE in vocational education such as that being undertaken in Virginia since teachers are assigned students for designated periods of time and are required to assign grades. The four standards adopted for CBE do not include this concept. Instead, grading procedures based on achieving more than 80 percent of the competencies for a given course, achieving at a higher level of performance than stated in the competencies, or a combination of these two are recommended.

CRITERION-REFERENCED MEASURES. The standards require that criterion-referenced measures be used to assess achievement of competencies. A number of task force groups worked to develop criterion-referenced measures for the terminal competencies listed in the secretarial, stenographic, typewriting, and related occupations course outlines. The outlines are cross-referenced to the V-TECS (Vocational-Technical Education Consortium of States) catalog for these occupations and the catalogs contain recommended criterion-referenced measures. However, the catalogs are based on tasks performed by experienced workers, and the measures they provide are not appropriate for most competencies in the outlines. In addition, a number of competencies that have been identified in the outlines are not in the catalog, especially in areas of emerging office technology and in the personal employability area.

The groups' initial efforts were directed toward the statement of performance objectives for each terminal competency. The objectives had to be stated in acceptable performance terms plus allow for the development of criterion-referenced test items that met the following criteria:

Does the item actually test for the competency?

Is the item structured to match the on-the-job situation?

Does the item test for achievement of the competency in the most efficient way?

Will all raters interpret achievement of the competency in the same way?

Are the materials required for the item manageable?

Three examples of terminal competencies along with performance objectives developed for them by the task force groups follow:

Competency: Accurately compute five net pay amounts including calculation of gross earnings and deductions.

Objective: Given the regular and overtime hours for five employees, marital status and exemptions for the five employees, an income tax withholding table, information for computing social security deductions, and previously determined optional deductions, compute the net pay for each employee with 100 percent accuracy.

Competency: Justify the most appropriate method of duplication—stencil, photocopy, or offset—for ten case situations.

Objective: Given ten case situations, select the most appropriate method of duplication (stencil, photocopy or offset) in five minutes with 100 percent accuracy. The following criteria will be used in selecting the most appropriate form of duplication:

(1) cost
(2) speed
(3) complexity of material
(4) quality of reproduction
(5) paper characteristics
(6) quantity

Competency: Prepare two transcripts from office-style dictation and transcribe in mailable form.

Objective: Given office-style dictation, prepare two mailable transcripts. Office-style dictation is characterized by variable rates with pauses and rapid spurts in dictation. Changes are made in the dictated material that include word additions, deletions, omissions, and rearrangement of syntax or copy blocks. Mailability is evaluated using the following criteria:

1. Deviations from that dictated do not change the meaning.

2. Format is correct.

3. Standard grammar, capitalization, spelling, and punctuation are used.

4. No noticeable corrections (from a distance of 18 inches).

Rate of dictation should be at that which the writer is capable of writing accurately, and transcription time is not a factor.

A well-prepared objective provides the basis for preparation of the criterion-referenced measure. The preceding examples show how details of test items are provided by clear and complete objectives. The task force groups prepared a number of test items from the objectives. Selected test items, those that meet the criteria particularly well, will be provided to all business teachers in Virginia along with suggestions for the preparation of criterion-referenced measures.

DOCUMENTATION OF ACHIEVEMENT. A number of systems exist for documenting the achievement of competencies. Systems recommended were selected on the basis of logic of format, simplicity, and ease of use. Provision exists for documenting achievement of a competency, exceeding a competency, and attempting but not achieving a competency. Local decision will determine the exact documentation system to be used and procedures for using the system.

The documentation system provides for the individual student the articulation of instruction within a school, from course to course, and from one school to another. Each student's record is a comprehensive profile of competencies achieved, exceeded, and attempted. In addition, the documentation system serves as a means of providing meaningful information to employers.

Why adopt the CBE approach. The major thrust of the CBE movement is to provide an instructional setting where each student can achieve to the maximum. Obviously, business teachers will need to make a number of changes, particularly in classroom procedures, to meet the four CBE standards adopted in Virginia. If the changes are to be warranted, then teachers and students must benefit.

ADVANTAGES OF CBE TO THE TEACHER AND THE STUDENT. By meeting the four standards, the classroom teacher will realize a number of advantages including management of the instructional program to meet individual needs; provision for communicating instructional intent to students, employees, and the public; and use of evaluation procedures directly related to competencies developed. In turn, students will benefit by learning of expected outcomes or competencies prior to instruction, by measurement of performance against predetermined standards rather than against other students, and through continuous opportunities for remedial instruction when competencies are not met.

THE TEACHER'S ROLE IN CBE IMPLEMENTATION. A key factor in the successful move to the four CBE standards is the acceptance of the standards by classroom teachers. The availability of recommended competencies for each course, sample criterion-referenced measures along with procedures for their development, and suggested documentation systems will assist teachers in the transition. However, teacher acceptance of achievement of competencies as a basis for determining student progress will be critical. Criterion-referenced evaluation procedures based on identification of role-relevant competencies are the backbone of the CBE movement.

119

CONCLUSION

Competency-based business education provides a method of describing the outcomes of programs. With clearly stated objectives which are measured with criterion-referenced measures, students will benefit. CBE provides a sound basis for communicating with the business community and more closely meeting the needs of this community. Students should be able to move vertically and horizontally within the education structure as they move from one institution to another without unnecessary duplication of instruction. Properly implemented, CBE will enable students to move more rapidly in their instructional program and make greater progress in achieving career goals.

CHAPTER 11

Selecting Appropriate Textbooks, Supplementary Materials, and Community Resources

MARY JANE LANG and **LONNIE ECHTERNACHT**
University of Missouri, Columbia

Most teachers today are enthusiastic about the abundance of instructional materials and aids in business education. At the same time, they are perplexed as to how to judge which materials are the most appropriate for implementing content changes and enhancing the teaching-learning process. Such movements as career education, consumer education, and metrication, as well as those resulting from the growing technological applications such as word processing, micrographics, and reprographics have challenging implications for the process of selecting appropriate teaching-learning materials. If we as business educators are truly committed to the belief that instructional materials are second in importance to the teacher in the total educational process, the significance of painstaking efforts in effecting suitable choices cannot be overemphasized.

SELECTING APPROPRIATE TEXTBOOKS

In the United States today, two practices for textbook selection are common: (1) state committee selection and (2) local district selection. In those areas following the practice of state committee selection of textbooks, local districts are generally provided a listing of three to five textbooks for each course from which a selection may be made. In those states specifying a definite period of time for which textbooks are to be selected, three to five years is a common practice. If the local district selection practice is employed, the specific procedure may vary from the small secondary school to the large school system. Selection by a committee composed of the teacher(s) responsible for the course and representation from the administration is more desirable than decisions by the principal, superintendent, business education consultant, or department head alone.

Regardless of the level at which the selection process takes place, this important task should be pursued with competence and concern. Although there are many unmeasurables in the matter of textbook evaluation, various authors have identified certain factors about which rather specific judgment can be made. Nanassy, Malsbary, and Tonne provide a listing of factors they deem important in the textbook selection process.[1] This listing appears comprehensive, though practical, and is reasonably representative of similar lists suggested by other business educators. The factors included are these:

Nature of the contents. The textbook should provide those topics of instruction important in the particular subject with a minimal amount of irrelevant material. Topics reflecting changing social, economic, and technological conditions must be included. The order in which the topics are presented should be examined also. Those participating in the textbook selection must ask themselves the question, will the topics included and the order in which they are presented facilitate the achievement of the behavioral objectives developed for the specific course for which the textbook is being considered?

Author. The ultimate value of a particular textbook can be assessed to a great extent by the degree to which the author is knowledgeable in the subject and versed in the instructional methodology of the subject. Nanassy, Malsbary, and Tonne condone the practice of joint authorship of textbooks, with one author a specialist in subject matter and the other an authority in teaching methodology.

Schools that use the text. If a textbook has been on the market for some time, it is advisable to seek firsthand reactions from teachers in reputable schools in which the book has been used. Knowledge of the number and quality of the schools using the textbook under consideration is indeed useful information in the selection process.

Date of publication or of revision. If a textbook is to reflect recent technological change as well as change in recommended instructional methodology, it must be revised at regular intervals. Those responsible for verifying that a particular textbook has actually been updated must examine the contents carefully. Some revisions are quite extensive while others include minor changes only. A late copyright date cannot, therefore, be accepted on face as evidence that a textbook has been updated substantively.

Language used. Nanassy, Malsbary, and Tonne have emphasized the importance of insuring that a textbook is readable, understandable, and interesting for the level of students who will be utilizing it. Consequently, it is imperative that the writing style, level of vocabulary, and size of print be considered. In addition, the wording should avoid sex bias and stereotyping.

Hasselriis suggests the administration of the Cloze Test by teachers of business courses—basic business subjects particularly—to determine the instructional reading levels of their students on material taken from a specific textbook or other instructional materials.[2] In devising a Cloze Test, a teacher selects a passage of material from a textbook or other instructional materials about which he or she may be inquisitive. The first sentence of the selection is typed verbatim. Beginning with any word of the second

---

[1]Nanassy, Louis C.; Malsbary, Dean R.; and Tonne, Herbert A. *Principles and Trends in Business Education.* Indianapolis: Bobbs-Merrill Educational Publishing, 1977. pp. 405-08.

[2]Hasselriis, Peter. "Strategies for Teaching Reading in Business Education." NABTE *Review.* 1971. p. 67.

sentence of the passage selected, a numbered blank is substituted for the word. This procedure is continued for every fifth word of the material until the fiftieth deleted word is replaced with a blank. The sentence containing the fiftieth omitted word is completed, and the sentence following is typed as shown in the material.

A copy of the test and a 50-blank answer sheet are prepared for each student. In administering the test, the teacher asks the student to try to provide the correct word in each of the numbered blanks after having scanned the selection to get some idea of what is being said.

The number of words replaced correctly constitutes the test score. Research has indicated that if a student replaces 20 or more of the missing words correctly, the material is at the instructional reading level of the student.

Textbook construction. Today's students are favorably impressed with and obviously prefer a textbook that is convenient in size and bound in attractive colors. An examination of recent textbooks in the various subject areas evidences the fact that publishers are responding positively to these preferences.

The quality of the paper and the durability of the binding are more important than general appearance, however. In various business subjects it is necessary to refer frequently to certain pages in the textbook for a form, a rule, a table, etc. Textbooks prepared for such subjects—typewriting and accounting, for example—should, therefore, be printed on very strong paper that will withstand such usage. While strong binding is desirable for textbooks generally, exceptionally durable binding is necessitated for typewriting textbooks since these books are folded back and must be flat when in use.

Textbook illustrations. In those subjects in which the textbook is the primary study reference for the student, effective illustrations can add substantially to the meaningfulness of the content. In evaluating the effectiveness of textbook illustrations, most authorities would subscribe to the following guidelines of Nanassy, Malsbary, and Tonne: be fairly numerous; be well printed; be of a reasonable size; relate to the text material; appear on the same pages with the principles they are supposed to illustrate, or at least on pages opposite the principles; have catchy, yet meaningful, captions so that they will arouse students' interest; be up to date; and fit the age level of the students. Textbook illustrations should be nondiscriminatory in terms of both sex and race; therefore, textbook evaluators should study pictorial presentations of individuals from those standpoints in addition to the foregoing guidelines.

Supplemental materials. Workbook materials accompanying the textbook make it possible for students to enhance their understanding of the course content by applying the concepts and principles they are studying. This practice is particularly effective in courses in typewriting, bookkeeping/accounting, basic business, clerical/secretarial practice, and shorthand. The utilization of workbooks eliminates the preparation of special forms by the teacher or the students for the completion of textbook learning activities. Attractively designed workbook forms also tend to encourage better penmanship and more attention to neatness and accuracy on the part of students. Shorthand workbook exercises, emphasizing auxiliary skills basic to the transcription process—spelling, vocabulary, grammar, punctuation, word division—are valuable supplements to the textbook in the teaching-learning process and should be evaluated as a part of the textbook selection process.

Instructional tapes, particularly those developed to accompany typewriting and shorthand textbooks, are especially valuable in coping with individual differences and in providing remedial instruction. Where a textbook with accompanying taped lessons is desired, it is important that those responsible for the selection insure that the quality of the tapes is satisfactory before a choice is made.

Tests to accompany textbooks are available from publishers of various business and office materials. In general, these tests consist of objective items carefully prepared, attractively presented, and easily scored. The evaluation of textbooks for a particular course would include an examination of these printed tests prior to making a choice.

The teachers manual accompanying the textbook is a valuable resource for the teacher. While the range of contents included in the manuals varies, suggestions for conducting the course, for teaching the different chapters or units of the textbook, and answers to the questions, exercises, problems, cases, etc., included at the end of chapters are normally provided. It is important that the teachers manual for each textbook being considered be examined before the actual choice is made.

Price. Regardless of whether the student or the school district is the purchaser, the price of the textbook is a factor in the selection process. Price must be considered in conjunction with the foregoing factors, however.

SELECTING APPROPRIATE SUPPLEMENTARY MATERIALS

Teachers who are genuinely concerned with serving students most effectively are aware that even the best textbook and workbook on the market do not provide a sufficient variety of materials for meeting the diverse needs represented in the usual classroom. Three such areas of need for additional materials—often referred to as "auxiliary" or "ancillary"— are apparent to most business teachers: (1) the reinforcement of specific skills through meaningful problem-solving and decision-making activities; (2) the acquisition of more realistic office experiences in working conditions, work production, and quality and quantity office standards within the classroom; and (3) the accommodation of individual differences and special needs.

Quality published materials directed toward the needs cited are advertised regularly in such familiar professional periodicals as *The Balance Sheet, Business Education Forum, Business Education World,* and *Journal of Business Education.* Information regarding instructional materials may also be obtained from publishers' catalogs and through the Education Resources Information Center (ERIC) network. Continued provision of new, and perhaps better, materials is insured through the strong concern of dedicated educators anxious to implement recent research findings in the development of instructional materials.

Many of these auxiliary or ancillary materials—visual (bulletin boards, charts, graphs, maps, transparencies, proofguides, silent filmstrips, slides, etc), audio (records, discs, cassette tapes, etc.), audiovisual (motion picture films, slide-sound presentations, etc.), modules, learning activity packets, practice sets, simulations, games, and others—are used extensively by business teachers in the promotion of improved teaching-learning. In the selection of specific published materials to augment the textbook (and workbook if used) in the satisfaction of any one of the areas of need identified, the following guidelines are suggested:

The content is pertinent to the behavioral objectives of the course(s) in which it is to be used. Only those instructional materials which contribute toward the achievement of the behavioral objectives of the course(s) should be included in the instructional program. Supplementary materials are certainly no exception. Indeed, the increasing emphasis upon the production of such materials magnifies the problem of the educator in identifying that which holds the greatest potential for assisting students in reaching established goals.

The content is accurate, up to date, and closely correlated with that of the textbook(s) with which it is to be used. In the selection of a practice set to reinforce basic accounting skills through problem-solving and decision-making activities, for example, the teacher must insure that the subject matter is correct, that the procedures and terminology are in accord with current, accepted practice, and that the content level of the set selected does not exceed the point of instruction at which the student(s) is working. Likewise, the content of professionally prepared transparencies chosen for use in conjunction with instruction on the "parts of a letter" to a special needs (low ability) group must be accurate in all details, reflect up-to-date and accepted practices, and be compatible with that of the textbook(s) with which they will be used.

The content is presented understandably. If instructional materials are to be effective in augmenting the textbook(s) utilized in the teaching-learning process—whether the target group be highly motivated, fast-learning accounting students or marginally interested, potential dropouts of a clerical office practice course, the materials must be carefully prepared. The visual component must be attractively formatted, easily readable, and void of racism and sexism. If procedural directions are a part of the materials, they should be clearly worded and on a vocabulary level appropriate for the population intended. Where an audio component is included, the various qualities pertinent to sound must be evaluated.

The time required for effective utilization can be accommodated within the instructional program. A teacher considering supplementary materials for assisting typewriting students with varied needs within an individualized instructional setting would likely have few restraints. It is highly probable, however, that this same teacher would experience less freedom if endeavoring to identify the most effective textbook enhancement materials for assisting typewriting students with varied needs enrolled in a group instruction class meeting 40 minutes daily.

The cost is consistent with the financial resources available. Regardless of how valuable a particular item of supplementary material might be to the teaching-learning process, it may be too expensive in certain situations and thus inappropriate for selection. Rarely does a school system have adequate funds for the purchase of all supplementary materials deemed desirable. Thus, priorities must be determined—the specific priorities to be those materials considered most likely to benefit the greatest number of students in their achievement.

In many situations, there is the policy that students purchase such consumable items as practice sets and job-stations simulations. Where this policy prevails, the cost factor may be a special concern.

SELECTING APPROPRIATE COMMUNITY RESOURCES

While business teachers recognize the need for bridging the gap between the classroom and the business community, they are generally unaware of the many educational possibilities that exist in their communities. Since the number and variety of resources will vary from community to community, teachers need to determine the specific resources available to them in their community and select those that can best be used to enrich and vitalize the business and office program.

When selecting community resources, the business teacher should consider various factors. In every community, large or small, there exists a wealth of educational resources that can be had and used simply for the asking. Improved learning occurs when the community serves as a laboratory and the scene for learning is extended beyond the limits of the classroom. The two alternative methods for utilizing community resources are to bring the resources into the classroom or to send students into the community. Contacts with business people and use of actual business forms and materials help to keep teachers informed of current developments in the field of business. Community and business contacts contribute greatly to successful school programs of career education and vocational guidance. The use of community resources in business classes improves school-community relationships and results in greater student interest. Even though business people are usually eager to cooperate with the schools, careful planning by teachers and students in the use of community resources is necessary.

Determining community resources. The most effective way to determine the nature and extent of community resources available for use in the business education program is to survey the businesses in the community. While it is recommended that the actual survey be conducted by students, the teacher's role in carefully planning and coordinating the survey is important. The method and scope of the survey must be understood by all individuals involved in the activity. The specific information sought should determine the types of questions asked, and consideration should be given the time required to conduct the survey. If all businesses are not included in the survey, extreme care must be exercised to ensure that those selected are representative of the various businesses in the community. The purpose of the survey—to determine specific business community resources available —should be clearly understood by all the participants. Publicity prior to and during the survey should be provided in both school and community newspapers.

In addition to the business survey, other means for determining community resources should be utilized by teachers. Newspapers can provide information about activities of community and business organizations, reorganization and expansion plans by companies, personnel changes in businesses, business exhibits, unusual merchandise, and cases illustrating legal principles. If filed and kept up to date, these newspaper clippings provide the teacher with useful information and are sources for community contacts.

Contacts through students and former students are important to the teacher in providing helpful information about the community. An advisory committee of representatives from management, employee groups, the professions, former students, and other interested citizens is an excellent source of information about community resources and their use in improving the program.

Participation by teachers in the activities of local business and professional organizations provides opportunities to meet and work with many different community leaders. These organizations usually welcome interest on the part of teachers and often have an education committee that is charged with the responsibility of maintaining a communication link with educators and supporting educational activities in the community.

Resource people. There is a variety of resource persons in all communities who, because of their special abilities and/or accomplishments, can provide valuable career information and greatly influence students. A resource person may be an elected or appointed governmental official, business owner, executive, employee with considerable experience, beginning worker, or a former student. When selecting a resource person, the decision should not be based necessarily on the position held by the individual but rather on the individual's accomplishments and ability to demonstrate and/or explain business procedures. To foster two-way communications, the sessions should be in the form of a demonstration or talk followed by questions, panel discussion with audience participation, small discussion groups, or round table discussions.

Both in-class and in-business discussions by resource people are useful for making course content seem more real to students. Whether the resource person should come to the school or the students visit the business will depend upon several factors. Some factors to consider are the type of demonstration or talk to be given, facilities and equipment needed for the demonstration or talk, kind of surroundings most desirable to involve the students actively, number of students, transportation facilities available, and wishes of the resource person.

To realize the maximum benefits from the use of community resource people, careful planning by both students and teacher is necessary if the following questions are to be answered in the affirmative: Does each student understand who the resource person is, what company he/she represents, and what the objectives are? Does each student understand the importance of courteous conduct and attention, and is each aware of his/her personal responsibility in this matter? Have the students formulated some questions to ask the resource person? Has the resource person been informed of the purpose of the talk or demonstration and the specific topics that the teacher and students want discussed? Has adequate information concerning the students to be addressed been given the resource person—type of class, age level, vocational objectives of the students, content already studied, etc.? Has a time limit been set, and is the resource person aware of it? Has a follow-up activity been planned so students will be able to relate what they learned to the classroom work? Will a courteous letter of appreciation be sent to the resource person?

Field trips. A field trip affords an excellent means of utilizing the community as a laboratory to supplement classroom experiences. Local business and government offices, as a rule, welcome the opportunity to conduct field trips through their operations. However, the effectiveness of a field trip is dependent upon the carefulness with which the trip is organized. A well-organized field trip can provide students with an unparalleled educational experience to meet business people, observe business activities in their natural setting, understand job requirements and employment possibilities, correct wrong impressions about business, and increase their understanding of the local business community. Field trips are also important for motivating interest, socializing, building group morale, and providing group planning experiences. Any field trip should correlate directly with the topic being studied and supplement text discussions. If students are to realize the maximum values from an educational trip, the teacher and students should plan and evaluate the trip and capitalize on the experiences gained.

For successful field trips the teacher should be able to answer the following questions in the affirmative: Will the field trip contribute sufficiently to the students' understanding of the topic being studied to warrant the expenditure of time and effort? Has the field trip been cleared with the administration; and if required, have signed consent slips from parents been obtained? Does each member of the class clearly understand the purpose of the field trip? Have students assisted in the planning and arranging of the trip and been sufficiently prepared to take the trip? Have arrangements been made with the business concerning the objectives of the trip, what is to be seen and done, time of arrival, and length of the tour? Have provisions been made for possible stragglers (a "buddy system" can avoid students getting lost or left behind)? Have plans been made for an evaluation of the field trip—what students did, saw, learned, and should have done that was not done? Will a letter be sent to the appropriate person(s) expressing appreciation for the opportunity to take the tour?

Business forms and materials. In a local community there are many different business forms and materials available that can be useful in the business education program. Even though textbooks and workbooks usually contain examples of business forms, those used in local businesses should also be examined and discussed. The use of forms from local businesses acquaints students with a greater variety and provides familiarity with forms they will be using if they obtain jobs with local businesses. Samples of accounting forms, inventory cards, purchase orders, invoices, sales slips, statements, application blanks, legal forms, cancelled checks, charts, graphs, letterheads, and correspondence from local businesses serve as excellent teaching examples.

Descriptive and informative pamphlets, bulletins, and booklets containing information about products, services, industries, and companies are distributed by government agencies, labor unions, civic groups, businesses, and business organizations. Prepared displays relating to products and services that can be exhibited at the school are sometimes available. These displays and materials help provide students with a better understanding of local businesses and help make them more intelligent consumers. Local businesses are frequently able to secure films and filmstrips for school use and will, when appropriate, lend films and other materials they use in training programs.

The selection of business forms and materials to be used in the classroom should be based upon affirmative answers to the following questions: Do the business forms and materials help meet the teacher's objectives, justify the time and effort necessary to arrange for their use, and supplement educational audiovisual aids? Are the business forms and materials available when needed and in sufficient quantities? Have arrangements been made to safeguard borrowed materials and return them in good condition?

Work experiences. A well-coordinated work-experience program for advanced students is an excellent way to use the business community to supplement and enrich classroom laboratory experiences. Cooperative work-experience programs have benefits not only for students but for the teacher, the school, and the cooperating businesses as well. In addition, a number of other students may be working part time for businesses. Their on-the-job experiences can be used to illustrate business procedures, and classroom activities can often be coordinated to good advantage with their work experiences. With the cooperation of local businesses, teachers can arrange one-day on-the-job programs to acquaint students with actual business and office procedures. In this type of program the student may perform actual office work or may observe only and is usually not paid for his/her work.

To obtain maximum results from work experiences of students, the teacher should be able to answer each of the following questions in the affirmative: Does each group involved with the work-experience program understand its purposes and values and support it? Have the necessary legal requirements and administrative problems related to the work-experience program been worked out satisfactorily? Have reasonable standards been followed in the selection of student participants? Has each training station been selected according to established standards? Has each student been provided assistance in securing a job and written instructions concerning what is expected of him/her? Do cooperating employers understand the objectives of the work-experience program and what is expected of them? Has a plan for evaluating students been developed, and is it understood by all individuals involved in the process?

CONCLUSION

Textbooks, supplementary materials, and community resources constitute the basic instructional materials and aids through which content changes are implemented. Their significance to the teaching-learning process is exceeded only by the teacher. There is at present an abundance of instructional materials and aids as well as assurance of their continued development and availability for utilization in meeting the increasingly diverse needs of the school population. With this increase of instructional resources and diversity of student needs, the task of selecting those resources most appropriate for coping with each area of need is a never-ending challenge.

CHAPTER 12

Determining Facility and Equipment Needs

CLEO MATTOX

University of Arkansas, Little Rock

Effective business education instructional programs can be further enhanced by modern, up-to-date facilities and equipment. Students respond in a more positive manner when they are housed in an attractive department with current office machines and teaching aids. However, many business educators do not find themselves in an ideal teaching situation and frequently are asked to "make do" with what is available. When this occurs teachers must create the best learning atmosphere possible through effectively utilizing what they have, while at the same time beginning an analysis process to determine what is required for improving the facilities and equipment.

The determination of facility and equipment needs is complicated by many variables. A few of the factors entering into the decision process are available space, extent of financial support, size of the student body, and local setting of the school (urban or rural). What are the needs in a particular area? Generally, a larger school has more offerings, while a smaller school has fewer offerings—perhaps only two or three courses in business education. How many students will be taking courses in the department? In very small schools, there may be fewer than 50 students. Enrollment will affect the number and size of classrooms needed. What is the projected student population for the next 10 years? Long-range expectations must be considered as well as current needs. Where do the graduates go? How can the school keep its instruction current with changing economic practices and technology?

Business education departments usually offer programs in two areas of instruction—general and vocational. The school's curriculum should be a primary concern when planning a department to house the business education offerings. Each subject area has specific requirements that must be met for maximum effectiveness. Shorthand, accounting, and general business courses should be taught in an area with minimum noise to facilitate concentration. Typewriting and office machines courses should be in an acoustically treated room or area to avoid disturbing other classes.

FACILITY NEEDS

Facility planning should be thorough and involve input from others who are knowledgeable about current business happenings and training programs. One of the first steps might be to consult with faculty members from other districts who have recently been through a building or remodeling project. On-site school visits to observe the good features and shortcomings of their facilities might be helpful. Ideas should be gleaned from as many people as possible. Every member of the department should participate in the planning activities. Business men and women should be brought into the planning process whenever feasible. The department's advisory committee should, of course, assume a major role in the planning process.

In planning physical space requirements, some of the factors to be considered include the following:

Enrollment. What is the present enrollment? What has been the growth pattern during the past 10 years? What is the anticipated growth for the next 10 years?

Physical characteristics of the space. Has the number of current rooms presented problems? Is the square footage of each room adequate? Does the lighting meet recommended standards? How satisfactory is the heating and air conditioning equipment being used? Do the rooms have acoustical ceilings and floor covering that adequately absorb noise? How many electrical outlets are in the room? Is there at least one outlet per student station? Do the outlets meet safety standards? Are there sufficient outlets for audiovisual aids such as overhead or film projectors? Is the placement of outlets satisfactory? Is there a master electrical switch in the typewriting/machines area? Is the location of the student desks appropriate in areas where sunlight will be a factor? Does the number of student exits per room and their placement promote good traffic flow and ensure security?

It is important to have adequate storage space within the department. Cabinets, shelves, or counters can be used, depending upon the overall plan and area available. A small room which could be utilized as a storage and machine repair facility might be included in the master plan. This would enable service persons to make machine repairs even when classes are in session.

Attention must also be given to any constraints that might affect the space planned. Can the space allocation be expanded to meet growing needs? Do financial limitations necessitate less-than-ideal facilities? Are there administrative policies that mandate a certain minimum size class? What constraints are caused by scheduling problems and the size of the faculty?

Curriculum. A major factor in planning facilities is the school's curriculum. One of the most difficult tasks is providing a simulated office environment for vocational course offerings. A thorough knowledge about the job market for graduates is essential. Comprehensive surveys of entry-level jobs in both large and small businesses will assist in determining specific needs for the training programs. Frequent contacts with graduates to ascertain how adequate they feel the present training programs are and actual visits to work sites would be helpful. Interviewing personnel directors is also recommended. The information obtained through these activities should facilitate a review of the present curriculum to see what revisions, deletions, or additions of courses and instructional units might necessitate changes in physical facilities.

Classroom arrangement. For optimum teaching and learning, the visibility of the teacher by students and vice versa should be ensured. In courses that require a great deal of individual supervision by the instructor, quick and easy access to each student station is important. Another factor to consider in a classroom arrangement is the ease with which student materials can be distributed.

In planning facilities, consideration should be given to safeguarding training equipment and audiovisual aids. Placement of department offices and classrooms should be reviewed carefully to assure that maximum teacher supervision will occur at all times, particularly in the office machines areas. Exits and corridors should not be located in areas where expensive office machines are housed if it is desirable that only certain trainees operate the equipment.

Some schools are experimenting with open space departments or areas similar to those found in modern office complexes. There appear to be mixed reactions from educators relative to this type of classroom arrangement. Some instructors function quite well and like the open laboratory environment while others feel more comfortable in a traditional "closed" classroom. Both agree that placement of office machines within the department is an important factor to consider during the planning process. Efforts should be made to soundproof office machines instructional areas through the use of acoustical tile, carpeting, and drapes so that students are not distracted in adjacent instructional areas.

After determining basic room needs, detailed floor plans including furniture arrangements should be drawn to scale for each classroom. This step will bring out such points as:

Location, direction, and accessibility of student desks and chairs

Placement of teacher's desk

Allowed space for peripheral furniture such as storage and file cabinets, dictionary stand, bookcases, etc.

Allowance for aisle space to permit easy entrance and exit of students

Placement of lavatory if room is to be used for typewriting and reprographics

Arrangement of auxiliary equipment such as duplicating machines and related furniture

Location of bulletin boards

Location of a master switch in rooms having electrical equipment

Placement of receptacles for plugging in equipment.

Special consideration should be given to the selection of appropriate electrical outlets and their locations within the rooms. A variety of multiple-type receptacles may be used such as floor conduits, strip wall outlets, or power poles. Placement of the outlets should be based upon the planned arrangement of student desks, office equipment, audiovisual aids, etc. When the basic wiring is completed, the arrangement of furniture and instructional equipment tends to become permanent. Therefore, ample planning time should be given to this task.

Another item to consider is that each student area has specific facility requirements which must be met if effective instruction is to occur. As some of the rooms will probably be utilized for multiple course offerings, sufficient flexibility should exist within them to assure changes can be made with minimal effort. For example, bookkeeping students need adequate writing space for texts, practice sets, workbooks, etc. By planning a room large enough to accommodate L-shaped desks, the instructor assures that the facility can be readily adapted for clerical-secretarial offerings as well as bookkeeping courses.

The business education department should be in an area where the rooms are closely connected or accessible. The facilities in one area must be located in proper relationship to the other rooms to facilitate traffic flow, reduce noise and confusion, and complement program planning. There must be easy accessibility to supplies and equipment.

The needs of handicapped students must be considered in planning the facilities. Government regulations mandate certain accommodations for school age handicapped persons. Among the special features to consider are the accessibility of rooms to handicapped persons and the availability of desks that can be used by individuals who are confined to a wheelchair.

Since facilities will likely remain as they are for a long period of time, research should be done to ascertain the kinds of new office equipment and instructional aids that can be expected to be used in future course offerings. Plan the rooms, if possible, to accommodate these predicted changes in equipment and instructional aids.

Business education has a broader variety of subjects than English, history, or mathematics, and many of the course offerings cannot be housed in a typical general classroom. Because of the diversity of equipment, furniture, and teaching aids required for the various course offerings, planning must include careful analyses of these distinct requirements so that adequate facilities can be provided.

In summary, every effort should be made to design the facilities with some flexibility, ensuring that the floor space and room arrangements can be adjusted to future student and curriculum needs. Care should be given to assure that adequate lighting is available and proper acoustic materials are utilized. Color schemes must be planned so a harmonious environment exists throughout the department. Student safety is of paramount importance. Therefore, careful consideration should be given to student traffic flow patterns within the department, the location of electrical outlets, and the placement of equipment. Planning functional business education facilities is a complex task; hence, extensive research and study should be undertaken. Always remember to seek input from advisory council members and others who have expertise about current business trends and employer needs so that the final plan assures modern, up-to-date facilities for the instructional offerings.

EQUIPMENT NEEDS

Equipment utilized in business education courses should be similar to that found in up-to-date offices, and this can be determined through surveys of offices and through consultation with business education advisory committees. The use of new equipment in offices has been increasing at an escalating rate during the past three decades. Businesses have moved from manual typewriters and operational procedures to fully automated offices where such terms as word processing, data processing, reprographics, and micrographics are used to describe the many technological processes that have been incorporated into daily operations.

Although there is some office equipment that schools cannot afford because of its excessive cost, much of the new electronic hardware is within many local districts' financial capabilities. However, careful study and comparisons should be made before any equipment is acquired. Because office machines will be used by many different students, quality is essential if downtime is to be kept at a minimal level. Equipment must be maintained after it is procured. Hence, the availability of prompt repair service is another factor of utmost importance.

Before recommending specific equipment for the department, business educators must be thoroughly familiar with the various brands and models available. They should be knowledgeable about the advantages and limitations of each item of equipment and should be able to prepare detailed comparison sheets delineating these factors.

Equipment performance requirements in a school situation may vary from that of a business office, and this should be considered in the final analysis. Nevertheless, the most important single factor when selecting office machines is what the employers who hire the school's graduates use. Students trained on similar equipment have a better chance of acquiring employment and enter the world of work with specific skills which allow immediate productivity on the job.

Enrollment. When projecting equipment needs, business educators must rely upon anticipated or pre-enrollment data to determine the number of specific items of equipment required for effective instruction. Obviously, in beginning skill classes such as typing, each student will need his/her own machine as a battery method of instruction will no doubt be utilized. In other secondary business education courses, student-machine ratios can be established if a rotation plan of instruction is initiated. For example, it may be determined in a clerical training class that one calculator for every three students is sufficient or a transcriber for every four trainees might be adequate if a well organized machines rotation plan is utilized. Hence, being knowledgeable about current enrollment expectations and anticipated changes is an important facet in the equipment planning process.

Cost. With increasing inflationary costs and declining enrollments, secondary business educators in many local educational agencies are being asked each year to operate their department on fixed or declining budgetary allotments. Hence, it is extremely important that equipment cost analyses be done periodically. Teachers must know about initial equipment acquisition costs as well as anticipated maintenance and supply expenditures. They must be prepared to determine what the cost per trainee will be over the expected use of the machine. By determining this kind of detailed information, more realistic decisions about the desirability of acquiring specialty items of equipment can be formulated.

Because of the short learning time required to operate some office machines, it may be more economical to take field trips to businesses or display rooms set up by machine companies where students can be given hands-on training. Many businesses are willing to include on-the-job training experiences on copiers, data-entry machines, and other expensive hardware to business education co-op students as part of their on-site learning activities.

Another factor to be assessed carefully is the anticipated changes in equipment within the next ten-year period. Some office machines are being updated very rapidly, especially equipment utilized in word processing and data processing. It usually is not advisable to acquire a new machine until it has been proven and accepted in the business world, nor should a model that has been on the market for five or more years be purchased, particularly

EQUIPMENT INVENTORY AND PLANNING GUIDE—BUSINESS EDUCATION[1]

Course	Proposed For Grade Levels	Estimated Number of Students Who Will Be Enrolled	Total Number of Students Currently Enrolled
____Accounting			
____Secretarial Office Practice			
____Clerical Office Practice			
____Cooperative Office Education			
____Data Processing			
____Distributive Education			
____Office Machines			
____Shorthand			
____Typewriting			
____Word Processing			
____Other			

Identify classrooms used for the various subjects:

Rooms	Subjects	Number of Sections	Grade Levels	Approximate Yearly Enrollments

[1] Adapted from *Arkansas' Guide for Business Education.* Little Rock: Arkansas Department of Education, 1975. p. 41.

Equipment Used for Student Training	Number	Date of Purchase	Located in Room Number	Needed for Minimum Requirements	Acquisitions Planned for: 1st Year	2nd Year	3rd Year	4th Year	5th Year
Typewriters:									
Electric									
Manual									
Long Carriage									
Mag Card									
CRT									
Memory									
Electronic									
Other (specify)									
Calculators/adders:									
Printing									
Display									
Programmable									
Dictation/transcriber machine									
Transcription machine									
Bookkeeping machine									
Postage machine									
Check writing machine									
Offset printer									
Stencil duplicator									
Spirit duplicator									
Electronic stencil maker									
Folding machine									
Collator									
Photo copier									
Mimeoscope									
Overhead projector									
File cabinets									
Recorder:									
Tape									
Cassettes									
Other _____									
Shorthand lab (specify)									
Data processing equip. (specify)_____									

What kind of telephone equipment/facilities are used for student training? If none, what are future plans?

when new technological changes are expected that will drastically alter the operation and capabilities of the equipment.

A study should be made as to the various types of equipment acquisition plans that are available from the vendors. Based upon the current departmental budget and anticipated financial condition of the local district, decisions should be made whether to purchase, rent, or lease the desired items of equipment. Most lease agreements require company maintenance on the equipment as the vendor is interested in keeping the machine in good condition for possible resale. If it is expected that the equipment will be used for five or more years, the most economical method of acquisition usually is an outright purchase.

Specifications. Because of the complexity and variety of office equipment available, business educators are frequently asked to assist administrators in developing detailed written specifications for bidding purposes. It is essential that the desired machine features be clearly outlined in the specifications so that vendors and local board of education members know exactly what is wanted. For example, in preparing a bid description for an electronic memory typewriter, detailed information should be included about the machine dimensions, print element and ribbon cartridge, print speed, variety of typestyles, keyboard, pitch selector, line selector, central logic unit, electrical characteristics, memory storage, visual display, and

MISCELLANEOUS EQUIPMENT AND SUPPLIES FOR BUSINESS EDUCATION[2]

Equipment and Supplies	Kind of Classroom			
	Typewriting	Shorthand	Accounting	Machines or Laboratory
Desks/tables	*	*	*	*
Posture chairs	*	*		*
Filing trays	*	*		*
Teacher's desk	*	*	*	*
Wastebaskets	*	*	*	*
Pencil sharpener	*	*	*	*
Overhead projectors	*	*	*	*
Transparencies	*	*	*	*
Bulletin board	*	*	*	*
Stapler	*	*	*	*
Record player	*	*		*
Tape recorder	*	*	*	*
Cassette player	*	*	*	*
Tapes	*	*	*	*
Dictionaries	*	*	*	*
Wall charts	*		*	*
Paper cutter	*	*		*
Secretarial handbooks	*	*		*
Copyholders	*	*		*
Demonstration stand	*	*		*
Stop watch		*		
Interval timer	*			*
Carbon paper	*	*		*
Art typing	*			*
Dial-a-Rate	*			
Certificates of award	*	*	*	
Flash cards		*		
Sten-O-Grader		*		
Stencil file cabinet	*			*

[2]Adapted from *Arkansas' Guide for Business Education.* Little Rock: Arkansas Department of Education, 1975. p. 55.

other automatic features pertaining to line justification, title centering, column layout, decimal tabulation, etc.

The bid specification should not only contain a thorough description of the desired items of equipment, but it should also request information from vendors about guarantees, maintenance contracts, single-call service agreements, and the availability of quick service. If local maintenance is not available or the company will not provide replacement machines while malfunctioning equipment is under repair, excessive downtime may result which would adversely affect the instructional offerings.

In requesting vendor price quotations, make certain that all possible acquisition plans are described in the bid. Prices should be acquired for outright purchase, lease-purchase plans, or rental agreements. Vendors should also be asked about the normal useful life of the equipment and anticipated technological changes that would cause obsolescence. All of these factors should be considered carefully before items of equipment are selected and methods of acquisition are determined.

MAJOR EQUIPMENT AND SUPPLIES FOR BUSINESS EDUCATION[3]

Equipment and Supplies	Kind of Classroom			
	Typewriting	Shorthand	Accounting	Machines or Laboratory
Typewriter— Manual	*	*		*
Typewriter— Electric carbon ribbon	*	*		*
Typewriter— Electric fabric ribbon	*	*		*
Typewriter— Automatic or magnetic keyboard				*
Typewriter— Long carriage	*			*
Pacer	*			
Shorthand lab		*		
Bookkeeping/billing machines			*	*
Display calculator			*	*
Printing calculator			*	*
Computers				*
Copy machine	*			*
Dictating/transcribing machine	*	*		*
Fluid duplicating machine	*			*
Offset duplicating machine	*			*
Stencil duplicating machine	*			*
Data-entry machines				*
Telephone equipment				*
Mimeoscope				*
Collator	*			*

[3]Adapted from *Arkansas' Guide for Business Education.* Little Rock: Arkansas Department of Education, 1975. p. 57.

Compatibility. If it is important that new items of equipment are similar in operation to other office machines within the department and that existing supplies and teaching aids be used, make certain that close scrutiny is given to catalog descriptions and manuals of operation. Too frequently, adding machines and printing calculators are purchased before determining what size paper tape or kinds of ribbons are required, thus necessitating that specific supplies be acquired for those machines. This prevents volume buying and increases departmental expenditures.

Other considerations. Despite the ease of instruction facilitated by having one brand of typewriter, most secondary business educators believe that since students may be exposed to several kinds of typewriters in the world of work it is advisable to have more than one brand in the classroom, particularly in the vocational training courses. However, when several brands of machines are used, dual service contracts are usually required which increase maintenance costs for the department. Because of these additional costs, many local districts are selecting only one brand of machine based upon input from its advisory committee, the availability of reliable vendors, and the cost of service agreements.

While the cost of most office machines has increased dramatically, electronic display and printing calculators have declined in price. These machines have become less expensive each year primarily because of a greater use of electronic technology. Although printing calculators are more expensive than display units, most business educators prefer these types of machines for classroom use. The paper tapes generated allow students to reexamine their work and permit instructors to analyze errors that are made.

There have been many changes during the past few years in dictating/transcribing equipment. Suppliers have moved from tapes and belts as recording devices to discs and cassettes. It appears that most major office machines manufacturers are now utilizing various sizes of cassettes for recording input. Because cassettes are relatively inexpensive and available through different sources, many business educators prefer cassette designed dictating/transcribing equipment.

Generally, buying new equipment is preferable to acquiring used office machines. New equipment will last longer and not become obsolete so quickly. However, should a decision be made to expend funds for used equipment, care must be exercised not to purchase discontinued models of equipment as their value usually declines rapidly while maintenance costs escalate. Before accepting any equipment that is being discarded by firms, careful study should be given concerning the employment potential for trainees on that specific office machine, time required to produce efficient machine operators, and cost of supplies and machine upkeep. Too frequently, maintenance expenditures and declining employment potential offset the fact that the equipment is made available without charge or for a minimal setup cost.

It is important that a systematic replacement plan for equipment be worked out to avoid excessive cost in any one year. Business educators should keep a comprehensive inventory of equipment and supplies by using an index card system or inventory sheets. Records delineating service calls, expenditures, and downtime on each machine should be maintained so that malfunctioning equipment can be traded or discarded as soon as possible. If adequate records are kept showing all maintenance costs and depreciation, often administrators can be convinced that a planned equipment replacement program actually saves the district money and assures that up-to-date equipment is available for student trainees.

The equipment inventory and planning guide shown on the following pages was published in *Arkansas' Guide for Business Education.* A few changes were made in the guide, but it is basically the one suggested for business teachers in Arkansas. Because business office needs and practices are similar elsewhere in the nation, the suggested equipment and supplies list can probably be used as a basic planning document for most business education departments.

A crucial element in equipment planning and acquisition is to have in classrooms those machines and supplies which graduates will encounter in the world of work. Recent technological advances have provided new equipment which enables business personnel to speed up administrative and clerical procedures, cut expenditures, and produce ·more effective and attractive business correspondence and records. In little more than a generation, offices have gone from a few standard typewriters and a handcranked adding machine to the marvels of electronic hardware. Every year more efficient equipment is introduced and put into use within the business world. Business educators through careful and farsighted planning can ensure that their programs are preparing graduates for entry-level positions in the challenging world of business.

CHAPTER 13

Choosing Various Instructional Methods
To Teach Skills, Knowledges, and Attitudes

THADYS DEWAR

East Carolina University, Greenville, North Carolina

Before a business teacher can choose an appropriate instructional method for teaching skills, knowledges, and attitudes, that teacher must consider the nature of the content to be taught in each given situation. The teacher must classify the specific objectives to be met into one of three categories—cognitive, psychomotor, or affective domain—and select a method that will best achieve the designated objectives, realizing that not only the learning style of the individual but the nature of the subject matter will, to a large extent, govern the choice of a method.

An understanding of the various alternatives available to the teacher is also necessary. No longer can the traditional approach be accepted as the one best approach. It must be weighed as one alternative among many. Or perhaps a combination of different methods, materials, or media would be the right choice. The proper mix of materials, media, and methods will generally produce more satisfactory results than instructional strategies that utilize a single method or medium.

No doubt, every teacher of business subjects has used what he or she termed a "successful method or device" for teaching. But how does one measure success in teaching? With today's emphasis on educational accountability, there must certainly be some evidence of the learner's having attained a level of competency based on the pre-established objectives. Performance criteria must be used to measure not only cognitive and psychomotor behavior but also to measure change in attitudes. Teacher educators should conduct and/or encourage creative research and use research findings. It is the responsibility of each business teacher to dream, to experiment, to design ways of enriching instruction so as to provide each learner a chance to experience his highest level of success.

Experience tells us that the teacher's knowledge of an innovation strongly influences the teacher's willingness to implement that innovation. It is, therefore, imperative that every teacher of business subjects be constantly alert to major content changes and effective innovative ideas for instruction, and be willing to experiment with new teaching ideas. Each teacher should realize that the strictly traditional methods of teaching used today are the result of someone's imagination, resourcefulness, and productivity in the past. Just as yesterday's educators conceived, designed, and implemented certain educational practices that are employed in schools today, so may today's teachers create and implement successful educational practices for tomorrow's schools. Sooner or later, all nontraditional methods cease to be nontraditional. They either become traditional or are discarded.

Business education subjects are readily adaptable to the innovative methods of learning, and many business teachers are introducing and using nontraditional approaches with success. In the pages that follow, a number of alternative methods of teaching business subjects, both traditional and nontraditional, are considered. Even though there are no research results to support the use of some of the techniques and strategies, there are strong proponents of each idea.

Before specific methods and/or techniques are presented, however, a comment should be made about the most important factor in learner success, no matter what the method—the teacher. Even the most widely acclaimed method can be catastrophic in the hands of a disinterested, inefficient teacher. Business education—as well as other subject areas—needs more truly dedicated teachers, teachers who look upon teaching as an exciting, challenging, and rewarding career rather than "just a job." The teacher is, indeed, the major influence upon learning in the classroom and, as such, is in a position to determine what is to be learned at any time, how it is to be taught, what kind of activities are to be engaged in by the students, and how outcomes are to be evaluated. Business teachers can assume a leadership role in strengthening the educational process by giving careful consideration to the various alternative methods of teaching, creating new ones as the opportunities are open to them. The subject demands up-to-date methods and effective implementation.

SIMULATION

For a long time, business teachers have been giving serious consideration to the vocational demands of the business world and have been attempting to teach the skills, knowledges, and attitudes necessary for students to secure gainful employment in the business world and to be wise consumers of goods and services. Recently, however, much attention has been given to providing even more realism in the classroom by including additional experiences that simulate actual work situations.

Any attempt to link classroom content to the business world by incorporating more realistic experiences for the students might be considered a simulated activity. In the typing classroom, the simulated business experience might begin when the typing teacher assigns letters or reports to be typed instead of straight-copy material. In the basic business class, realistic experiences might be provided through the use of mock trials, case problems, role-playing situations, or games. Practice sets have long been used in bookkeeping/accounting classrooms and are used quite extensively in the office practice classroom. As the trend toward providing more realistic experiences in the business classroom continues to grow, simulation becomes a more viable method of teaching to meet student needs. In the discussion that follows, various ideas for incorporating simulated activities into different

143

business classes are presented. Business teachers need not be reluctant to experiment, because any business class holds potential for the effective use of simulated activities. Though simulation may not always be the answer, the wise teacher will consider it among the alternative methods of teaching.

Although simulations can be effectively used in any business class, they are perhaps more widely used in secretarial/clerical classes. Once the typing students have gained experience typing letters and reports, the teacher adds more realism by having them take production tests consisting of business letters or forms to be typed within a given period of time.

Considering the fact that composition at the typewriter is deemed to be the third most-used activity in the business office, business teachers should use every opportunity to teach students to compose at the typewriter. Not only will the acquisition of this skill enable office workers to increase office productivity, but it will also prepare students for the time when, according to some experts, a typewriter keyboard on the desks of management personnel will be considered essential. The typewriter keyboard will be needed for composing at the typewriter and for interacting with a computer to call up needed documents and reports.

Using findings from two recent studies about a composition emphasis in beginning typewriting, Robert E. Gades and Barbara Dougal report that the composition approach during the first semester of typing is an effective method for developing speed in composing at the typewriter. In the experiment, the students who learned typing using a composition approach typed straight-copy materials as fast as those who learned using a noncomposition approach. They also had significantly fewer errors on straight-copy timings than those who learned typing using a more traditional approach. These authors report that a composition emphasis is not an effective method during the second semester of typing.

Other efforts at providing more realistic experiences for office training include the use of task simulations, integrated exercises, job simulations, and LAP's (Learning Activity Packages). More extensive treatment is given to these teaching methods in the section devoted to cooperative education.

A discussion of simulated training for office work would be incomplete without some reference to the use of in-basket exercises. In-baskets, by replicating the form and content of actual business documents, give students a chance to make decisions regarding what to do with the typical business documents that are received daily, how to do what needs to be done, and the order in which they should do it. Obviously, the use of in-baskets is increasing because it provides an opportunity for students to experience in an educational laboratory setting certain aspects of the world of work that they would otherwise not experience until actual employment, which sometimes is too late.

A summary of recent research conducted by Stamps and reported by Dean R. Malsbary shows that the in-basket exercise method of instruction is a better method of teaching production typewriting skills than the traditional textbook method. He found that the traditional textbook method restricts decision-making skills to the mechanics of the tasks.

144

Other business classes in which simulation can be used effectively are bookkeeping/accounting, introduction to business, marketing, business law, business management, consumer economics, and communications. Gordon W. Brown considers role playing a "natural" for teaching business and consumer law. He concludes that students enjoy acting out lifelike situations and that their participation in a role-playing situation helps them remember what they have learned. Other advantages cited by teachers include fun in learning, attitudinal changes, involvement of quiet and shy students, and utilization of current subject matter.

A variation of the role-playing methodology is the use of the mock trial. The mock trial is usually developed for a business law class, and teachers claim that students have lasting memory of the trials and the applicable points of law. In marketing classes, role playing can be effectively used to teach the proper techniques to be used in sales presentations.

Because business managers have voiced concern that young people entering the business world today are not adept at problem solving, the use of cases for instructional purposes is gaining acceptance. As in actual practice, students are required to identify, from the bulk of information given, the basic principles upon which decisions are to be made. The case-study method has been proven an effective method in transmitting values as well as knowledge.

A type of simulation that has been effectively used in bookkeeping/accounting classes for many years is the practice set. Through the use of the practice set, students are able to see how each phase of accounting fits into the total accounting function. In bookkeeping/accounting, students are given an opportunity to reinforce their learning by completing exercises and projects that require them to apply the theoretical principles that have been learned. The practice set can be used in other business classes as well as in bookkeeping/accounting.

An outgrowth of the case problem approach to learning is the games approach, which is rapidly receiving recognition at all levels of business education. To stress this point, Robert L. Jacobson, in a recent article in *The Chronicle of Higher Education*, says, "Give some professors a pair of dice, poker chips, and some old golf tees and they are ready for the classroom."[1] In his description of game players and game designers of the academic world, Jacobson explains that the game players and game designers admit that what they do is "fun," but they also do it because they sincerely believe that some of the most effective learning takes place when students get a chance to act out what they are studying in a game or special environment designed to simulate a part of the real world.

According to current literature, games are used at all educational levels and range from the very simple to the complex. While there does not seem to be any conclusive evidence that the use of games leads to better acquisition of cognitive skills, there are many enthusiastic proponents of instructional gaming, and many of the academic gamers predict that an educational

---

[1]Jacobson, Robert L. "Teaching with Games." *The Chronicle of Higher Education* 19:1, 19; November 26, 1979.

revolution could be in the making because of the tremendous potential of the gaming concepts. The fact that there is no concrete evidence that the more traditional methods and techniques are superior to the gaming method may be construed as evidence that the gaming method is a worthwhile alternative.

There is ample evidence that business teachers have been using competitive games in business classes for many years. Many teachers are firmly convinced that games provide motivation for the students and help to build better attitudes toward school work. Crossword puzzles, bingo, tic-tac-toe, and various adaptations of television games such as Concentration are examples of competitive games that are used in business classes. Most of these games are designed to reward students for their ability to recall facts previously presented, thereby serving as a review for them.

The business games that account for much of the recent surge in the popularity of the gaming concept of teaching are those which simulate problem-solving and decision-making activities that go on in business. Advocates of these problem-solving techniques and activities tell us that they provide an opportunity for students to put theory into practice, stimulate interest in the subject, and change the classroom environment from a dull, monotonous one to one that is vibrant and exciting. Teachers who have used the decision-making games indicate they are very effective in management, economics, business law, and accounting courses. Computerized business games are being used rather extensively at both the high school and college level, and it appears that enthusiasm for this approach to teaching continues to grow.

Perhaps the most comprehensive effort to bring realism into the business classroom is that which is exhibited in the model office concept of teaching. Model office simulations are being used successfully in many high schools and, on a more limited scale, in four-year college business programs. To implement the model office concept, the teacher must be willing to spend many extra hours planning the office layout, organizing the materials, arranging the furniture and equipment, and preparing for the on-going office operation. Based on comments by students who have participated in a model office simulation program and teachers who have used this method of teaching, however, the rewards are worth the effort.

The simulated model office provides excellent opportunities for students to get the feel of the real office and to conduct business as it is done in the business world. Once the teacher has determined that the established objectives can best be met by utilizing the model office concept of teaching, he or she can either create a model office or adapt one of the commercially prepared packages to the needs of the students.

The technique employed when the model office idea is used is to place students in a reproduced, real-life situation and have them carry out office operations by completing tasks required in each job assignment. The input from customers provides a full cycle of work flow, beginning with the purchase of goods or request for service and continuing through the different departments until the orders are filled, payment has been received, deposits

146

have been made, and the bank statement has been received and reconciled. In addition, administrative and clerical activities must be completed.

In one particular case, a commercially prepared package provides the input and suggests the basic organizational structure for the arrangement of the office, while additional office experiences are provided for through the addition of a telephone switchboard that connects the various departments, a time clock, a word processing center, and a centralized dictation system that connects each department to the word processing center. Additional positions created for the purpose of teaching the word processing concept are the correspondence secretary position and the administrative secretary position. In the word processing center, there is a magnetic card selectric typewriter and the IBM 60 typewriter. As students learn about word processing, they are provided opportunities to refine their communications skills by composing and dictating letters and memos, typing business letters and forms, proofreading correspondence that has been typed, and judging communications for mailability.

The extent to which the simulated office can bring realism into the classroom is limited only by the imagination of the teacher. The preparation of the payroll can be expanded to include such deductions as group insurance premiums, savings, and charitable contributions, in addition to the usual FICA and income tax deductions. Before the extra items are added to the list of payroll deductions, certain individuals can be assigned to study different types of insurance coverage or different savings plans and make reports to the employees so that the employees themselves can approve or reject them.

By working in the simulated office, students are able to see the practical use of such forms and records as balance sheets, income statements, sales analysis reports, inventory records, and journals and ledgers. Actual figures are used in the determination of net profit. Through the use of realistic figures, students are better able to understand how the cost of goods sold is figured, how inventory affects business operations, and how to increase net profit by reducing operating expenses. The people who work with sales have an excellent opportunity to prepare advertising, conduct sales campaigns, and develop marketing strategy in order to increase the volume of sales. With a telephone system connecting the different departments and the outside world, students can be taught the proper telephone response for both the inside call and the outside call.

One of the greatest benefits that the model office offers is in the area of human relations. While some attempt should be made to equalize work loads, the employees should realize that each person has a responsibility to assume his or her share of the load. This realization should bring with it an understanding that, in certain circumstances, the most valuable employees are those who are willing to "go beyond the call of duty" for the sake of the company.

Obviously, the model office concept should be used in high school in a capstone business course. The block courses provide an excellent opportunity to incorporate such training into the program. The model office idea can accommodate students with different levels of ability as well as students with varied vocational interests. Students who take shorthand can be assigned to jobs that involve the use of shorthand dictation while those interested in accounting can obtain realistic experience by working in the accounting department.

In a recent article on research for business teachers, Dean R. Malsbary reported on Edward G. Thomas's study of three approaches to the teaching of office practice at the secondary level. The three approaches included in the study were the cooperative approach involving coordinated work-study experiences, the simulated office practice class in which simulated office experiences are used alternately with traditional teaching-learning experiences, and the model office which involves extensive simulation on a daily basis for the entire school year and in which students are employed in positions within a company. Thomas concluded that the office practice course has a positive impact on student's knowledge and attitudes and that the three frequently used approaches are equally effective methods of teaching.

To get a fair idea of the expansion of the simulation and gaming concept of teaching specific knowledges, skills, and attitudes, one need only consider the sizable body of literature that has recently been published on the subject. A ten-year bibliography recently published by the ERIC Clearinghouse on Teacher Education contains approximately 1,600 entries on games and simulations in 70 different categories. Considering the acclaimed merits of the use of simulated experiences in the business classroom, one might readily agree with the suggestion made by many business teachers that the route of simulation may be the way to go.

COOPERATIVE EDUCATION — WORK-STUDY EXPERIENCE

Closely related to the concept of using simulated activities to teach knowledges, skills, and attitudes needed by students to competently enter the world of work is the cooperative education method of teaching. While simulation provides a certain degree of realism, cooperative education gets the students one step closer to the real world by having them engage in a school and work program in which the student-learners receive supervised work experience as part of the school curriculum. Through a cooperative arrangement between the school and business employers, the student spends a part of the day in school and part at a training station (business firm) and is paid for his/her services.

The objectives of the cooperative programs are:

1. Occupational orientation and job counseling, together with related instruction in school

2. Coordination of school and work activities through job visitations by the teacher-coordinator

3. The systematic progression of skills and techniques through a definite pattern of learning experiences on the job

4. Cooperative school and employer development of appropriate classroom work and job experiences

5. School credit for combined employment training and related schoolwork.

Since the passage of the Vocational Education Act of 1963 and the succeeding amendments, cooperative education has received an increased emphasis in vocational education. The cooperative education program at the high school level is designed for senior students who have specific vocational career objectives. On the job, the student is supervised by the teacher-coordinator from the school and by a job sponsor from the business where he/she is training. The teacher-coordinator makes frequent visits to the cooperating business to evaluate the student's work and to plan meaningful learning experiences for the trainee. These visits to the business community by the coordinator enable the teacher-coordinator to provide more pertinent classroom instruction in the related class as well as in other business classes.

At the college level, cooperative education offers students the opportunity to alternate periods of academic study with periods of off-campus employment related to the students' academic majors or career goals. The program represents a working partnership in which students, faculty, and staff join with public and private employers in a structured relationship which provides benefits to all participants. The increased importance of occupational work experience in education is being recognized, and the cooperative education program serves to bridge the gap between in-school training and the world of work.

Many educators are predicting phenomenal growth of the cooperative education method of providing appropriate instruction for students in the 1980's. Congress has cited cooperative education as a priority area in recent legislation. Cooperative education may be referred to as a "sleeping giant" because of its tremendous potential in the training of today's youth for the future.

In a recent issue of *The Chronicle of Higher Education*, William M. Birenbaum, president of Antioch University, expressed the opinion that the establishment of a relationship between formal education and problem-solving areas in the world of work has never been more vital than now and that further development of such a relationship through cooperative and internship programs is essential. Educators should grasp the opportunity to combine their human talents with the sophisticated technology that is available to enhance the process of training students for the world of work. Applied learning gained through the professional work experience, integrated with related classroom performance, supplements and reinforces the academic content of any curriculum.

Arthur Eidson, an East Carolina University philosophy major who completed his cooperative education experience by working in Senator Robert Morgan's office in Washington, D.C., said, "Learning in a real-life situation offers experiences which would be almost impossible to simulate in the university classroom. The opportunity to serve with Senator Morgan and his staff has provided invaluable insight into the American political system." Ann Holland, a business education major who worked with the Social Security Administration in Gastonia, North Carolina, writes, "This job increased my self-confidence and added many experiences to my personal development. I was very satisfied with the experience and plan to make this type of work my career."

Listed below are some of the major advantages of cooperative education to the student:

1. Coordination of work and study increases student motivation.
2. Theory and practice are more closely integrated and the student finds greater meaning in his or her studies.
3. The student in cooperative education develops greater skills in human relations.
4. Work experience contributes to a greater sense of responsibility.
5. Cooperative education helps to orient the student to the world of work.
6. The student's earnings contribute to financing his or her own education.
7. The student usually experiences a smoother transition into full-time employment because of the undergraduate experience.

Since one purpose of the cooperative education program is to orient students to the world of work, the program should be built on a competency base. While space does not permit a full treatment of the subject, some of the most significant techniques and procedures to be followed in initiating and conducting a competency-based program are discussed below.

The cooperative vocational education program must be based on the needs of students, as determined from information relating to the career objectives of and personal qualifications of students. Certainly, cooperative education will prove to be unsatisfactory if it fails to meet the specific needs of the students. Continuous and careful planning is required if the potential of cooperative education is to be realized as a viable alternative of providing instruction. The basic components of the coordination effort are the career objectives of students, in-school instruction related to paid on-the-job work experience, and youth club activities.

In order to assure the best career results for students, care must be exercised in the selection of a training station for the on-the-job work experience. The cooperating employer (the training sponsor) may not have the same perception of the goals of the cooperative education program as the student or the teacher-coordinator. Although the employer's main goal in hiring is to earn a fair profit for the firm, that employer, by agreeing to participate in the cooperative education program, assumes some responsibility for helping the student-trainee acquire needed competencies. A good way for the teacher-coordinator to ensure that competency-based education becomes a part of the cooperative education experience is to specify, in the training agreement, the competencies that are to be developed and indicate the employer's contribution to the development of such competencies.

The training plan is a very significant part of the cooperative education instructional method of teaching skills, knowledges, and attitudes. Both the teacher-coordinator and the employer must give careful consideration to its preparation. The employer needs to be aware of the competencies required for the tasks that the student-trainee must perform and his or her role in the development or refinement of those competencies. The teacher-coordinator must also use job descriptions and task analyses to assist in planning appropriate classroom experiences for the student-trainees. It is important that task performance be taught in small segments. In the classroom, job skills can be developed or refined by using integrated exercises, task simulations, job simulations, LAP's, or a combination of these methods.

Learning activity packages can be developed by the teacher, or they may be purchased from commercial sources. Activities included in the learning activity packages should be matched to the student's interests and ability level.

An exchange of visits by the teacher-coordinator to the training station and the employer to the classroom, whenever possible, should serve to strengthen the employer's role in the training process. It is recommended that the schedule of training experiences be attached to the training agreement with the employer. The experienced coordinator is acutely aware of the fact that each student-trainee has different needs which must be met if the program is to be successful.

The individual components of a successful cooperative education training program do not automatically fall together into a perfect pattern. Careful planning must be done, and special consideration must be given to each aspect of the program. As is true with any instructional method, the teacher is the component that determines its success or failure. Nowhere is this more true than in the operation of a strong cooperative education program. If the cooperative method is to be successful, the teacher must be totally committed to its worth and willing to expend the effort necessary for it to succeed. Certainly it is a *viable* alternative for the business teacher to consider.

YOUTH GROUP PROJECTS

In most schools, a youth club program is an integral part of the cooperative vocational education program. Because the activities promoted by the youth organization provide opportunities for the students to demonstrate and refine competencies required in their respective occupational areas, all vocational education students are encouraged to join the club and participate in its program. Some states have one club for all cooperative vocational education students while other states have clubs for each program field or area. Vocational/occupational student organizations are fostered by professional associations and by agencies of government at federal and state levels. State educational agencies usually encourage student organizations and provide help for teachers who wish to organize new chapters. In most situations, the advisor of a local student organization is the teacher-coordinator of a cooperative program.

Among the youth organizations to which students aspiring to careers in business may belong are Distributive Education Clubs of America, Future Business Leaders of America—Phi Beta Lambda, and Office Education Association. All of these organizations have both secondary and postsecondary divisions.

Some of the general purposes of the youth organizations are as follows:

1. To assist students in establishing occupational goals
2. To develop leadership ability
3. To provide students more confidence in their own ability
4. To stimulate more interest in understanding American business enterprise
5. To encourage members to develop individual projects which contribute to the development of job competency and the welfare of the business community
6. To develop character, foster patriotism, and prepare students for useful citizenship
7. To encourage efficient money management
8. To assist students in making the transition from school to work
9. To foster liaison between student, school, and community
10. To encourage business leaders to support business education by providing training stations and participating in other supporting activities.

In addition to promoting membership among cooperative vocational education students, the advisor correlates the activities of the club with the vocational education program and seeks to assure that the club activities assist in achieving the goals of the individuals and the vocational program as a whole. Involvement in local, state, and national activities is strongly encouraged. Members' participation in competitive events at local, state, and national meetings serves to motivate students to work more diligently on the development of competencies in specified areas. Future Business Leaders of America—Phi Beta Lambda competition is held in almost every phase of business education including accounting, economics, general business, business law, secretarial skills, parliamentary skills, and many more. Distributive Education Clubs of America competitive events provide opportunities for students to demonstrate competencies across the broad competency areas, thus serving as culminating experiences which grow out of the instructional program. These events provide realistic evaluation of learning as well as awards and recognition for student participation and achievement. Competitive events for Office Education Association include those involving vocational skills and personal development and leadership contests.

To accomplish their established goals, these student youth groups participate in meaningful school and community projects. Some examples of worthwhile projects that students take part in are conducting surveys for the chamber of commerce for a town or city, participating in fund-raising drives for charitable organizations, securing speakers from the business community for club programs, engaging in simple research projects to find out what is going on in the business world concerning the kinds of equipment used, the organization of the work areas, the kinds of records management systems in use, the qualifications that employers look for in employees, etc. In many cases, the club members assume the responsibility for operating the school store. All of these projects serve to tie the classroom to the community and to the world of work.

A very worthwhile project initiated by Future Business Leaders of America—Phi Beta Lambda is called "Project Awareness." This project was started to familiarize business students with America's free enterprise system and to help them understand the competitive economic society. Learning packets on the free enterprise system are distributed to local FBLA and Phi Beta Lambda chapters. As a result of this endeavor, billboards promoting the idea of free enterprise have gone up across the country, and many business firms have shown an interest in the project by providing support in various ways.

Projects, both individual and group, provide students the opportunity to participate in related experiences, both simulated and real, which lead to the accomplishment of their educational and occupational objectives. Oftentimes, students who are not involved in regularly scheduled cooperative employment develop predetermined competencies through their participation in an assigned project.

Many advisors for youth groups have testified that students have definitely been motivated and developed a spirit of group loyalty through participation in organization activities. Some teachers believe that student youth organizations are as important as related classes and training stations. Surely the merits of youth group projects and activities justify the inclusion of these options in the list of alternative methods to be considered for providing instruction for business students.

MISCELLANEOUS METHODS AND TECHNIQUES AS ALTERNATIVES

Among the various instructional methods of teaching business subjects that a business teacher might consider are the following (in alphabetical order): brainstorming, business games (including computer-assisted instruction), buzz session, case study, committee, conference, contest, cooperative education, debate, demonstration, dialogue, discussion, dramatization, drill, field trip, guided discovery, lecture, panel, problem solving, programmed instruction, project, question and answer, reading, report, resource speaker, role playing, seminar, self-analysis and evaluation, simulation, skit, student tutor, team teaching, and creative writing. Because of the increased attention that educators are giving to some of the more recently introduced methods of instruction, most of this chapter is devoted to a discussion of simulation, cooperative education, and youth group projects. Others are considered to be "traditional" methods and are already familiar to the business teacher. Still others occupy an "in-between" position and perhaps do not fit into either category. A brief discussion of some of these techniques is included in the remaining part of the chapter. In addition, comments and suggestions that might be helpful to a teacher regardless of the method being used are included in the discussion.

Generally speaking, many of the instructional methods that are being advocated today are those that promote active student participation in the instructional process. While there are some teachers who still prefer a teacher-centered (lecture) approach to teaching, many are suggesting that teachers move the students to center stage and get them involved. This suggestion simply gives reinforcement to the idea that all instruction should be centered around the student, a concept that has resulted in more extensive utilization of individualized strategies.

While it is true that the concept of programmed instruction has, in some cases, been abused, individualized instruction or programmed learning is being used effectively in many business classrooms, and predictions are that this method of instruction will experience considerable growth in the future and will be instrumental in helping individuals meet the demands for competent workers. The individualized approach to teaching certain business subjects seems to be feasible and appropriate. The primary difference between individualized instruction and the traditional methods is that it removes the restrictions of time and space that have been imposed by the latter. It permits mastery learning regardless of the time required to reach the mastery level. Business teachers must recognize its merits and become innovative vanguards of teaching by adapting and combining teaching strategies in such a way that the best of several methods might be employed to "hit a new high" in effective instructional methodology.

An innovative adaptation of the individualized instruction concept that is rapidly being integrated into instructional programs at all educational levels is computer-assisted instruction. The application of the computer to the educational process has resulted in a variety of instructional techniques never before possible in schools. The computer can be programmed to present instructional material to the student and then analyze the student's performance based on a previously established criterion. As a criterion is reached for each objective, the student is allowed to proceed to the next objective. Because of the computer's capability to analyze vast amounts of data in a very short time, it has made a reality of the individualization of instruction. It appears that a new application of computer-assisted instruction is initiated almost every day, and possibilities for future adaptations seem unlimited. Computer-assisted instruction is being successfully used in the teaching of typing, business mathematics, business law, business English, accounting, economics, marketing, shorthand, and other subjects. In the discussion of games and simulations as an alternative method of teaching, it is noted that the use of the computer has resulted in extensive use of the gaming concept.

Mr. Branscomb of International Business Machines Corporation says that, in the United States, computer-assisted instruction has been adopted more readily by industry than by educational institutions. Some 10,000 employees of International Business Machines Corporation's engineering division, which deals with maintenance of data processing equipment, spend 90,000 student-days per year taking computer-aided courses at their offices. He indicates that just the savings resulting from avoiding the travel expense and per diem cost associated with a more traditional classroom approach exceed the cost of the data processing equipment by a considerable margin. Mr. Branscomb says:

If computers, communications, and electronics can bring educational services into the home, office, and factory, if they can make education more gratifying and less threatening, if they can greatly increase access to education without increasing its costs, then the evident need and the emerging capabilities will reinforce each other and a new plateau in our national life might be achieved.[2]

To attempt to select a teaching method without giving some consideration to present-day technology would be unrealistic. Modern technology has changed the office and the business world in general, and business teaching must reflect these changes. It is predicted that the school environment of the twenty-first century will be a center of electronic marvels. Even today, teachers are able to greatly enhance the instructional process through the use of educational media ranging from the chalkboard to books, maps, films, filmstrips, slides, videotape, cassettes, television sets, text-editing equipment, the electronic chalkboard, and the computer. For the business teacher, the challenge is to recognize the potential inherent in various media and integrate them into the teaching-learning process. A survey of the literature on instructional methods suggests that many business teachers are experimenting successfully with integrating media usage into the instructional process.

One teacher advocates the use of cassette tapes on a rather broad scale in the teaching of business subjects and suggests ways in which they might be used effectively. Another tells of success in the use of the videorecorder for teaching typewriting. A multimedia system for teaching typing is used by another business teacher. In a particular school, bookkeeping/accounting instruction is enhanced by the use of the overhead projector. A business teacher uses the electronic calculator to teach flowcharting. These are just a few of the examples of media usage that typify what creative business teachers are doing in an effort to combine media and methods to make the teaching/learning process more effective for all students.

SUMMARY

The task of selecting appropriate instructional methods to teach attitudes, skills, and knowledges in the business classroom is challenging. The trend toward choosing instructional techniques and procedures that provide more realistic business experiences in the classrom is growing. There is more emphasis on individualized instruction and learning systems. Modern technology is changing the educational environment and enabling teachers and students to do things that, in the past, have been impossible to accomplish. The challenge is to effectively combine media, materials, and methods in such a way that the specific learning goals will be achieved. In the final analysis, the choices that the business teacher makes will have to prove their validity by the effectiveness of the learning outcomes in meeting the needs of the individual, the business world, and society in general.

---

[2]Birenbaum, William M. "Forward to the Basics." *The Chronicle of Higher Education* 19:56; December 3, 1979.

CHAPTER 14

Informing Administrators, Guidance Counselors, Students, Parents, and Community About Curriculum Revisions

ROBERTA N. STEARNS
Westbrook High School, Westbrook, Maine

TED D. SPRING
Thomas College, Waterville, Maine

Business educators recognize the multitude of challenges that are present in today's educational arena. These challenges are continually brought about by progressing technology and by a broader awareness of the ever-changing complexity of our clientele—our in- and out-of-school youth in need of employable skills; the emotionally, mentally, and physically handicapped students; students with language barriers; adults in need of training and retraining to upgrade skills; persons incarcerated in state and federal institutions; the chronically unemployed, as well as the underemployed; and a myriad of others who lodge demands on our programs. Conquering these existing challenges and preparing to meet the future demands of this diversified array of publics call for a professional commitment to curriculum change that must become commonplace if business educators are to continue meeting the needs of their publics.

Historians will reflect on the seventies as a period of accelerated change and alteration in business education. However, merely developing new programs is not sufficient. Business educators must design a vehicle to disseminate to their publics information concerning the revised curriculum. To insure that their publics are aware of the most recent and vital services, it is essential to keep them regularly and accurately informed.

An effective school-community relations program is one that functions each day of the year building a solid foundation of community rapport. Disseminating program information and sharing data with the various publics about revised curriculum offerings are components of such a school-community relations program. It is not the intention of this chapter, however, to design a comprehensive school-community relations program, but rather to describe several effective techniques used in conveying business program information to administrators, guidance counselors, students, parents, and the community. Seven techniques designed to assist the business educator in a variety of communication situations are the open house, promotional brochure, television and radio presentations, promotional displays, news releases and articles, meetings, and presentations.

OPEN MINDS THROUGH OPEN HOUSE

A technique which allows the dissemination of information to any number of publics during a specified time frame is the open house. An open house may be schoolwide in design, with the business education department comprising only one important component. Conversely, the open house may be more narrowly designed, allowing a small group access to the business education department exclusively. For example, the department may wish to invite parents of special needs students to the school to acquaint them with the available programs, facilities, and equipment. On the other hand, school administrators, guidance counselors, teachers, school board members, students, and parents may be invited to an open house to learn more about the business education program.

Advantages and limitations. The open house technique provides some advantages as well as limitations to the business educator in disseminating program information. Among other things, the open house allows the business educator an opportunity to communicate—

Advantages of participation in courses and programs in business education

Advantages of occupational work-experience programs

Advantages, purposes, and need for FBLA or OEA

Needs for facilities, equipment, and instructional support

Changes in the business education curriculum.

However, careful planning, organization, and delivery are key components to a successful open house program. A poor performance at an open house may damage the image of the business education department.

Cooperation among the faculty and learning experiences for the students can be skillfully orchestrated by involving the faculty and students in the planning process. Faculty and students should have a comprehensive understanding of the purposes and objectives of the open house as well as an appreciation of the advantages that may accrue as a result of a successful open house program.

Planning an open house. A series of meetings should prove effective in coordinating faculty and student responsibilities for the open house program. Time lines can be developed to aid in meeting deadlines. Additionally, program content and program coordination can be finalized at regularly scheduled meetings.

It is important that the plan for the open house be comprehensive. Appointing a program chairperson, depending on the scope of the open house, to coordinate open house activities will help to assure a successful program. Other chairperson responsibilities might include the following: program, publicity, social activities, facilities, display, cleanup, and administrative matters.

PROGRAM CHAIRPERSON. The responsibilities of the program chairperson should include—

Providing for the general coordination of events of all chairpersons

Selecting student guides for escorting guests through the department

Assigning students to demonstrate equipment and to make presentations

Providing assistance in developing and reviewing presentations with each speaker

Serving as a faculty liaison with the school administration

Having emergency telephone numbers available.

PUBLICITY CHAIRPERSON. The major responsibility of this chairperson should be to publicize the approaching event. Coordination of newspaper, radio, and television coverage, as well as the development of exhibits, bulletin boards, displays, and brochures to arouse interest, is an important undertaking. In some cases, the publicity chairperson may wish to send special invitations to select people.

SOCIAL CHAIRPERSON. Building an atmosphere which allows for cooperation, understanding, and an exchange of ideas is paramount. Responsibilities of the reception chairperson should include—

Providing a guest book for visitors

Greeting each arriving guest and making appropriate introductions

Providing student guides for the guests

Providing for refreshments during the open house

Providing and coordinating exiting procedures.

FACILITIES CHAIRPERSON. The duties of the facilities chairperson should include—

Arriving early to make certain the assigned rooms are prepared and arranged

Making sure special equipment has been acquired and is in working order

Making certain special attention is given for access of all persons including the handicapped

Insuring that safety precautions are taken to avoid accidents to guests.

DISPLAY CHAIRPERSON. The duties of the display chairperson should include—

Planning and coordinating displays

Maintaining control over design and preparation of displays

Assisting in the collection of materials to construct displays

Being responsible for seeing that displays are erected and dismantled.

CLEANUP CHAIRPERSON. The cleanup chairperson should make certain that cleanup activities are completed by those assigned to specific tasks, i.e., publicity, facilities, displays, refreshments. However, the cleanup chairperson must take additional responsibility for—

Making sure that all rooms assigned to the business education department are in order

Removing and discarding debris from the room(s)

Securing unclaimed equipment and/or materials.

ADMINISTRATIVE CHAIRPERSON. The duties of the administrative chairperson are to oversee all the activities of the open house and to be ready to provide expertise and support when required.

POWER IN THE WRITTEN WORD

Program information can be distributed through the use of promotional brochures. Brochures are usually unbound, folded, and carry an important single message for a specific purpose. Business educators believe that although other media are effective in sharing program news, the brochure communicates the message with special impact at the most appropriate time.

Advantages and limitations. Using the promotional brochure carries advantages and limitations.

ADVANTAGES. A well-planned brochure utilized by the business education department may—

Inform the public about changes in curriculum

Report accomplishments of programs, such as placement and job information

Encourage support of a special program, such as cooperative education

Describe opportunities in the field of business education

Tell the public about a community service the business education department provides.

LIMITATIONS. Limitations can plague an attempt to communicate program information. Some limitations of the brochure are as follows:

Brochures reach a limited public.

Brochures may be discarded without being read.

Printing costs are spiraling.

Planning a brochure. The essence of any brochure is its simplicity. Designing a plan to formalize the development of the brochure is fundamental. Use the following plan as a guide:

Establish the need for and purpose of the brochure.

Identify the publics for whom the brochure is to be designed.

Discuss ideas and plans for the brochure.

Arrange meetings with the school administration to obtain approval and to secure funding.

Prepare a draft and rough layout of the brochure.

Meet with a printer, illustrator, and/or publications specialist to discuss ideas.

Revise and refine the plans and layouts as necessary.

Get reactions on drafts from colleagues.

Prepare final copy of the brochure.

Print the brochure.

Distribute the brochure.

Prepare a file on the brochure for future reference.

Funding a brochure. Funds to cover the costs of developing and distributing the promotional brochure may be secured through the public relations department, principal's contingency fund, school and community organizations, or advisory committees. It is important that the promotional brochure be a combined effort of many persons. Recruit the assistance required from professionals with expertise to help make the brochure a success.

TARGETING SIGHTS AND SOUNDS TO ASSIST THE PROGRAM

Other techniques used to disseminate business education program information are television and radio presentations. Television and radio provide a unique opportunity to promote business education to an immense and varied audience. These media can be used to create for a significant segment of the public an *awareness* of and *support* for business education programs.

Advantages and limitations. It is important to be aware of some of the advantages and limitations of communicating program information via television and radio.

ADVANTAGES. Advantages of television and radio presentations are as follows:

Television and radio presentations become economical because they reach large audiences.

The audience may not be familiar with programs in business education. This technique affords an opportunity to create awareness and interest among a new public.

Broadcast programs provide an opportunity to enlist the cooperation of community and business leaders.

Preparing television and radio presentations provides excellent learning experiences. Students can become involved in planning, writing, and broadcasting.

Faculty involvement may lead to new levels of motivation.

LIMITATIONS. There are, however, the following limitations to television and radio presentations:

Television and radio are one-way communications, and it is difficult to receive feedback.

Because of the varied nature of the audience, the message may be interpreted in different ways. Possibly, the audience will misinterpret the message and some people may be alienated.

Media choices. Radio, commercial television, and educational television/radio are three choices available to the business educator to disseminate information over the air.

RADIO. Usually, AM and FM radio stations are available. AM stations reach larger audiences because the receivers are less expensive and more common. FM stations tend to reach smaller audiences. The type of station selected depends on the anticipated audience. AM signals can be picked up by wide-area audiences; FM signals are generally more limited.

COMMERCIAL TELEVISION. Television unites sight, sound, motion, and color. When these elements are combined with a well-written script, the impact is powerful. The development of a television presentation is more demanding and more expensive than a radio presentation, but television coverage of events taking place can be dynamic.

EDUCATIONAL RADIO AND TELEVISION. By their nature, educational radio and television devote frequent coverage to education. Almost every geographical area has an educational radio and/or television station, and debates and general discussions are welcomed. Also, short announcement spots are usually available at no cost.

Presentation choices. Several types of presentations to promote business education on television and radio are available, including spot announcements, news items, panel discussions, guest appearances, debates, demonstrations, interviews, and other creative expressions.

SPOT ANNOUNCEMENTS AND NEWS ITEMS. Spot announcements and news items are often the easiest to obtain because the preparation time and the air time are limited. A spot announcement is effective in announcing new appointments, an open house, FBLA/OEA winners, and other brief items. The station may run these spot announcements as free public service announcements, or time may have to be purchased. News items should include the WHO, WHAT, WHEN, WHERE, WHY, and HOW of the event. Stay alert for human interest stories, success stories of graduates, speakers in the department, contests, or displays.

Preparing a news release for television or radio requires a slightly different approach than a news release to the print media. Keep in mind the following:

Use the KISS principle: Keep It Super Short.

Refrain from using over 100 words (this is about 45 seconds of reading time).

Triple space copy beginning each line at the horizontal center of the page, allowing adequate space for the speaker's written comments.

Spell out difficult names phonetically.

Do not abbreviate.

Spell out dollar amounts, dates, and numbers.

PANEL DISCUSSIONS. Panel discussions are well-suited for television. The audience has an opportunity to see and to identify with the presenters. Administrators, teachers, students, advisory committee members, and others can be featured on the same program, presenting a wide range of views concerning the business education program.

GUEST APPEARANCES. When business students, teachers, or administrators have a message which can be best communicated if delivered directly to the public, a television or radio guest appearance may be the best medium.

DEBATES. Debates can quickly arouse the public's interest in business education programs, especially when covering controversial topics.

161

Debates, although usually a contest of ideas, can be powerful, particularly when the debate leads to a well-balanced understanding of the business education program.

DEMONSTRATIONS. Demonstrations given by business students or business graduates create interest in business education programs. Television provides an excellent opportunity to demonstrate student accomplishments.

INTERVIEWS. Interviews with business administrators, teachers, parents, and students provide interesting radio and television programs. Business educators may be interviewed or they may conduct interviews with outstanding business students. Also, business graduates may discuss the benefits of the various business programs.

When selecting the most appropriate medium, consider the following:

The purpose of the presentation

The audience

The amount of air time available

The visual and sound effects needed

The money, as well as the time, effort, and personnel available for developing the presentation.

USE PHYSICAL SPACE FOR ADVERTISING

A promotional display can be an effective technique to communicate information and to solicit support for business education programs. The displays may be as simple as a bulletin-board announcement or as complex as a major display in a shopping mall. Displays are effective in reaching students, parents, administrators, guidance counselors, and others in the community.

Advantages and limitations. Using the promotional display as a medium for advertising has several major advantages and limitations.

ADVANTAGES. Some of the advantages of promotional displays are as follows:

A display utilizing color, pictures, objects, and movement can be forceful.

A display can reach an audience not ordinarily reached—people who do not read brochures or news releases, or listen to radio, or watch television.

A display using students' work or students themselves can carry an impact not easily achieved with another technique. Information can be imparted and attitudes may be changed with effective promotional displays.

LIMITATIONS: Advertising by means of the promotional display, however, does possess some limitations:

A display can be expensive to develop and difficult to maintain.

A display can be time-consuming to prepare.

A display in a shopping center may be competing for an audience with displays prepared by professional advertising people.

A display needs a simple theme. Complex themes are difficult to handle with this technique.

Planning a display. Before constructing the display, four basic questions must be answered: Why the display? Who will be the audience? What will be said? How will the message be presented?

Developing a display. A plan to develop a display emerges after formulating responses to the four basic questions mentioned above. Proper clearance needs to be made with school officials before making a commitment. School officials will be interested in answers to the following questions:

What is the purpose of the display? What is its theme?

What will the display look like?

Where will the display be located, and how long will it be displayed?

Will the display interfere with the normal activities of the program?

Will the display create any hazards?

Who will provide materials for the display, and who will pay for them?

Who will set up the display and when?

What are the plans for staffing the display, providing security, and dismantling the display?

What will be the bottom-line costs?

The display may be the most effective technique to use if (1) the message is simple and direct, (2) there is a dramatic way of presenting the message, and (3) the help is available to construct, maintain, and dismantle the display. Developing promotional displays allows teachers and students to work together outside the classroom to promote business education programs.

EXTRA! EXTRA! READ ALL ABOUT IT!

Business educators may find their local newspaper an invaluable source for disseminating program information. News releases and feature articles can effectively inform the public about business education programs. A news release is a news story written in a specified style that meets newspaper criteria and standards. Articles refer to a completed piece of professional writing that may be found in a newspaper feature section, magazine, newsletter, trade, and/or professional magazine.

Advantages and limitations. In addition to being relatively inexpensive as a communication technique, news releases and articles offer many advantages. However, limitations of this technique also should be addressed.

ADVANTAGES. Advantages of utilizing news releases and articles are as follows:

They provide a flexible tool for reaching a specified public.

They allow a means of effectively communicating complex topics, subtle concepts, and any number of facts and figures.

They provide an effective and inexpensive means of informing the public about the current program including changes and revisions in the curriculum.

They are effective in influencing the public about the program.

163

LIMITATIONS. Some of the limitations of using the news release and article are as follows:

News releases and articles are time-consuming for teachers to develop.

Getting news releases and articles accepted for publication is time-consuming and sometimes frustrating.

Communications of this nature reach only the reading population.

Planning a news release. It is important when writing a news release to answer the following basic questions:

What do you want to communicate to the public?

Whom do you want to inform—a broad cross section of the population or a specific segment of the population?

Why do you want to inform the readers about your business education program?

Tips on writing a news release. When writing a news release, it is helpful to follow a guideline. The following list of suggestions can be used by the business educator in developing.a news release:

Use the KISS principle: Keep It Super Simple.

Write your own headline. It might catch the news editor's eye.

Capture and hold the reader's attention with the opening paragraph.

Clearly state the WHO, WHAT, WHEN, WHERE, WHY, and HOW of the story making sure to be specific on names, places, dates, and other matters of importance.

Continue with important but less essential details.

Close with miscellaneous information that might add some interest.

State the message briefly and succinctly.

Type the story on 8½ x 11 white bond, double-spaced, using one side of the paper.

If the story continues to a second page, end the first page with a complete paragraph and type "more" at the bottom of the page.

Indicate the end of the story with ###.

Type the name, address, and telephone number of the writer in the upper left-hand corner of the page.

Be sure to date all releases.

Tips on writing an article. Writing an article for publication is a challenging undertaking. It provides the business educator an opportunity to use organizational skills in writing as well as an opportunity to study a particular subject in greater detail. Planning carefully what is to be communicated, organizing and completing a comprehensive outline of the article, representing points in logical order with supportive details and data, and providing a logical summary based on the information provided in the article will require effort and skill.

Consider these four general rules when writing an article for any publication.

BE CONVERSATIONAL. It is most important to communicate to the readers what you intend to communicate. Express ideas as simply as possible using appropriate terminology.

BE VARIED. Vary your choice of phrases and words. It is wise to keep sentences short for clarity, but try to vary syntax to keep the reader involved and interested.

BE LOGICAL. If you have thought through what it is you are trying to express, you should be able to express it logically. If your writing is somewhat cloudy, rethink the problem, and try restating your ideas. Eliminate flowery phrases or sentences that sound good but do not add to the article.

BE ACCURATE. Make certain that the content is flawless. Check the final copy for errors in spelling, punctuation, and grammar.

Plan ahead. Pick a magazine that would be interested in your topic and submit the idea for an article to the editor for consideration. If it is of interest to the readers of that magazine, the editor may give you the "go ahead" and offer some advice about the development of the article.

TÊTE À TÊTE BRINGS RESULTS

Meetings provide business educators opportunities to communicate directly with administrators, advisory groups, counselors, parents, students, teachers, and other select groups.

Advantages and limitations. Communicating directly with persons about important concerns within the business education department provides advantages unique to face-to-face communication. Likewise, direct contact has its limitations.

ADVANTAGES. There are advantages to informing the school community of curriculum revisions through meetings. The advantages are as follows:

People are given an opportunity to participate.

Meetings offer an opportunity to develop understanding, support, and interest in business education.

Meetings permit participant feedback.

LIMITATIONS. Using a meeting as a technique to disseminate program information may have the following limitations:

Meetings that are poorly organized and that last too long turn off participants to the subject under consideration.

Lack of leadership in conducting a meeting opens the door to "soap box" oration from participants, which lessens the productivity of the group.

All publics might not be able to attend because of time conflicts.

Meeting procedures. Each meeting should be designed to meet the varied needs of the group; however, common elements of effective meetings can be identified and should be incorporated into each meeting. These common elements include preparing for, running, and ending the meeting.

PREPARING FOR THE MEETING. Follow these steps to prepare for a successful meeting:

Prepare and mail the agenda (copies of the agenda should also be available at the meeting).

Send information and background documents with the agenda if you seek action at the meeting.

Send a reminder note (or telephone) if the meeting notice is more than two weeks old and if the meeting is not a regularly scheduled one.

Identify the meeting room with a sign outside the meeting-room door.

Arrange to have business department teachers greet the guests.

Arrange for name tags.

Design the seating plan.

Check out the public-address system.

Plan for refreshments, if appropriate.

Predetermine the adjournment time, if possible.

RUNNING THE MEETING. The presiding person has the following inherent responsibilities:

Begin on time.

Plan for recording the discussion.

Make clear the purpose of the meeting.

Introduce everyone.

Involve everyone.

Initiate agenda items for the group to consider.

Keep the discussion focused on one agenda item at a time.

Facilitate the deliberations and actions of the group.

Listen better than anyone else.

Use Robert's Rules of Order.

Summarize, clarify, and restate motions or discussions.

ENDING THE MEETING. Exiting procedures include the following:

Plan for the next meeting.

Announce the next meeting (purpose, date, time, place).

Close the meeting on a high point of interest rather than when the people are exhausted and impatient to leave.

Assign a staff member the responsibility of listing all the matters requiring follow-up action.

Assign responsibilities for implementation.

Set target dates and deadlines.

Inform the members of procedures to be followed.

Conduct an evaluation of the meeting.

Variety of meetings. A by-the-book, standard, formal meeting may be the most appropriate format to use for meetings of large groups. When meeting with advisory committees, administrators, counselors, students, or parents, a varied meeting format may be more appropriate.

ALTERNATIVE SEATING ARRANGEMENTS. The traditional seating design of formal meeting rooms with chairs in rows and columns may be appropriate when the purpose of the meeting is solely information dissemination. However, chairs arranged in rows and columns tend to limit communication. A formal seating arrangement is awkward when people try to communicate with those sitting behind them, beside them, or in front of them. Meetings have flopped because the members were not seated in participatory relationships.

INFORMAL FORMATS. When the purpose of the meeting is to informally share information and to solicit input from the group, alternative formats such as buzz groups, brainstorming, and the personal agenda may be considered.

Buzz groups. People who come to a meeting together tend to sit together, to think alike, and to agree on most points. By restructuring seating arrangements into new groups, the opinions in the groups may become mixed. When utilizing a buzz-group format, consider the following:

Arrange the group so it consists of people with different ideas.

Arrange the chairs in small circles.

Tell the group their task *before* forming the group.

Tell them how much time they have.

Tell them to select a person to summarize their discussion and to report for the group.

Brainstorming ideas. Brainstorming is an excellent process for soliciting imaginative ideas from a group. There should be a minimum of six people in each group. Five brainstorming rules must be rigidly observed.

1. The idea must be positive.
2. The idea must be briefly stated.
3. No comments will be allowed on any idea presented.
4. Every person is encouraged to express ideas regardless of how bizarre the idea may seem.
5. Every person is encouraged to present ideas as rapidly as they come to mind.

At the end of the time, an idea originator may give a detailed explanation of the idea if it is questioned. Then the ideas should be prioritized and the top ideas taken back to the large group.

The personal agenda. The personal agenda gives individuals a chance to speak about their concerns and priorities. When utilizing the personal agenda technique, consider the following:

Arrange the group (ideal size: 15) in a circle with everyone facing the center.

Inform the group that each person will have an opportunity to do *one* of the following.

167

Ask a question to get factual information: e.g. "What is the unemployment rate of secretaries in this county?"

Ask for help in solving a problem: e.g. "The business department needs more training stations, and we need your help."

Make a statement: e.g. "I think we are dragging our feet in recruiting males into our secretarial program, and. . . ."

Make it clear that each person must choose to do only one, and each person will be given only two or three minutes to ask a question, make a statement, or receive help from the group.

Begin with someone who is ready. Call "time" at the end of the person's time.

Repeat the process until everyone has had a turn.

AUDIENCES CONTAIN INTERESTED PUBLICS

An effective technique for promoting business education programs is the *live* presentation. This technique gives the business educator an opportunity to bring the program to the public on a personal level.

Advantages and limitations. As previously mentioned, most information-dissemination techniques have identifiable advantages and limitations.

ADVANTAGES. Advantages of live presentations are as follows:

The personal approach is direct and simple.

Presentations offer a unique opportunity to develop understanding, support, and interest in business education.

Presentations permit audience feedback.

Presentations can pave the way for future community contacts.

Presentations permit adapting the information to the type of audience being addressed.

LIMITATIONS. Limitations of live presentations may be—

A poor presentation leaves a poor impression of the program.

A speaker may be uncommunicative and not skilled at dealing with questions and, therefore, lose the opportunity to enlist the support of the group.

Identifying speaking opportunities. Communicating through live presentations improves relations with the school personnel, community, and parents of students in the program, as well as familiarizing students with the business program. Groups that might be interested in presentations are business organizations, faculty, counselors, administrators, professional organizations, school boards, advisory committees, parent organizations, service organizations, and students.

Identifying the audience. The purpose of a live presentation is to impact on the audience. The content, slant, and intensity of the presentation depend on the characteristics of the audience. Acquaint yourself with your audience prior to your presentation. Characteristics that can be identified are (1) average age, (2) educational level, (3) occupations, (4) knowledge of the subject, (5) membership in special organization, and (6) interests and concerns.

Planning the presentation. After obtaining support from the school administration, proceed with planning the presentation. Organizing, delivering, and providing supporting materials for the presentation are areas to consider in planning.

ORGANIZING. A written outline facilitates a well-planned, well-organized presentation. Outlining involves (1) breaking the topic into its parts and sequencing these parts, (2) deciding on an introduction and a conclusion, and (3) determining the supportive evidence to be used in developing the topics.

DELIVERING. Basic public speaking principles should be followed when making the presentation. Points to be considered include: (1) speak clearly, (2) project your voice, (3) be natural, (4) maintain eye contact with the audience, (5) refrain from reading the presentation, (6) project enthusiasm and sincerity, (7) use gestures, and (8) maintain good posture and attractive appearance.

SUPPORTING MATERIALS. The effectiveness of the presentation may be enhanced with the use of supporting materials such as visual aids, illustrations, handouts, statistics, or examples. Supplementing an explanation with a visual aid such as a transparency, slide, or chart can clarify the point as well as help the audience remember it. Statistics can be effective; however, sometimes approximations are less overwhelming to an audience than exact figures. A flip chart, bar graph, or handout can help to clarify and explain statistics and free the presenter to concentrate on the meaning.

Public speaking offers the business educator an opportunity to involve the school community on a personal basis. This technique allows limitless opportunities to clarify purposes and objectives of the program as well as to deliver information about the varied services of the business education program.

CONCLUSION

The professional commitment to curriculum redesign will become commonplace among business educators as they continue to meet present and advancing challenges of the 1980's. The array of publics lodging demands upon business education programs must find the curriculum relevant, flexible, and able to meet their individual needs and requirements. How quickly we educate our publics to our most recent and vital services becomes a function of each individual business education program. Planning for a systematic information-dissemination program utilizing the many techniques available and implementing such a system will do much to speed our services to those who so desperately require them.

NOTE: The writers wish to acknowledge and to thank the National Center for Research in Vocational Education at The Ohio State University and the American Association for Vocational Instructional Materials (AAVIM), University of Georgia, for allowing us to make use of the materials in the PBTE Modules in Category G, School-Community Relations, of their Professional Teacher Education Module Series in preparing this chapter.

Part IV
CHANGING SECONDARY BUSINESS EDUCATION CONTENT TO MEET SPECIAL NEEDS

CHAPTER 15

Making Content Changes for the Physically Handicapped

ELAINE F. UTHE

University of Kentucky, Lexington

Two concepts are consistently emphasized in the American way of life—concern for the individual and a free education for all. All citizens are equal and have the right to life, liberty, and the pursuit of happiness.

The goal of vocational educators is to prepare productive workers who will contribute to the economic well-being of the nation and who can lead worthwhile lives as individual citizens. Major efforts are now being made to extend this concept of vocational preparedness to a broader spectrum of the citizenry each year—the disadvantaged, the bilingual, the mentally handicapped, minorities and women, and now the physically handicapped.

Physically handicapped refers to individuals who have visual, hearing, speech, orthopedic, neuromuscular, neurological, or other health conditions that limit or prevent occupational employment. Persons who have serious emotional problems, are mentally retarded, or are classified as having "learning disabilities" are not included in the physically handicapped term for this chapter. The term "impairment" refers to a handicapping condition; the terms "disability" and "disabled" refer to employment capability.

Mainstreaming refers to the practice of enrolling those students with physical impairments or handicaps in a regular class situation with the nonhandicapped students.

CURRENT EMPHASIS ON EDUCATION FOR THE HANDICAPPED

One of every 11 adults is handicapped according to the President's Committee on Employment of the Handicapped. Also, the number of physically handicapped youth in the United States (over six million between 6 and 19 years in 1976 as reported by the National Advisory Committee on the Handicapped) indicates the need for concern for an appropriate education —and an education that includes vocational education so that many of these individuals become self-sufficient. When the lifetime cost of providing welfare or an institutional life for a physically handicapped individual is measured against the cost of providing occupational training, it quickly becomes apparent that providing occupational training is a better investment.

The emotional cost to the physically handicapped person who is not an independent-living, self-supporting individual is an unmeasurable one.

Furthermore, the individual rights of all American citizens are the same—an equal opportunity to life, liberty, and the pursuit of happiness—whether or not that person is handicapped or nonhandicapped.

Relevant legislation. The concept of equal opportunity has been emphasized in legislation in recent years. The Civil Rights Act of 1964 mandated equal opportunity for all citizens regardless of sex, nationality, race, age, or religion; it relates to the handicapped as well although no specific citation is made in the act.

The Architectural Act of 1968 mandated that all public buildings be accessible to the handicapped.

The Rehabilitation Act of 1973 included mandates in five major areas: (1) requires employment of handicapped individuals in the federal government; (2) creates an Architectural and Transportation Barriers Compliance Board; (3) requires firms that contract with the federal government to agree to affirmative action in recruiting, hiring, and promoting qualified handicapped individuals for entry to federally assisted programs or activities and covers all programs in terms of employment practices at the elementary, secondary, and higher education levels; and (5) prohibits discrimination in recruitment, hiring, compensation, fringe benefits, job assignment, and classification of qualified handicapped individuals.

The Education for All Handicapped Children Act of 1975 spells out some major requirements:

1. A free and appropriate education must be provided for all handicapped children from ages 3 to 21.

2. Special education and related services (including vocational education) to meet the unique needs of these students must be provided.

3. The education must be in the "least restrictive environment" possible.

4. An individualized education program (referred to as an IEP) must be developed for each individual and must be updated yearly. This IEP must include assessment of the handicapped student, long-range or yearly goals, short-term goals, statement of specific vocational services to be provided, date the services are to begin, and description of the evaluation process used to determine if the objectives are being met.

5. Supplementary aids and services are to be provided at no cost to parents.

6. Parents are assured of participation in the planning, review, and revision of the IEP.

7. The rights of the individual must be protected using due process of the law— that is, specific procedures must be designed and promulgated for planning programs, assessing the handicapped student, making class/course enrollment decisions, and evaluating progress.

Review committees and "grievance procedures" must be available if there is disagreement between the student (or parents of a minor) and the school.

Under Public Law 94-482, the *Vocational Education Amendments of 1976*, vocational education programs that receive federal assistance must be accessible to the physically handicapped by 1980; such programs must be consistent with the federal and state requirements under the Education for

All Handicapped Children and other acts. An individualized education program (IEP) must be developed for every handicapped vocational student. The handicapped student must receive the same quality of instruction and the same instruction (to the extent possible) as the nonhandicapped student. Modifications in equipment, curriculum, and standards may be justified for the handicapped student; supportive services that are "extra cost" items (that is, above the cost of providing the same instruction to a nonhandicapped student) may be reimbursed from vocational education funds when approved by the state department.

These legislative mandates affect business education programs in many ways: accessibility to programs, modification in curriculum and/or standards, and flexibility and variations in instructional techniques.

ACCESSIBILITY

Access to business education programs must be provided in four ways to the physically handicapped student: access to the building and classroom, access to or accommodation of equipment and furniture, access to enrollment in courses or programs, and access to instruction.

Access to building/classroom. Architectural barriers to the school building itself as well as the classroom must be removed. For example, the typewriting course may be taught in a second floor room; if a student in a wheelchair enrolls and there is no elevator, the course needs to be transported to the first floor—either by moving the entire class or providing individual instruction.

Accommodation of equipment/furniture. Chairs, tables, and other furniture may need to be modified and/or changed to accommodate students with specific handicaps. For example, a student in a wheelchair may need a higher or different table so that the wheelchair arms go under it; also, additional space is needed so that the student can maneuver the wheelchair through the aisle and up to the table.

Equipment may need to be modified—or special equipment may be necessary. A student with weak fingers or arms may need an electric typewriter which has an easier touch. In some cases, special arm rests may be necessary to support the typist's hands.

Vocational education funds may be available for "extra costs" in providing such accommodations—that is, the costs over and above furnishing the same instruction/equipment to the nonhandicapped student. Discuss this procedure with the local vocational education director and/or special education teacher and obtain guidelines for making application to your state department of vocational education prior to the student's entry to the class.

Access to programs/courses. All students should be given information about occupations available to them, and care must be taken to avoid prejudice, stereotyping, and misinformation. The business education program is open to all students—handicapped and nonhandicapped, male and female, minorities—in both traditional and nontraditional roles. Some guidelines to observe are:

1. Make unbiased information about all business education programs available to all groups; include all business teachers in the recruitment process.
2. Recruitment should be based on the student's occupational objective, interest, and aptitude rather than on the basis of race, color, national origin, handicap, and/or sex.
3. Make information about nontraditional as well as traditional role models available, especially at recruitment time; show handicapped models performing various types of office work, for example.
4. Involve parents in reviewing information and making course selections for the physically handicapped student—a step which is required during the IEP development process.
5. Prepare physically handicapped students for course prerequisites and requirements in a *positive* way—concentrate on what they *can* do rather than on what they cannot do.

Again, handicapped students are to be placed in the least restrictive environment possible and one in which they can benefit and succeed. The handicapped student may be mainstreamed in only one regular class per day—such as typewriting—or two or three classes, or the full day.

Access to equal instruction. The physically handicapped student should receive quality instruction; however, some modifications may be necessary in course content, teaching methods, time allotments, instructional materials used, and evaluation procedures.

Various types of supportive services, supplementary instructional services, and part-time special class services should be used for achieving equal instruction as well as modifying it. These services include such items as large-print books, teaching aides, individualized instructional programs, and even translators. Again, the need for these services should be discussed during the IEP development; the business teacher should be aware that such services are available when justified and then be able to justify this need.

MAKING CONTENT CHANGES

The Education for All Handicapped Children Act advocates a positive approach by mandating that handicapped students be educated with the nonhandicapped—the mainstreaming concept. The EHC Act does *not* mandate that the course/program content or standards be changed *if they are essential*—only that curriculum modifications and/or adaptations be made to aid the individual in overcoming a handicap. For example, a recent court case upheld a postsecondary program's decision to deny enrollment to a deaf person who wanted to enroll in a practical nursing program because of the essential need for the LPN to *hear* patients' cries for help.

But many questions arise concerning business programs and courses! What content is *essential* and what is important and or desirable? What are reasonable performance objectives and criterion for handicapped and nonhandicapped alike? How do you vary teaching techniques for the various types of impairments? What alternate forms of testing/evaluation are appropriate? How does the business teacher equate performance on a decreased number or different objectives and a final grade when the content is modified, adapted, or changed?

Business education programs should be based on a sound philosophy and specific educational objectives. For the vocational part—the job training purposes—a job/task analysis approach (Figure I) is functional. For what jobs does the business program prepare students (e.g., clerk-typist, secretary, accounts payable clerk)? What jobs/tasks are performed on that job (list of tasks taken from the DICTIONARY OF OCCUPATIONAL TITLES) and the level of importance for each one? What learning activities and/or what courses are prescribed for each task? These curricular decisions are appropriate for both handicapped and nonhandicapped business students.

Perhaps a look at the process of developing the IEP and ways to vary teaching methods will provide some clues for working with physically handicapped students.

DEVELOPING THE IEP

The IEP includes many items, and forms may vary somewhat from school to school and state to state. Only specific parts will be explained here. The IEP used in the Fayette County (Kentucky) Schools (Figure II) includes a 'Total Service Plan"—summaries of present levels of performance on various assessment tests, annual goals in order of priorities, regular class placement, and deadlines.

Selection of courses. The review committee, the physically handicapped student and parent(s) of a minor, and the vocational teacher should cooperatively establish annual goals and priorities after reveiwing the student's career objective and need for specific vocational courses. Consideration should be given at this time to type of impairment and essential content. Any special services and necessary supplementary aids should be identified at this time so that they are available when the student first enters the class.

What if the accountant aspirant has a visual handicap? Would it be better to place the student in a recordkeeping class because the pace is slower and the content is less complicated? Think again! Recordkeeping is designed for slow learners—those who are less capable academically; its content is different from that of accounting. Neither is it a prerequisite for accounting. The visually impaired student must not be considered mentally handicapped unless assessment data on the IEP indicates so. Therefore, the accountant aspirant should enroll in the accounting class and supplementary aids (such as large-print books or tape-recorded lessons) and different teaching methods and evaluations should be provided.

Selecting content and objectives. The second part of the Fayette County IEP (Figure III) is actually an "Individual Implementation Plan." For each business course a series of criterion-referenced short-term objectives must be stated; each one must include action or observable form, the conditions under which the task is to be performed, and the evaluation criterion. In addition, instructional strategies and materials must be identified, and the date the student is to be enrolled and review times must be indicated. Interestingly, evaluation is based on progress—the difference between pretest and posttest scores.

174

FIGURE I. Job/Task Analysis Approach to Development of IEP for Vocational Education

Job Title and/or Course Title:					
Projected Job Tasks (from DOT or . . .)	Level of Importance				Prescribed Learning Activity or Materials (CBVE, text, and . . .)
	Essen-tial*	Impor-tant	Desir-able	If time permits	

Each vocational education course should have a list of job tasks (topics—including skills, knowledges, and attitudes) prepared in advance and available for *all* students. When a physically handicapped student is enrolled, a selection of these job tasks and objectives is easier and will be made according to what is offered to all students.

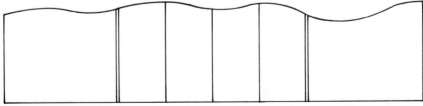

*"Essential" means that this task is absolutely required for employment at this job title; most tasks will probably be rated as "important" or lower. Also, serious consideration should be given to the possibility of job redesign (eliminating the job task) in the actual employment situation.

FIGURE II.

INDIVIDUAL EDUCATION PROGRAM: TOTAL SERVICE PLAN

INDIVIDUAL EDUCATION PROGRAM: TOTAL SERVICE PLAN
(I.E.P.)   (T.S.P.)

Child's Name _____ School _____ Date _____

Birthdate _____ Age _____

Summary of Present Levels of Performance: (Psychological and Educational Evaluations)

I.   Test: _____ | Date _____

Strengths: | Weaknesses:

II. Test: _____ | Date _____

Strengths: | Weaknesses:

III. Test: _____ | Date _____

Strengths: | Weaknesses:

IV. Test: _____ | Date _____

Strengths: | Weaknesses:

***See Attached Sheet For Test Results

Prioritized Annual Goals:

1. _____

2. _____

3. _____

4. _____

5. _____

6.

Regular Class Placement	Hours per day	Committee Members Present
1.		1. _____ Principal
2.		2. _____ Parent's signature
3.		3. _____ Regular class teacher
		4. _____ Special class teacher

Specific Special Services:

Date Start	Projected Review Date	Program	Related Services	
				5.
				6.

5. _____
6. _____

White copy to the Department of Special
   Pupil Services
Blue copy to the Special Education Teacher
Yellow copy to the Chairman of the School
   Based Admissions & Release Committee
Pink copy to the parent

INDIVIDUAL IMPLEMENTATION PLAN (I.I.P.)
Fayette County Public Schools

Date _____

STUDENT'S NAME	SCHOOL:	PERSON RESPONSIBLE:

INSTRUCTIONAL AREA: _____

ANNUAL GOAL: _____

CRITERION REFERENCED SHORT TERM OBJECTIVES	INSTRUCTIONAL STRATEGIES AND MATERIALS	DATE START	EVALUATION								REVIEW DATE
			PRE-TEST			MASTERY	POST TEST				
			DATE	RAW SCORE OR COUNT	CRIT. %	DATE	RAW SCORE OR COUNT	CRIT. %			

ANNUAL REVIEW STATEMENT FILED ON FORM EC/IEP-14

White Copy: Special Pupil Services
Blue Copy: Parent
Yellow Copy: Chairperson, School Based Admissions and Release Committee
Pink Copy: Special Education Teacher

REVIEW RECOMMENDED AT EACH GRADING PERIOD

Admissions and Release Committee

1. _____ , Principal
2. _____ , Parent's Signature
3. _____ , Regular Class Teacher
4. _____ , Special Class Teacher
5. _____ ,

FIGURE III.

177

In some courses, such as shorthand and accounting, the content is sequential in nature—and little or no selection is possible. However, learning time may be adjusted. In others, such as office procedures and basic business courses, some selection of content is possible. For example, a hearing impaired student may not be able to operate a transcription machine and perhaps cannot use the telephone. Therefore, some other topic or area should be substituted; perhaps an essential area should be studied in more depth. The substitution of another topic for the transcription machine is often made for a nonhandicapped student who cannot spell (actually, another form of "handicap"!). Although the hearing impaired student may not be capable of answering the phone, he/she may be capable of performing three or four other clerical tasks extremely well; incapacity in one area should not bar the individual from enrollment in the office procedures class.

Setting performance objectives. Performance objectives should reflect community standards for employment and the school's grading scales; they should be the same or nearly so for both physically handicapped and non-handicapped students. No students should be misinformed about these standards; neither should they be unrealistic.

Modifications in course content and the performance objectives may be made by (a) eliminating nonessential topics, (b) varying the length of assignments according to the impairment, (c) allowing more time to complete assignments, and (d) using oral recitations or tests for those who have difficulty in writing. The business teacher should be involved in discussions about enrollment in specific business courses and should determine course content and the short-term behavioral/performance objectives.

VARYING TEACHING TECHNIQUES

Business teachers should observe these guidelines when working with the physically handicapped student and the IEP:

1. Encourage the physically handicapped student to explore career clusters while assessing interest, ability and capabilities, and motivation levels.

2. Modify the curriculum as needed (and if appropriate) so that the physically handicapped student acquires as many occupational competencies as possible in order to succeed in finding employment.

3. Observe the physically handicapped student for tasks and jobs that he/she *can* do rather than for what cannot be done.

4. Be empathetic but not sympathetic; be reasonable and realistic, placing the emphasis on the student's capabilities—or potential capabilities.

5. Visit with the physically handicapped student prior to the time he/she comes to the class if at all possible.

6. Treat the student in the same manner as the nonhandicapped students in terms of discipline, attitude, and performance.

7. Observe the student to determine needs and capabilities. When adjustments in procedures/operations are necessary, remember the principle underlying the technique/action but work out a compromise with the student; i.e., typewriting speed is built on the principle of continuously using the same

finger on a key; if a finger is missing, substitute another but insist that the student use the *same* finger each time the key is struck.

8. Let the physically handicapped student know in advance what is to be learned, how it is to be learned, and how well it must be learned—via behavioral objectives.

9. Adjust the time allotted and/or shorten routine assignments where possible and if deemed necessary because of the student's impairment.

10. Provide encouragement when needed and give criticism when due. Make the student part of the group when asking questions, conducting discussions, assigning chores, and encouraging friendships.

Suggestions and guidelines for the various types of physical impairments are provided here. A general description of symptoms will be provided first, and then specific suggestions will be made. Remember, however, that each individual may have the impairment to a differing degree of severity than anyone else and it is not possible to suggest specific, detailed suggestions for each type of symptom/impairment here. Therefore, the business teacher should select the teaching techniques that are appropriate.

If questions arise, the business teacher should consult with the special education department, the parent if the student is a minor, and/or others.

Teaching suggestions—visual impairments. Students with visual impairments may have one or more of the following *symptoms* related to visual impairments:

May see distance objects but not nearby ones

May write quite small and be unable to locate details in a picture

May have good vision one day but not the next

May not be able to differentiate colors

Eyes may be sensitive to light (noticeable squinting and efforts to shut out light)

May have involuntary rapid movement of eyes due to disease

May lose place in work

May see only fragments of words or phrases

May not be able to distinguish light and dark

May have problems with depth perception

May have difficulty in writing—poor spacing, staying on the line

May hold reading materials too close or too far away

May have difficulty moving around the building if the impairment is severe.

The business teacher should acquaint the student with a severe visual impairment with the room, the equipment, and the furniture. The handicapped student should be instructed to take hold of the nearest moving person and move quickly during fire drills. When taking the class on a field trip, notify the company and make arrangements if possible for the visually handicapped student to view the items/activities closely and/or be permitted to touch the objects.

The extremely farsighted student (even when wearing corrective glasses) may need a bookstand so the textbook can be placed at a distance; in some cases, the instructions may best be placed on an overhead projector. This student may have difficulty doing close work so use of chalkboard, overhead projector, flip charts, and oral instructions are recommended.

The extremely nearsighted person has little or no difficulty with close work but has difficulty seeing objects in the distance. This student needs to be given oral instructions, also. Study materials may need to be enlarged— some publishers give permission for doing so on an enlarging copier when requested to do so. Large-print textbooks are available for some courses from the American Printing House for the Blind, Inc.

Since students with visual impairments may be slow at reading, the length of the assignment may need to be shortened, the materials may be recorded on tape for listening, or the teacher may share lecture notes that summarize the salient points.

A number of special devices or adaptive materials are available; only a few will be identified here:

Nonoptical aids—bookstands, felt tip pens (black), acetate in yellow to lay over a printed page to darken print, large-type books, bold-line paper, page markers and reading windows, sun visors, braille writer, raised-line drawing board, abacus, templates and writing guides

Auditory aids—cassette tape recorders, talking books, variable speed attachments to tape recorders, speech compressors, talking calculators

Optacon—transforms print into letter configurations of vibrating reeds that are read tactually, and *closed circuit television* that electronically enlarges the print

Optical aids—glasses with special prescriptions, magnifiers, telescopic aids.

The visually impaired student may also be helped by sitting in the front row; others may want to avoid windows because of the light glare. The business teacher may request that instructional materials such as tape recorders be purchased; these "extra costs" may be paid from vocational funds if prior approval is obtained.

Some tools have raised markings that the visually impaired student can feel. Just recently a typewriter manufacturer announced a "talking" typewriter that mechanically "reads" the typewritten material aloud, a boon to the visually impaired. The central office of a large company employs a totally blind individual as a telephone operator, using "talking" directories and recording phone calls with a braille writer.

These suggestions, aids, and guidelines are only a few of the many that may be useful in working with students who have lost a little, some, a good deal, or even all of their ability to see. Contact different agencies and associations for additional and more detailed suggestions.

Teaching suggestions—hearing impairments. Students with hearing impairments may have one or more of the following *symptoms and/or problems.*

May have difficulty hearing directions

May have difficulty participating in class discussions

May lack self-esteem; may show frustrations

Has difficulty hearing bells, fire drills, announcements

Distracting sounds are amplified over hearing aid

May have speech problems

May appear to be inattentive and lost in daydreams.

The business teacher may sometimes find it necessary to recommend a hearing test as a student may be compensating for the hearing loss—or the loss may be a recent one. Depending on the severity of the hearing loss, adaptations may include moving the student's seat to the front of the room, providing some of the instruction on tape recorders that can be amplified without disturbing others, and speaking directly to the student. Auditory and visual distractions should be removed or lessened if possible. If the student speechreads (reads lips), the teacher should stand about six feet in front of the student when speaking and should speak naturally in a normal tone of voice without exaggerating lip movements.

New vocabulary should be introduced both orally and in writing. The teacher should encourage the hearing impaired student to ask questions and should be willing to repeat and rephrase questions and comments when asked.

Use as many visual aids in the instructional process as possible. Using transparencies on an overhead projector is a good procedure; simply writing out directions is also good.

Teacher demonstrations are essential. If the student is totally deaf and being mainstreamed, an interpreter may be necessary on occasions ("extra cost" if prior approval is obtained).

Some types of equipment may need to be modified for safety reasons and/or to permit efficiency in using it. For example, a deaf person working in a warehouse that uses forklift trucks will not hear a horn; therefore, the forklift truck should be equipped with a bright light that can be flashed as a warning signal. In typewriting class a bright light is attached to the typewriter as a signal when the carriage is at the right margin. The newer electronic typewriters with automatic carriage return may be best.

In some situations the teacher may wear a cordless microphone that the student's hearing aid will pick up. Visual aids of all types, outlines of main points, and amplified recordings are all recommended.

It is important—and sometimes difficult—to encourage the hearing impaired student to participate in group discussions, especially if the hearing loss is quite apparent. The other students need to develop an awareness of the problem as well as basic techniques in helping to overcome it. Small group discussions should be used, with the group more or less facing the hearing impaired student. Specific questions should be directed to this student when the teacher is leading a discussion—in this case, call the student's name first to ensure his/her attention for the rest of the question.

Some curriculum modifications may be necessary at times for the hearing impaired student when hearing is essential for the task—such as answering the telephone in a business office. If the hearing loss is a total one, the telephone unit may be dropped and another more appropriate unit of instruction added for this student.

Equipment modifications—or simply the use of special equipment—may be necessary in an employment situation. For instance, in a business office an amplifier from the telephone company can be attached to the phone used by the worker with some hearing loss.

Teaching suggestions—speech impaired. Speech impairments may take several forms: inability or difficulty in producing speech sounds, language disorders and lack of development, articulation or voice disorders, and others. Stuttering may also be a problem. Most speech impairments require special teachers trained in these areas. However, most speech impairments are usually detectable early so that the business teacher will seldom find it necessary to refer a student to a specialist.

For those who do have speech difficulties—especially stuttering—the business teacher may need to be "acceptant" of the student and patient in conversing with him/her. Eye contact and encouragement are essential. In working with the stutterer the teacher must be patient, listen attentively, let the student finish what he has to say, and avoid any form of ridicule. The teacher should not try to avoid the problem—or talking with the student about it—as the problem cannot be avoided. The speech impaired student should be encouraged to work on improvement of speech patterns and communication skills.

Teaching suggestions—orthopedic impairments. Students with orthopedic impairments may have one or more of the following symptoms or problems:

May be self-conscious and embarrassed at times

May have poor self-esteem

May show frustration at times

May have a problem with physical mobility

May have impairments in other areas

May wear prostheses or orthotic devices (braces, artificial limbs).

In some cases, the impairment does not hinder the student's ability to do the work or acquire the occupational skill. However, the business teacher may find it necessary to work out creative or different ways for the orthopedically impaired student to achieve competency in certain tasks. Frustration may cause more problems for the student than for the teacher.

Occasionally special tools or equipment may be necessary so the orthopedically impaired student does not lose balance or become overly fatigued. Vises and clamps may be necessary to hold work and/or materials in place while the student works on them. Some of the same devices and aids described in the neuromuscular/neurological teaching suggestions may be useful for this group also.

Teaching suggestions—neuromuscular/neurological impairments. Individual differences are great with this group and therefore each student should be considered as an individual. Only suggestions for cerebral-palsied individuals will be made here. As a group, they are very responsive to others and tend to be self-conscious, excitable, and distracted; they may also lack motivation.

The cerebral-palsied individual may have weak wrists so a handrest is useful when typing. Two types may be used: (1) at the bottom of the keyboard as a rest for hands and arms, or (2) over the top of the typewriter so the student can rest the hands and type from above. This student may also have difficulty inserting paper into the typewriter; a guide that extends above the typewriter table may serve as a funnel for inserting the paper without having a firm grasp on it.

SUMMARY

Business teachers may expect increasing numbers of physically handicapped students in their courses. Success depends not only on the student's own ability and motivation but also on acceptance and effective instruction from the teacher.

Additional teaching techniques for a specific type of impairment may be obtained from readings, consultants, and special education teachers; they will in most cases need to be adapted to business education courses. New equipment adaptations are already in existence, such as the talking typewriter for the blind; others will be forthcoming, no doubt.

Barriers? Yes! Insurmountable? No! But we must all cooperate in providing high-quality, appropriate business education instruction to the physically handicapped as well as nonhandicapped individuals in our schools. We must also convince employers that the business-trained, physically handicapped graduate will be an efficient worker.

CHAPTER 16

Revising Content for the Economically, Culturally, and Educationally Disadvantaged

MERLE WOOD

Oakland City Schools, Oakland, California

The disadvantaged students are still there—by the millions. They are still waiting for someone, anyone, to develop an educational system that meets their needs. They are identified as the economically, culturally, and educationally disadvantaged. In reality, this term is redundant. To qualify in one of these three categories generally qualifies students for the other two. The most common element in the profile of the disadvantaged student is poverty, the lack of economic power. Of course, it is true that there are some students who suffer from disadvantagement because of problems that have absolutely no relationship to poverty: physical or mental disability, emotional problems, severe family situations, and so forth. However, the great common denominator among disadvantaged students, of any age, lies in their lack of economic security. Poverty is passed on from generation to generation and fosters the feeling of despair and a lack of a feeling of self-worth, self-fulfillment, or hope.

It is tempting to suggest that by simply providing some sort of economic support we would solve the problems of the disadvantaged. Yet, based on various financial support programs that have been offered, this has not seemed to work. Providing stipends to disadvantaged students and even monetary support to families has not resulted in long-term solutions for the majority of such students and families. Indeed, there are many reasons why make-work programs and giveaway schemes are actually damaging.

Rather than providing doles to the disadvantaged and economically insecure, we must attack the root of their problem. We must stop the cycle that continues to generate more and more individuals who are not educationally, emotionally, or psychologically able to cope with the world as they find it. This can only be done by providing such persons with the tools to earn their own money, to help them to become contributing and productive members of society, and to provide them with an opportunity for self-fulfillment. Literally, they must have an opportunity to gain the dignity that comes from being self-sustaining. This is what most disadvantaged persons want, and they should be provided with that opportunity.

PERCEPTIONS

Many see the disadvantaged student as unclean, uncaring, defiant, sullen, unmotivated, and unresponsive. Some of these perceptions are indeed true for many students. To a large degree, these qualities are reflections of a society in which the young person feels unwanted and unable to succeed. Some students are defiant. Others become sullen and seemingly uncaring. Yet, in their defense, there are justifications. Some of these young people are unclean simply because they have no way to keep clean and no particular reason to make the effort that would be necessary. Most of what society sees in the disadvantaged person is what has been sown there. And, it is sadly true, large numbers of disadvantaged students have beome so damaged and are so belligerent that they are beyond the help of most classroom teachers. Nevertheless, many more can be helped. We must begin somewhere.

Disadvantaged students have a perception of themselves. They generally see themselves as failures. They sense the feelings of institutions and the people who operate them. There is great validity in the self-fulfilling prophecy. If we see these students as failures, they tend to become failures. If we see them as worthwhile, valuable, and potentially successful people, they tend to fulfill that prophecy. One only has to talk to skillful teachers of disadvantaged students to know the magic that can be worked once such students begin to believe in their teachers, the schools, and in their own worth. Certainly this is a key, perhaps the only real key, to bringing positive change in the instructional program for the disadvantaged. Motivation comes from success.

WHO ARE THEY AND WHERE ARE THEY?

It is commonly held that the disadvantaged student is located in the inner city and that, by and large, these students are members of the various minority groups. Yet, by total count, more disadvantaged are white than minority, and more are located in suburban and rural areas than in our cities. Thus, dealing with the disadvantaged student in business education is the job of all of us—in the city, or village. Disadvantagd students exist at all ages, from early elementary through high school and beyond. They come from all races. The most common element in their backgrounds is poverty.

A sample group. Here, using an example from a city school system, is a profile of a group of 300 middle school students entering a nearby high school as ninth graders. Their reading and mathematics scores on nationally normed tests are ample evidence of the fact that they do not have well developed basic skills.

READING

a. 227 students at 0-6.0 grade level 76%
b. 59 students at 6.1-8.0 grade level 20%
c. 14 students at 8.1+ grade level 4%

MATHEMATICS

a. 211 students at 0-6.0 grade level 70%
b. 68 students at 6.1-8.0 grade level 23%
c. 21 students at 8.1+ grade level 7%

185

ADDITIONAL ANALYSIS REVEALED

a. 87 students were reading from the 1-3.9 grade level 29%
b. 140 students were reading from 4.0-6.0 grade level 47%

There is further information about these test scores; however, this is sufficient evidence to suggest that the receiving high school needs to develop strategies to provide special help to these entering ninth graders. Incidentally, this school system is located in a city where in excess of 39 percent of all students come from families that are on some sort of welfare. Further, the 300 students feeding into this particular high school are from one of the poorer sections of that community and represent an even higher percentage of welfare income.

These young people are *not* stupid. They simply are not educated to grade level in basic skills. They do not have the tools to succeed in traditional business education programs, or in any other kind of traditional program of instruction. Some of these 300 students will enroll in beginning typing. At the end of one year of instruction, they will not be typing 30 words per minute—they will still not be able to *read* thirty words per minute! Absenteeism for this group of students will tend to run about 20 percent or more each day. Many of these ninth grade students are already well on their way, indeed some of them already are doomed, to academic, social, and economic failure. But let us leave this sample group for now and return to them later.

Negative descriptors. As one reads the literature dealing with the disadvantaged student, one finds a thread of commonality in the terms and descriptions. There are words and phrases pointing out negative qualities, such as rejects school, has low morale, is defiant, has negative attitudes, often absent or tardy or truant, places high value on physical power, has unrealistic occupational goals, has low skills, knows that he or she will fail, has low communication skills, cannot express abstract ideas, has low cognitive skills, is unable to follow directions, has little imagination, avoids trying, is not conditioned to seek extra help, is used to studying at a slower pace, has little skill in self-direction, feels unwanted at school, is defiant, acts indifferent, does not see the value of what he or she learns, finds that most school-imposed goals are not attainable, is not oriented to the present, etc.

By reviewing lists of such negative descriptors we certainly can gain some insight into what it is that disadvantaged students need in order to begin to succeed. Certainly, we are not going to overcome years of inadequate study, poor personal habits, and negative attitudes in a short period of time. Yet, we can begin. An effective tactic is to prepare a formal listing of solutions to each of the negative factors that tend to describe the disadvantaged student. For example, if a student feels unwanted at school, then we must find techniques and procedures that will cause the student to feel wanted; this can only come about if the student *is* wanted. One thing we know for certain is that these students are not easily fooled. They are quick to detect insincerity and shams.

Specific needs of the disadvantaged. In the same literature dealing with the disadvantaged we find words and phrases that describe their needs. Among the many items listed we will find that these students need recognition, a positive self-image, status, success, acceptance by peers, physical activity, rewards, encouragement, acceptance by authority figures, a chance to be heard, fair discipline, relevant content, time to learn, teachers to whom they can relate, short assignment units, realistic personal objectives, tutoring, opportunities to evaluate their own progress, a secure home, opportunities to lead, to have people care, to have a feeling of belonging, to have understandable objectives, to have fun, to know that they are succeeding, to learn how to study, to have pocket money, to have hope, to get credit for things they already know, to have decent school clothes, to have friends at school, to receive praise.

The needs listed here are certainly reasonable. These are the kinds of conditions that anyone would expect to find in any school population. The fact that disadvantaged students do need these conditions and environments is a guide we can use to solve their educational problem. Since they need such things, it is obvious that they are not supplied. We have to ask ourselves as teachers why they are not available and, even more importantly, what we can do for these young people to cause them to begin to say, "School is great!" . . . "I really like school" . . . "I'm learning a lot." Until we supply solutions to the needs, however, we are going to have very few disadvantaged students making these kinds of exciting claims.

BASIC CONSIDERATIONS FOR CURRICULUM REDESIGN

Before we can redesign business education curriculums to meet the needs of the disadvantaged students, we must be certain that our own attitudes as teachers are positive. We must not blame the students for their lack of ability. These young people did not choose to be disadvantaged. Their problem is generally one that they inherited. We need to see in them the potential for growth and improvement. We must believe that what we might do for them can and will make a difference. In early experimental use of new curriculum designs we can expect that disadvantaged students will continue to display a lack of interest and enthusiasm. They must be given time to experience some success in school before they will become motivated to try and to succeed. As one person stated rather cleverly, ". . . we must remember that parents send us the best students they have." And then we must move from that point.

A further guide to our curriculum redesign is not to fall into the trap that this "homogenous group" is homogenous. The students are definitely different. While there are many similarities, these young people are as different as any other group of students who might be selected out of a school population. Some will, to be sure, lack native ability. Others will be deficient in language skills, or math skills, or both. Some students will be lazy, and others will be overactive. Some will be extremely verbal while others will be quiet and withdrawn. The point is that we must look at each student as an individual, with individual needs, strengths, and potential.

Patricia Cross, writing in *The College Board Review,* in the spring 1976 issue, used the clever title "Beyond Education for All—Toward Education for Each." We must adopt this philosophy—teaching each student, as well as teaching all of them.

Costs and traditions. As modifications are made in the instructional program to accommodate the disadvantaged, we must recommend those procedures and strategies that we believe will work and not restrict ourselves to staying within the traditional system of instruction. We need to remember that the traditional system has already been proven to be of little worth to these students. If it takes additional time, smaller groups, different bell schedules, independent study, modular credit, aides and tutors, special materials and equipment, or special facilities, then we must recommend those procedures.

It costs money to teach and educate the disadvantaged student. We cannot expect to succeed with these special students using our standard school district per-pupil cost ratios. Their needs demand expenditure of added resources. More time will be needed for many of these students to learn; teacher/student ratios will tend to be smaller; special resources and materials will be needed; and so forth.

Our districts must answer the question, Are the disadvantaged students worth a special investment? This is really an emotional question, but it is a fair one. What is each child worth? If staff and other costs for a one period special class for 20 disadvantaged business students totaled $8,000 or $9,000 for a year, would that cost be justified? Further, suppose that only one single student in that small class was "turned around" and became a motivated, productive student. We would have to admit that this class was not cost effective from an administrative standpoint. Yet, the investment, when looked at by the successful student and his or her family, would be reasonable indeed. As one person has stated this situation, "If you are able to turn one disadvantaged student into an excited, motivated, optimistic person during the year, you have earned your entire salary for the year—particularly if the child we are speaking of was *my* child." We must remember that each child does indeed belong to someone.

When we move from the emotional level to purely economic considerations the results are much the same. We *must* make an investment in the disadvantaged, even though only one student out of a class of 20 is "saved" at a cost of $8,000 or $9,000. At least two economic factors should be considered: that student will probably not be drawing public welfare payments for a lifetime; just as significantly, that student will be producing, earning, and paying taxes through a lifetime of work. This, of course, says nothing about the fuller, richer, happier life that will be available to the hypothetical student.

Individualization. We are going to need to work with students at their own level. We cannot give students tenth grade materials and programs just because they happen to be in the tenth grade. When the tenth grader is reading at fourth grade level, we must begin at that level. If we cannot do so, we should not accept such students and claim that we have a program for them. A student who has little or no background in basic math will not succeed even in a "simple" recordkeeping program. The program is anything but simple, to such a student. Students who do not know the alphabet will not succeed with even a basic filing exercise. Students who cannot read with ease cannot type with ease.

Thus, it is important to develop some sort of assessment system for entering students and to start them on units where they can succeed. We must provide reachable goals. Surprisingly advancement comes quickly to disadvantaged students who become motivated. A part of the frustration expressed by disadvantaged students is due to the fact that many of them know they have ability and also know they have academic deficiencies. Once they begin to succeed, they can and frequently do move ahead at a rapid rate.

There must be great flexibility in any learning laboratory designed for disadvantaged students. Students may be working on different projects and at a variety of paces. Individualization of instruction is virtually a necessity due to varying interests, abilities, and attendance patterns. This method of instruction demands a wealth of resources and materials.

Discipline. Discipline must exist in teaching the disadvantaged. No one can work successfully with these students, or any students, without control. One formula that describes the successful teacher is one who is "fair, firm, and friendly." While this may be overly simplified, it is a usable description. Teacher/student rapport is essential in any teaching situation. It is critically important when working with disadvantaged students. Discipline is necessary and must exist. Upon discovering that they are learning in a class, disadvantaged students are responsive to fair discipline. Standards of conduct and performance must be developed and administered. Regardless of the quality of the teacher and resources available, instruction will not take place unless there is an environment where learning is possible. It is distressing, but nonetheless true, that students who disrupt instruction or refuse to study and cooperate must be removed from the class in order to provide for the learning of others. There are some students who are simply beyond the point where they can be helped in a classroom setting.

NEED-BASED CURRICULUM MODIFICATIONS

Most decisions that we make in education relative to curriculum are based on two factors—needs and constraints. Sometimes we are unable to do things we wish to accomplish because of inadequate staff, facilities, equipment, or operating funds. In such cases, we modify our curriculum decisions to fit the situation that exists. However, our success is and always has been, on making curriculum decisions based on needs. Thus, with the disadvantaged we can use this same criteria, needs, as the basis for decision making. The needs of disadvantaged students are different from average students. Based upon some of the needs commonly identified in the profile of disadvantaged students, content and methods can and should be modified to meet the special requirements of these students. You can develop similar recommendations for the many needs of these students in addition to those listed here.

Recognition. Place on the tack board 3 x 5 cards with the name of mini-units at the top of each. (These need to be mini-units on which students can succeed.) As students successfully complete a unit have them print their names on the appropriate card.

Positive self-image. When students are successful in their work, improve their deportment or attendance, or distinguish themselves in any way where you can honestly compliment them, do so. Depending upon the particular student, you may be able to do this within the hearing of other students and help build not only a positive self-image but status with their peers as well.

Physical activity. Build into your program premeditated systems where students must move about. For example, have their study folders at one end of the room and their check-in sheets (where they check in work that is completed) at another part of the room. Place needed forms and papers in another location within the room. You will, of course, have to establish some basic rules relative to moving about the room, but meaningful movement is better than students getting up and wandering. Many disadvantaged students do need to break the routine of sitting at a desk and working, and you can actually prevent disruptive movement if you will design meaningful movement into your instructional program.

Success. Have small but attractive certificates for successful performance. For example, if you are using small modules of instruction, combine into meaningful groups and issue a small certificate for completion of each group of activities. The certificates can be billfold size and still be effective. One teacher recently issued attractive billfold size typing certificates for 10, 20, 30, 40, and 50 words per minute to her students. These students would never have tried to reach a standard 40 or 50 wpm certificate, yet they competed for the lower level certificates and worked hard to gain them. An honor roll was also kept and each student who got one of the minityping certificates had his or her name typed in bold primary type on the various honor rolls. To some students this was the first recognition they had ever experienced for successfully doing something at school.

Rewards. Along with certificates you can give special awards for disadvantaged students who perform well in selected areas. For example, for two weeks of perfect attendance (and that would be a *real* record for many) you can give a special pass to the library or simply let the student read a book of his or her choice for a period in class. Attainable goals can be set where you identify a block of work and upon its completion the student is given a simple, inexpensive gift. Even a candy bar will work with many students! One teacher recently discovered (upon noting that many cassettes were missing) that blank cassette tapes are a sought-after prize.

Encouragement. Many disadvantaged students are desperately in need of someone to encourage them. This means that you need to be circulating about the room frequently. As you identify students who appear lost or are having trouble, stop and help them. Show signs of concern for them. Every one of us wants to have people interested in us, willing to help us, and showing they care about us. These students are no different.

Fair discipline. Set up fair standards of conduct for your classroom. Be certain not to make any disciplinary statements that you cannot administer or back up. If you are working with students who are loud, crude, and difficult to handle, it is particularly important to develop a degree of rapport before suggesting a formal disciplinary system or behavior code. Be fair and unswaying in the administration of discipline. Some teachers have successfully worked with students by cooperatively developing classroom rules. When this is possible, the students feel they are a part of the system and tend to cooperate to a higher degree. In fact, they also assist in maintaining discipline since they helped to develop the system.

Relevant content. If you are working with modular material (and even a thick, hardback text can be used in a modular way), try to have alternative assignments. Until students actually begin to feel success, they may balk at some assignments because they feel the instructional materials are "dumb." The first step is to get the students to participate and experience success. Let them, when you can, skip a unit that annoys them. You can often reassign those "dumb" units and students will do them without complaint once they begin to feel success. If we cannot defend why a particular unit is in a course when we are challenged by a student, then perhaps the student is right. It is far better to have a student studying content out of sequence and still trying and learning than to have a confrontation which drives the student away from instruction altogether.

Time to learn. Certainly a major adjustment that all of us must make in working with disadvantaged students is to give them adequate time to learn. Some of us learn more slowly than others. The objective for disadvantaged students is to keep them moving ahead, to get them motivated, and to let them succeed. Many of these young people complain that they can't do an exercise because they have to rush so much. Rather than debate the issue they simply will do nothing. Therefore, as long as a student is working on a unit, he or she should be given the time that is needed to do the work. Then they can move on.

Know they are succeeding. Look for opportunities to tell students how well they are doing. Have a system where you, with your students' knowledge, will write a memo to the principal each month listing those students who have not been absent or tardy more than one time (or six if that is your criterion). Let those whose names are in the memo have a copy of it. Use minicertificates and honor rolls when you spot noteworthy effort. Compliment students aloud so that their peers can hear your congratulatory statements.

To have fun. Disadvantaged students like to have fun just like anyone else. For some you need to be very careful or they may become a bit too enthusiastic. However, you can help to build an atmosphere of pleasantness and fun in your room. As teachers, we do set the tone. One teacher, for example, set aside the first school day of each month for celebrating everyone's birthday for that month. Students got involved in planning and

191

carrying out details, and this turned out to be a rich, enjoyable learning and social situation. Various instructional units can be entertaining, and you should take advantage of all such opportunities.

Consider establishing competitive "teams" who compete to see which group gets a certain number of units completed by a certain date. Keep the bulletin board full of current cartoons and jokes. Students will stop and read them. Be willing to share brief amusing stories and anecdotes with your class and let them participate in such sharing too. Look for ways to make the classroom a pleasant place to be.

Short assignments or units. Even if you are using a standard text you can shorten assignments. Give them three pages to read rather than ten if you detect that they are unable to cover ten pages in an assignment. If there are 30 problems in math at the end of the unit, break the assignment down. Assign the first five problems as the basic assignment (if you feel that is a just assignment). Call it assignment A. Call the next five problems assignment B. Let that be an extra credit assignment.

Recording accomplishments. Give credit, and a mark, for every mini-assignment you give. If you will break assignments down into very tiny parts and identify each with some sort of number or code, these students may be able to do two or three assignments each day—and they can mark this in their individual progress record as you mark it in your class record book. This lets the students know they are moving ahead. It is honest accomplishment—and it works.

Perhaps the most sage advice available for dealing with disadvantaged students is to remember the quotation from Emerson, "What is true in your private heart is true for all men." Whatever you feel, your students feel. Whatever you want, they probably want. They would like to be treated as you would like to be treated. This measuring stick seldom fails in dealing with disadvantaged students—or with anyone else for that matter.

300 STUDENTS

Let us now move back to those 300 students entering that neighborhood high school. These are real people. They exist. This year the ones who have survived are seniors. Most of them, however, will not have continued their education to the senior class.

First, we cannot simply blame their prior education and teachers. There is little value in blaming their homes and their families. It is fruitless to blame their poverty. We must pick up such students and, based on their needs and the constraints that exist, begin teaching them. Remember that over one-fourth of this entering class are reading at the first through 3.9 grade level. Another 47 percent are reading at grade level 4.0 through 6.0.

Text material in the business subjects at such reading levels is virtually nonexistent. There will be some of these ninth grade students entering typing and introduction to business courses. If you were the department head or a teacher in the receiving school, what would you do?

The instruction in typing would have to be undertaken with the lowest level text available and even that should not be used initially. Teacher demonstrations would be needed to teach the keyboard. Drills should be from teacher prepared materials which are carefully selected. As students move toward typing sentences, extreme care would need to be taken to select content that was virtually at the Dick and Jane level. As the teacher discovers that these students can be motivated and successful, more complex assignments could be developed. If these students were typing, using good techniques, at 20 words per minute at the end of the semester and enjoying their typing class, the teacher would surely deserve a star in his or her crown.

The point here is that we should not strive for standard performance from a nonstandard group of students. They may, with special care and attention, develop into typists if they are given the time. It would be most helpful if a reading consultant could work in cooperation with the teacher as assignments were developed for student drill. Ultimately, these students can successfully move on to selected junior high typing text material.

A standard text in the introduction to business course would serve only as a picture book for such students as they would not be successful with the materials. Assignments need to be carefully discussed and illustrated. Homework or classroom work should consist of teacher-made materials. The course should contain nontraditional content in order to cater to the interest of the students, and progress would be slow.

EXPERIMENT OR ABANDON?

The suggestions just made will, to some teachers, seem ridiculous. Such work compounds a teacher's already impossible day. Too many schools are not able to assist a teacher with a demanding assignment such as that just outlined. In many schools, there are no reading specialists available to assist teachers. There may not even be duplicating equipment on which to run copies of the study sheets and the loose-leaf text. The alternative is to hand them a standard text and, while modifying the course as much as possible, teach.

This is what most often happens to such students. They are abandoned because we are unable to deliver the kind of service they so desperately need.

The cost, in both labor and added funds, for teaching the disadvantaged is severe. Yet this task cannot be accomplished in any way except by meeting their special needs. If they are ever going to be helped and brought up to grade level, it must be accomplished slowly while building their belief in themselves and improving their self-motivation. This can only come through their having success—and little success will occur if we treat them as regular students, give them standard texts, and assign them standard work.

In your own business classes there may be one or two students that you would identify as disadvantaged. There may be so few of these that your school is considered to be made up of average and above-average students. However, there are probably a few less able students there, quietly enduring the agony of knowing they are failing.

As each of us teaches, we need to look for the disadvantaged. We need to individualize our instruction to meet the needs of these students. We need to get them to see that we do have some understanding and that we do not hold them responsible for their lack of skill and ability. We need to get them to understand that we care and that we will help them. When resources are lacking, we simply must do the best that we can with what we have. Yet, great value can come from the simple discovery by these young people that someone they know cares about them.

SUMMARY

The latest government figure states that there are some four million disadvantaged and unemployed youth in America today. There are approximately 100,000 business teachers in this country. If each of us were personally able to help one of these young people become a motivated, successful student—then there would only be three million, nine hundred thousand left—and the correct word is "left"—left out of the mainstream of life in so many ways because of educational disadvantagement that the schools were unable to solve due to lack of resources and commitment. For we *do* know how to help them. Let us never give up trying to meet this obligation.

CHAPTER 17

Eliminating Sex Bias, Stereotyping, And Discrimination

C. B. STIEGLER

Northern Kentucky University, Highland Heights

With the passage of the Vocational Education Act of 1963, business educators were given the opportunity to receive funding for occupational preparation programs. These programs have been instrumental in bringing about the phenomenal enrollment growth in vocational education. As of 1979, approximately 50 percent of the high school students in the United States were enrolled in vocational programs.

Vocational education has become big business as greater public acceptance occurred and labor market needs justified the volume of training. Recognizing the opportunity to correct past inadequacies and bias practices, new federal and state laws have been enacted to assure that all students have an equal opportunity to prepare for demand occupations within the labor market.

To prepare students for business, office, and distributive education positions in the 1980's, today's educators must—

1. Be aware of the factors which contribute to the present status of vocational education.

2. Know the laws which affect vocational personnel, the training environments, and the students.

3. Consciously develop and practice strategies for "sex fair" vocational recruitment, training, and placement.

STATUS OF VOCATIONAL EDUCATION

The status of vocational education can be described in terms of three factors—social/economic environments, employment demands, and vocational enrollments.

Social/economic environments. The United States has changed from an agricultural society to an industrial and technical one. As this change has evolved, the roles of men and of women have changed in at least seven ways.

1. An increasing number of women are entering the paid work force. Approximately 60 percent of all women between the ages of 18 and 65 work outside the home, and they make up about 41 percent of the total work force.

2. Women are increasing their years of formal education. As of 1979, they equal men in completing an average of nearly 11 years of school. And in undergraduate collegiate education, women make up about half of the student enrollment.

3. Women are having fewer children. The birthrate and the size of families in the United States has been steadily declining.

4. More women are joining the ranks of men as heads of households. Changing economic opportunities, changing viewpoints about marriage, increasing divorce rates, and increasing numbers of single adults have increased the number of females who head households.

5. Men have less responsibility for the full financial support of the family. The rising cost of living and the increasing desire of women to work have caused men to more readily accept shared financial responsibilities.

6. Men are assuming more responsibility for household work and for child care. As a single parent or as a partner in a two-career family, men are beginning to disregard role stereotypes.

7. Men and women are beginning to enter nontraditional occupations. Technological advancements constantly create new jobs and drastically change existing ones. Technology now makes it possible for both men and women to be trained and employed in practically every type of work.

In addition to these social changes in the United States, an evolution has also occurred in the legal concepts of justice and discrimination. Laws in the 1960's and in the 1970's have defined discrimination, structured guidelines for equal opportunity, and identified sex fair employment and educational requirements. A brief summary of these laws is presented in the next section of this chapter.

The legal system in the United States is committed to the support of equal opportunities for males and for females in all facets of social and economic environment. And, of course, the evolution in the legal principles related to discrimination and to equal opportunities has affected and will continue to affect employment and educational environments. Not only must businesses and educational institutions follow equal opportunity guidelines but they must also achieve a certain representation of males, females, and minorities in their number of workers and of students.

Employment demands. In terms of labor market needs and employment growth, total employment in the United States is expected to increase by 20 percent in the years between 1974 and 1985—from 85.9 million to 103.1 million. The number of white collar workers is expected to increase by 28 percent from 1974 to 1985—from 41.7 million to 53.2 million. The number of service workers is also expected to increase about 28 percent—from 11.4 million to 14.6 million.[1]

In addition to filling the need for more workers in particular occupations between 1974 and 1985, businesses are also concerned about the balance of males and females in the supply of qualified workers. Because of equal opportunity legislation on both national and state levels, labor supply needs have to be met on the basis of equal opportunity employment. Employment

---

[1]*Occupational Projections and Training Needs.* Washington, D.C.: Bureau of Labor Statistics, 1976.

figures have to show sex fair recruitment and employment. This means that employment needs in the 1980's will involve increased emphasis on recruitment of men and women into nontraditional vocational occupations.

As of 1978, nearly 70 percent of working women and a similar percentage of working men were employed in three occupational groups.

Women	Men
Clerical	Professional/Technical
Service	Operatives
Technical	Craft/Kindred Workers

Statistics concerning the composition of the labor force seem to indicate that there is an undersupply of qualified men and women to enter nontraditional occupations. Occupational sex segregation has been characteristic of the labor market for many years in the United States. Sex segregation, a very large number of one sex filling particular kinds of jobs, hurts both men and women as it closes off occupations in which they might be extremely productive and occupationally satisfied. Such segregation also has a tendency to trap women into typically low-paying, low status jobs. This tendency is due largely to the reluctance of employers to overlook the traditional myths about female workers.

The undersupply of qualified workers for nontraditional occupations is explained on the basis of such factors as the following:

1. Career counseling which follows traditional career paths for either males or females.

2. Ineffective career orientation information. People are not aware of job opportunities in particular fields for male and female workers.

3. Apprenticeship training programs which have previously limited participation to one sex.

4. Attitude beliefs that there are jobs which should be performed by only one sex, that women are less competent than men, and that a woman's place is in the home.

5. Low wages associated with traditional female occupations.

6. Limited educational program options in traditional female occupations.

7. Extensive educational program options in traditional male occupational programs.

8. Exclusive enrollment by a particular sex in specific vocational programs.

9. Traditional concentration of female students in three areas of vocational education—home economics, health, and office work.

10. Traditional concentration of male students in three areas of vocational education—agriculture, technical, trade/industrial.

11. Physical isolation of classes—female course work in one building or area; male course work in some other place.

12. Insufficient number and visibility of nontraditional role models. Vocational education staffs are sex segregated. Nearly 100 percent of agriculture teachers and about 97 percent of technical education teachers are male. Over 97 percent of home economics teachers, about 85 percent of health occupation teachers, and over 70 percent of office/business education teachers are women.

There are many reasons for the undersupply of qualified nontraditional workers in vocational occupations; however, this undersupply problem has to be solved in order to meet labor supply needs for the 1980's. The employability of people with vocational skills and the greater emphasis on nontraditional employees makes it necessary for educators to recruit and to train nontraditional vocational students at the secondary level of education.

Vocational enrollment. Vocational enrollments for the nation for 1978 are shown in the following table.

Vocational Education Enrollments, 1978[2]

Program	Nation	Females	Percent	Males	Percent
Agriculture	1,600,542	173,824	17.2	1,426,718	82.8
Distribution	962,009	495,738	51.5	430,271	48.5
Health	758,808	591,764	77.9	167,044	22.1
Home Economics	3,659,441	2,946,101	80.5	713,340	19.5
Office Education	3,312,475	2,506,368	75.6	806,107	24.4
Technical	527,681	93,001	17.6	434,680	82.4
Trade/Industrial	3,402,722	527,142	15.4	2,875,580	84.6

This distribution differences between females and males in vocational education programs correlate with the composition of the labor market:

Dominance of females in traditionally female occupations.

Dominance of females in traditionally female vocational programs.

Dominance of males in traditionally male occupations.

Dominance of males in traditionally male vocational programs.

Vocational occupation hiring practices and worker attitudes encourage dominance of traditional work types.

Vocational education program recruitment practices and leadership attitudes encourage dominance of traditional work types.

There is a definite correlation between equal educational opportunities and equal participation in the job market. Therefore, myths, stereotypes, customs, and mores have to be reoriented to gear up for the accomplishment of vocational education's responsibilities in the 1980's—(1) a sufficient number of qualified vocational graduates and (2) an adequate number of qualified nontraditional vocational graduates.

LEGISLATION

Since the 1960's, Congress has enacted a host of civil and equal rights laws, and each President has issued Executive Orders addressing social parity and equal rights. Even though several laws and Executive Orders have been addressed to the improvement of opportunities for minorities and for women, vocational educators have only recently become sensitive to the program implication of these laws and orders.

Equal opportunity in employment and equal opportunity in vocational education are often viewed as two separate concerns in our society; however, it is difficult to have one without the other. Employment opportunities are

---

[2]U.S. Department of Health, Education, and Welfare, Office of Education, Washington, D.C.

not likely to truly open unless the avenues to those opportunities are present. And avenues to opportunities will seldom be used unless the opportunities themselves are known to be real.

To provide quality business, office, and distributive education programs, vocational education personnel have to be familiar with employment legislation—to monitor the implementation of laws prohibiting sex discrimination in hiring, firing, and promotion procedures in their schools. They must also be concerned with the ways in which equal opportunity legislation affects vocational education students—to provide sex fair vocational recruitment, training, and placement.

As you read the discussion of the following legislation, please notice that the laws really apply to all people, both men and women of various ethnic, racial, and religious background—not just women.

Equal working rights. There are four basic legal orders which guarantee equal rights in employment for women and other minority groups. They are the Equal Pay Act, the Civil Rights Act, Executive Order 11246, and the Education Amendments of 1972. A chart is provided on pages 200-202 for convenient reference in comparing the provisions of most of these laws.

The Equal Pay Act of 1963 was the first piece of federal legislation forbidding sex discrimination in employment. This act, which is an extension of the Fair Labor Standards Act, is designed to prevent discrimination because of sex in the payment of wages. Until 1972, most persons in education were exempt as were executives, administrators, professional employees, and outside sales personnel. The Act essentially provides for equal pay for equal work; however, the definition of equal work is left with the courts. As amended in 1972, the Act prohibits sex discrimination in salaries and most fringe benefits. It also covers all employees of educational institutions and agencies.

Title VII of the Civil Rights Act of 1964, as amended in 1972, makes it illegal for private employers, labor unions, employment agencies, state and local governments, and employees of educational institutions to discriminate on the basis of race, color, religion, sex, or national origin. Specifically, it is unlawful to use discriminatory practices in—

Recruitment, hiring, firing, layoff, recall

Wages, conditions or privileges of employment

Classification, assignment, or promotion of employees

Use of facilities

Apprenticeship training or retraining

Promotion opportunities

Sick leave time and pay

Overtime work and pay

Medical, hospital, life, and accident insurance coverage

Optional and compulsory retirement age privileges

Application or referral procedures

Printing, publishing, or circulating advertisements relating to employment.

Federal Laws and Regulations Concerning Sex and Race Discrimination[3]

	TITLE VI OF THE CIVIL RIGHTS ACT OF 1964	TITLE VII OF THE CIVIL RIGHTS ACT OF 1964 as amended by the Equal Employment Opportunity Act of 1972	EXECUTIVE ORDER 11246 as amended by 11375	EQUAL PAY ACT as amended by the Education Amendments of 1972	TITLE IX OF THE EDUCATION AMENDMENTS OF 1972
Coverage:	All agencies and institutions receiving Federal assistance.	All employers with fifteen or more employees, employment agencies and labor organizations.	All organizations holding Federal contracts or subcontracts of $10,000 or more. NOTE: All organizations, agencies, and institutions holding Federal contracts or subcontracts of $50,000 or more are further covered by the Order's requirement for development of a written affirmative action program.	All employers.	All education agencies and institutions receiving Federal assistance.
Prohibitions:	Discrimination against students on the basis of race, color, or national origin, including: denial or differential provision of any aid, benefits, or services; segregation or separate treatment relating to the receipt of services, financial aid, or other benefits.	Discrimination against employees on the basis of race, color, religion, sex, or national origin (including hiring, upgrading, promotion, salaries, fringe benefits, training, and all other terms and conditions of employment).	Discrimination against employees on the basis of race, color, religion, sex, or national origin (including hiring, upgrading, promotion, salaries, fringe benefits, training, and all other conditions of employment).	Discrimination against employees on the basis of sex in the payment of wages, including fringe benefits.	Discrimination against students and employees on the basis of sex, including: • admissions and recruitment of students (with some exceptions), • denial or differential provision of any aid, benefits, or services in any academic, extracurricular, research, occupational training, or other education program or activity; • any term, condition, or privilege of employment (including hiring, upgrading, promotion, salaries, fringe benefits, and training); • financial aid or other benefits.

[3]Vetter, Louise; Burkhardt, Carolyn; and Sechler, Judith. *A Guide for Vocational Education Sex Equity Personnel.* Columbus, Ohio: National Center for Research in Vocational Education, 1978. p. 50.

Complaint Procedures:	Charges may be filed by individuals on their own behalf and/or by organizations authorized to act on behalf of an aggrieved individual(s). The complaint may be filed with the national or regional Office for Civil Rights (OCR), Department of Health, Education, and Welfare (HEW) within 180 days of the alleged violation.	Charges may be filed by individuals on their own behalf and/or by organizations authorized to act on behalf of an aggrieved employee(s) or applicant(s) for employment. The charge must be made in writing and filed under oath with the district office of the EEOC or a recognized State or local deferral agency within 180 days of the alleged violation.	Charges may be filed by individuals on their own behalf and/or by organizations authorized to act on behalf of an aggrieved employee(s) or applicant(s) for employment. The written complaint may be filed with the national or regional Office of Federal Contract Compliance Programs (OFCCP), the Department of Labor, or the Office for Civil Rights (OCR), Department of Health, Education, and Welfare (HEW) within 180 days of the alleged violation.	Charges may be filed by individuals on their own behalf and/or by organizations authorized to act on behalf of aggrieved individuals. They may be filed by letter, telephone call, or in person to the nearest office of the Wage and Hour Division of the U.S. Department of Labor. There is no official time limit for filing complaints, but recovery of back pay is limited to 2 years for a non-willful violation and 3 years for a willful violation.	Charges may be filed by individuals and/or by organizations authorized to act on behalf of aggrieved individual(s). The complaint may be filed with the national or regional Office for Civil Rights (OCR), Department of Health, Education, and Welfare (HEW) within 180 days of the alleged violation.
Enforcement:	If attempts to secure voluntary compliance fail, OCR may institute administrative proceedings which may result in suspension or termination of Federal assistance and the denial of future awards, or OCR may refer the case to the Department of Justice with a recommendation for court action to compel compliance without jeopardizing Federal assistance. OCR may also delay final action on application for new Federal assistance upon instituting administrative proceedings.	If attempts at voluntary settlement fail, EEOC or the U.S. Attorney General may file suit. Aggrieved individuals may also file suit after obtaining a "right to sue" letter from EEOC. Courts may enjoin the employer, labor organization, or other covered organization from engaging in unlawful acts, order appropriate affirmative or remedial action, reinstate employees, and award back pay and/or attorney's fees.	If attempts to secure voluntary compliance fail, OCR may institute administrative proceedings to suspend or terminate Federal contracts and to bar future contracts. OCR may also delay new contracts while it is seeking voluntary compliance.	If attempts to secure voluntary compliance fail, the Secretary of Labor may file suit. Aggrieved individuals may also file suit when the Secretary has not done so. Courts may enjoin the employer from engaging in unlawful acts, order salary raises and back pay, and assess interest.	If attempts to secure voluntary compliance fail, OCR may institute administrative proceedings which may result in suspension or termination of Federal assistance and the denial of future awards or OCR may refer the case to the Department of Justice with a recommendation to compel compliance without jeopardizing Federal assistance. OCR may also delay final action on application for new Federal assistance upon instituting administrative proceedings.

Confidentiality and Protection of Anonymity:	Although the identity of the complainant is kept confidential if possible, it is sometimes impossible to investigate a complaint without the identity of the complainant becoming known. If court action becomes necessary, the identity of a complainant is likely to become a matter of public record.	Charges or related information are not made public by EEOC. If an aggrieved person files a charge personally, the name is divulged to the organization against whom charges have been filed. If an organization files on behalf of any individual, only the name of the organization is divulged. EEOC charges or information may be made available to the charging party. If court action becomes necessary, the identities of the parties become a matter of public record.	The identity of a complainant is kept confidential, if possible. It is sometimes impossible, however, to investigate a complaint without the complainant's identity becoming known.	The identities of a complainant and an employer (and labor organization, if involved) are kept in strict confidence. If court action becomes necessary, the identities of the parties become a matter of public record.	Although the identity of the complainant is kept confidential if possible, it is sometimes impossible to investigate a complaint without the identity of the complainant becoming known. If court action becomes necessary, the identity of a complainant is likely to become a matter of public record.
Harassment/Retaliation:	Covered agencies and institutions are prohibited from discharging or discriminating against any employee, student applicant, or student applicant because he/she has made a complaint, assisted with an investigation, or instituted proceedings.	Covered agencies and institutions are prohibited from discharging or discriminating against any employee or employee applicant because he/she has made or threatened to make a complaint, assisted with an investigation, or taken any action that indicates opposition to discrimination.	Covered agencies and institutions are prohibited from discharging or discriminating against any employee or employee applicant because he/she has made a complaint, assisted with an investigation, or instituted proceedings.	Covered agencies and institutions are prohibited from discharging or discriminating against any employee or employee applicant because he/she has made a complaint, assisted with an investigation, or instituted proceedings.	Covered agencies and institutions are prohibited from discharging or discriminating against any employee, employee applicant, student, or student applicant because he/she has made a complaint, assisted with an investigation, or instituted proceedings.
For Further Information Contact:	Office for Civil Rights, Department of Health, Education, and Welfare Washington, D.C. 20201 or your regional Office for Civil Rights, Department of Health, Education, and Welfare	Equal Employment Opportunity Commission 2401 E Street NW Washington, D.C. 20506 or your regional Equal Employment Opportunity Commission	Office for Civil Rights, Department of Health, Education, and Welfare Washington, D.C. 20201 or your regional Office for Civil Rights, Department of Health, Education, and Welfare	Wage and Hour Division Employment Standards Division U.S. Department of Labor Washington, D.C. 20210 or your field, area, or regional Wage and Hour Division office, U.S. Department of Labor	Office for Civil Rights Department of Health, Education, and Welfare Washington, D.C. 20201 or your regional Office for Civil Rights, Department of Health, Education, and Welfare

Title IX of the Education Amendments of 1972 prohibits sex discrimination in all federally assisted education programs. Specifically, discrimination is forbidden in the following employment policies and practices:

Access to employment
    recruitment policies/practices   application procedures
    advertising   testing/interviewing practices

Hiring and promotion
    selection practices   layoff, demotion, termination
    nepotism policies   tenure

Compensation
    wages/salaries   extra compensation

Job assignments
    position descriptions   seniority lists
    lines of progression   assignment/placement

Title IX takes on unique importance because its procedures differ a great deal from those of Title VII and of the Executive Order. Title IX is enforced by the Wage and Hour Division of the Employment Standards Administration of the Department of Labor. Reviews can be conducted without prior complaint, and the complaint procedure is very informal. Unlike Title VII, which requires a notarized complaint, the Wage and Hour Division will investigate an establishment on the basis of a letter or even a telephone call. Also, the Wage and Hour Division does not reveal the name of the complainant to the employer unless permission is given by the complainant.

Executive Order 11246 as amended by Executive Order 11375 covers only those institutions which hold federal contracts. It prohibits discrimination in employment and does not cover students unless they are employed by an institution. The Executive Order is not a law but a series of rules and regulations which contractors agree to follow when they accept a federal contract. The main provision of the Order is that the contractor must not only cease discrimination but also have a written plan of affirmative action, including numerical goals, to remedy the effects of past discrimination and prevent continuation of current discrimination. Since most elementary and secondary schools have grants rather than contracts, they are not usually affected by the Executive Order.

Equal educational rights. Stereotyped ideas of women's work and men's work still exist although certain pieces of legislation are helping to make it illegal to exclude anyone from training programs on the basis of sex. Title IX of the Education Amendments of 1972 (Higher Education Act) and Title II of the Education Amendments of 1976 (Vocational Education Act of 1963 and the Vocational Education Amendments of 1968) are two such pieces of legislation; both of these acts prevent discrimination against students on the basis of sex.

Title IX of the 1972 Education Amendments. Title IX forbids discrimination on the basis of sex in all federally assisted education programs. It covers virtually all areas of student life—admissions, course offerings, activities, financial aid, health financial assistance, dress, conduct, marital and parental status, provision services, sports, testing, differential rules and regulation of school facilities, counseling programs and techniques, etc. Some of the school practices prohibited by Title IX include the following:

1. Refusing to admit students to courses on the basis of sex
2. Maintaining sex segregated interest clubs
3. Employing counseling procedures—tests, career materials, counseling techniques—which discriminate on the basis of sex
4. Denying financial aid, benefits, or services to students on the basis of sex
5. Discriminating on the basis of sex in providing work-study opportunities and placement of students in employment
6. Bestowing student honors on the basis of sex.

If a particular class or course of study has a substantially disproportionate number of individuals of one sex, the school must take action to assure that this disproportion is not the result of sex discrimination—by either administrators, teachers, or counselors. Nothing in this regulation requires or prohibits the use of particular textbooks or curricular materials.

Education Amendments of 1976, Title II. There are many references included in Title II concerning the need to eliminate sex stereotyping and sex bias from all vocational programs. The provisions stated in this law establish priorities and programs which affect the design and implementation of vocational programs at national, state, and local levels.

At the national level, the commissioner of education is required to investigate the extent to which sex discrimination and stereotyping exist in all vocational education programs and to set up a data reporting system for national vocational education. The commissioner is also authorized to use 5 percent of available funds for state grants for model programs and for research. And, appropriate representation of both sexes is mandated on the National Advisory Council and State Advisory Council for Vocational Education.

Each state must have a five-year plan to assure sex fair vocational education. A full-time person has to be designated in each state to assume responsibility for eliminating sex bias in programs, with a minimum of $50,000 to be spent for this purpose.

Among the provisions of this Title, every state is mandated to do the following:

1. Provide counseling and job placement services for nontraditional students
2. Develop nonsexist curriculums
3. Develop exemplary and innovative projects to give priority to reducing sex stereotyping
4. Provide support in-service training of teachers and other staff concerning the elimination of sex bias in educational programs
5. Develop guidance and testing materials designed to overcome sex bias in programs.

Implication of laws. This brief review and summarization of the legislation and Executive Orders give some feeling for the scope of the concern that has been expressed by Congress and the Executive Office for equal opportunity in education and employment. While business, office, and distributive education teachers and students may be affected in various ways by all of the mandates, it is Title II of the Education Amendments of 1976 that brings the equal opportunity mandate close to home. It places the charge of eliminating sex stereotyping and bias squarely on the shoulders of the educators. It is now incumbent upon vocational educators to know what is expected of them under legislation.

To provide sex fair vocational education in business, office, and distribution programs, educators have to—

Be knowledgeable themselves about problems of sex stereotyping and bias and ways to reduce such problems.

Create awareness of problems of sex stereotyping and bias (in both school and community environments).

Use sex fair recruitment and placement procedures in programs/courses.

Disseminate data on the status of men and women in the labor market.

Design recruitment and counseling procedures/materials to get and keep nontraditional students in particular programs/courses.

Identify existence of bias in programs.

Monitor and keep up to date on implementation of laws concerning equal working rights and equal educational rights.

Provide support services for nontraditional students.

Review and revise curriculums and other materials to ensure sex fair content and illustrations.

Develop and refine sex fair teaching techniques.

Work with counterparts in business, industry, and general public (parents, civic groups, legislators, etc.) to assure that students completing nontraditional courses will have employment/advancement opportunities.

As of 1980, it is no longer a matter of whether or not to provide sex fair vocational education; it is mandated by law. Congress has made it very clear that we must all serve as advocates for equal opportunity for all students!

STRATEGIES FOR SEX FAIR VOCATIONAL EDUCATION

There are many techniques which business, office, and distributive education teachers can use to promote sex fair vocational education in their work with students. Because of space limitations, selected activities for recruiting, teaching with biased materials, creating sex bias awareness, adopting nonsexist teaching strategies, and retaining students will be given as examples of such techniques. A representative bibliography will also be presented for additional strategy and technique ideas.

Recruiting. Even though efforts are being made legislatively and academically to provide sex fair vocational training, enrollment figures indicate that there is a need to actively recruit students into nontraditional areas. To counter socialization patterns which prevent men and women from getting the job training that would best fit their talents and do them the most good, a variety of recruitment strategies are necessary to effect any appreciable change in enrollments.

Before beginning recruitment strategies, it is necessary to determine recruitment needs. Information from the Title IX self-evaluation may help determine such needs. The self-evaluation document, which should be on file and available for your use, evaluates your school's policies and practices concerning admission, enrollments, treatment, and placement of students.

Once the evaluation of the existing situation is completed, then a master plan can be developed to recruit nontraditional students for particular programs. Such a master plan includes steps, activities, and timetables for the recruitment effort. The plan would, of course, have to be approved and supported by the school administration. It would also require the support of school counselors as they work with students to reinforce career options, provide role models, develop nonbiased attitudes, administer sex fair tests and career inventories, and distribute career literature.

Specific activities for the recruitment of nontraditional students might include some of the following:

1. Educate parents and community members about the need to remove barriers to nontraditional occupations—open house, parent meetings, addresses to community groups, mass media exposure, AV presentations, informational brochures.

2. Share career information with counselors to make them aware of job opportunities for both sexes.

3. Publicize nontraditional career options—design sex fair vocational brochures, arrange tours of classrooms, conduct a career fair, use bulletin boards to inform students about jobs, and use auditorium programs to emphasize nontraditional opportunities.

4. Review clubs and interschool organizations to be sure that membership criteria are sex fair.

5. Encourage development of a career resource center which contains a range of self-instructional counseling resources such as filmstrips, interest inventories, vertical files containing occupational information, reference materials, and games.

6. Organize guided consciousness-raising groups to help students gain knowledge, set career/life goals, overcome occupational sex role stereotypes.

7. Offer special selective courses geared to attract nontraditional students.

8. Provide tours of a variety of classrooms and industries to convey advantages and disadvantages of various occupations.

9. Assist student organizations in designing and implementing an awareness training workshop.

10. Communicate information about job trends and needs for nontraditional workers.

11. Provide big sisters and big brothers to new students in nontraditional vocational education programs.

12. Change course titles and descriptions to encourage participation of all students.

13. Publicize student success in nontraditional classes.

14. Publicize teacher efforts to recruit, train, and place nontraditional students.

15. Use guest lectures by individuals who are nontraditional workers.

16. Develop simulated job experience programs to give students experience in nontraditional roles.

17. Include nontraditional workers on advisory committees.

18. Select males and females to serve on the departmental advisory committee.

Teaching with biased materials. Many of the vocational education materials currently in use in today's schools are sex biased. Such bias limits the scope of occupations which are presented to males and to females; the traditional roles and occupations these materials present to females do not realistically prepare them for careers that will enable them to be self-sufficient adults, and many males are prevented from realizing their full potential. However, because of economic reasons, schools will probably continue to use biased materials. For that reason, educators have to be capable of creatively using such biased materials in a nonbiased way.

Perhaps one of the most effective ways to overcome bias and stereotypes in educational materials is to deal with it directly. This means that textbooks and other materials themselves should become the topic of classroom discussion and learning activities. One way to increase the students' awareness of bias and stereotypes is to have students evaluate their materials. The following checklist is appropriate for such an exercise.

A Checklist for Evaluating Materials

ITEM	YES	NO	NA
Language:			
1. Is the generic *he* used to include both males/females when sex is unspecified?			
2. Is the generic *she* used where the antecedent is stereotyped as female?			
3. Is a universal male term used when the word is meant to include both sexes—mankind?			
4. When referring to both sexes, does the male term consistently precede the female—he, she; men and women?			
5. Are occupational titles used with man as the suffix—chairman?			
6. When a woman or a man holds a nontraditional job, is there unnecessary focus on the person's sex—woman president, male typist?			
7. Are nonparallel terms used in referring to males and females—Mr. Jones and his secretary Ellen?			
8. Are the words "women" and "female" replaced by such terms as girls, fair sex, ladies?			

A Checklist for Evaluating Materials (continued)

ITEM	YES	NO	NA
9. Are women described in terms of their appearance or marital and family status while men are described in terms of their accomplishments or titles—Senator Kennedy?			
10. Are women identified by their husband's names—Mrs. F. D. Roosevelt?			
11. Are women presented as either dependent on or subordinate to men—John took his wife on a . . . ?			
12. Does the material use nonsexist language initially and then slip into use of the generic he?			
13. Is the issue of sexual equality diminished by lumping the problems of women with those of minorities—". . . equal attention will be given to the rights of the handicapped, blacks, and women"?			
Roles:			
14. Are occupations presented as appropriate to qualified persons of either sex?			
15. Are certain jobs automatically associated with women and others associated with men—personnel manager, female; director of marketing, male?			
16. Are housekeeping and family responsibilities still a prime consideration for only females in choosing and maintaining a career—flexible hours, proximity to home?			
17. Is it assumed that the boss, executive, professional, etc. will be male and the assistant, helpmate, "gal Friday" will be female?			
18. In addition to professional responsibilities, is it assumed that women will also have housekeeping tasks at the place of business?			
19. Is tokenism apparent—an occasional reference to women or men in nontraditional jobs while the greatest portion of the material remains job stereotyped?			
20. Are men and women portrayed as having sex-linked personality traits that influence their working abilities—the female bookkeeper's loving attention to detail?			
21. Are only females shown as passive and inept?			
22. Are only females shown as lacking a desire to assume responsibility?			
23. Are only females presented as gossips?			
24. Are only women shown as vain and especially concerned about their appearance?			
25. Are only females presented as fearful and in need of protection—"she should not walk home alone"?			

208

A Checklist for Evaluating Materials (continued)

ITEM	YES	NO	NA
26. Are only males shown as capable, aggressive, and always in charge?			
27. Do only males consistently display self-control and restraint?			
28. Are opportunities overlooked to present a range of emotional traits for females and males?			
29. Are women and men assigned the traditional roles of males as breadwinners and females as caretakers of home and children?			
30. Is a woman's marital status stated when it is irrelevant and when the same information about the man is not available?			
31. If a couple work together in a business, is it assured that *she* will assist *him*?			
32. Is information included about family relationships which is not relevant to the tasks—"Jane Dawson, mother of four, is the new supervisor"?			
33. Are both men and women shown in nontraditional occupations?			
34. In historical and biographical references, are women adequately acknowledged for their achievements?			
35. Are quotes and anecdotes from women in history used as frequently as those from men?			
36. Is there acknowledgement of the limitations placed on women in the past—women could not put their names on literature, inventions, etc.?			
37. When a historical sexist situation is cited, is it qualified when appropriate as past history no longer accepted?			
Physical appearance:			
38. Are females described in terms of their physical appearance and men in terms of accomplishment or character?			
39. Is grooming advice focused only on females and presented as a factor in being hired?			
40. Is a smiling face considered advisable only for a woman in many occupations?			
41. Are only men presented or described in terms of accomplishment or character rather than appearance?			
42. Are only men presented as rarely concerned with clothing and hairstyle?			
43. Are men shown taller and more vigorous and women as smaller and more fragile?			
44. Are women presented as more adroit with a typewriter than a saw?			

A Checklist for Evaluating Materials (continued)

ITEM	YES	NO	NA
45. Are men presented as dextrous and at ease with tools and machines and baffled when confronted with a filing cabinet?			
Audiovisual materials:			
46. Are only male voices used consistently to narrate audio materials?			
47. Are female voices used only when dealing with traditionally female occupations?			
48. Do illustrations of males outnumber those of females?			
49. Do the illustrations represent mainly young, attractive, and preferred-body types both in composite pictures as well as in the body of the materials?			
50. Is the text inconsistent with the illustrations—sex fair content with sexist graphics?			
51. Are women and men commonly drawn in stereotyped body postures and sizes with females shown as consistently smaller, over-shadowed, or shown as background figures?			
52. Does the artist use pastel colors and fuzzy line definition when illustrating females and strong colors and bold lines for males?			
53. Are women frequently illustrated as the cliché "dumb broad"?			
54. Are bosses, executives, and leaders pictured as males?			
55. Is only an occasional token woman pictured as a leader or as serving in a nonstereotyped role?			

Other creative strategies for using biased materials in a nonbiased way are listed below.

1. At the beginning of the school year or term, devote one or more classes to an analysis of the textbook.

2. As resource materials are used in the course, point out and discuss such language factors as the following:

   a. Masculine generic terms.

   b. Masculine pronouns which theoretically represent both males and females.

   c. Gender nouns that denote occupations—businessman, salesman.

   d. Inconsistencies in the language of materials—"Both men and women will find excellent job opportunities in the secretarial field. The secretary . . . she. . . ."

   e. Descriptive words which affect student role perceptions—cute secretary, attractive nurse.

f. Stereotyped occupational roles—only males as boss, only females as secretaries or clerks. Discuss physical and mental requirements which would limit either sex from having a certain occupation.

g. Statements that tie vocational choice to social roles.

h. Personal traits which are sex linked. For example, do the case studies show women being more vain and emotional or less assertive and competent than men?

i. Representation of men in both primary roles and women in secondary occupational roles.

3. Consider a unit on "Do Words Make a Difference?" Have students study the difference between negative, demeaning, and neutral language and find examples in the resource materials.

4. Ask students to bring pictures of males and females in expanded roles which might be used as illustrations in the text materials. Such pictures could be used on the bulletin boards.

5. Have students analyze trade journals and other materials ordinarily used in class for the purpose of eliminating biased and stereotyped language and illustrations.

6. Encourage students to write textbook and other publishers explaining how they have analyzed their materials and what they found.

Creating sex bias awareness. Most students are not aware of their own attitudes and biases concerning sex fair occupational work and training. There are techniques which teachers can use to help raise the consciousness of students to the sex stereotyping which we have all been taught. The following strategies are examples of such techniques.

1. Prepare a list of human characteristics. Write each one on a separate piece of paper. Place the papers in a "Personality Sack" and let each student draw a characteristic. The student should act out the characteristic, and the class will identify the characteristic as male or female. Then discuss why the characteristic was classified that way.

2. Prepare a list of issues related to sex roles. Assign to students pro, con, or neutral position for each issue. Have students debate issues as assigned.

3. Use two filmstrips concerning the same topic—one out of date and one which is very current. Discuss changing roles.

4. Ask students to list jobs as "male" and "female"; discuss whether each job could be done well by a woman or by a man.

5. Have students bring in Dear Abby and Ann Landers columns dealing with male and female behavior, sex roles, and relations. Have students write nonsexist responses.

6. Have students observe and discuss how teachers stereotype students; e.g., boys carry boxes, are supposed to be good at math, are good athletes; girls decorate bulletin boards, write neater papers. How do students react to this stereotyping? To what degree do students accept and/or encourage this stereotyping?

7. Have students list as many job titles as possible. How many titles have the implied sex of the job holder (repairman)? Develop nonsexist titles.

8. Hold a contest for the "Sexist Ad of the Year" with each student bringing an entry and the class voting on the winner.

9. Collect and share correspondence received to illustrate sexist and nonsexist terminology. Assign rewriting/retyping of sexist letters into nonsexist language—and use them on the bulletin boards.

10. Have students search out people in magazines and TV shows who depart from traditional sex roles.

Adopting nonsexist teaching strategies. Much sex stereotyping in the classroom is not the result of conscious behavior on the part of teachers. Educators do not purposefully set out to teach boys that it is more masculine to do things that require great strength. Teachers unconsciously stereotype students by sex because teachers have been socialized and taught stereotyped attitudes and biases.

Business, office, and distributive education teachers have to be aware of their unconscious or unintentional bias in teaching strategies. Since students learn much more in school than factual information, teachers must consciously strive to reinforce sex fair occupational choice, training, placement, and advancement. Nonsexist teaching strategies are illustrated in the following activities:

1. Create bulletin board displays and posters showing nontraditional workers in business, office, and distributive occupations.

2. Have students use evaluation sheets concerning sex equity when they design and put up bulletin boards or exhibits.

3. Collect illustrations which show nontraditional role models.

4. Have students participate in a panel discussion concerning barriers to and problems in entering and training in sex fair vocational education.

5. Evaluate student papers for sex bias and stereotyping.

6. Have students redesign charts, bulletins, and other materials that are sex biased.

7. Organize an occupations fair with student-developed posters designed to attract nontraditional students into exploring business, office, or distributive occupations.

8. Research field trips carefully to be sure that professionals are a mix of males, females, and/or minority groups working together and succeeding in the occupation.

9. Train students to edit materials for sexist terms.

10. Provide a copy of DOT (Dictionary of Occupational Titles) for class use.

11. Integrate group discussions, class seatings, and project work for equal representation of males/females.

12. Practice using gender-free terms—students, pupils, assistants, class.

13. Assign writing skits on small group basis—several people portraying people in nontraditional roles and several in traditional roles—with suggested themes.

14. Outline techniques for students to use in coping with sexist interviews.

15. Teach telephone techniques to emphasize nonsexist behavior and language.

16. Assign leadership and clean-up classroom tasks equitably to female and to male students.

17. Develop case studies or role play situations dealing with work adjustment, human relations, and communication—cast characters in both traditional and nontraditional roles.

18. Organize an occupational treasure hunt which enables students to meet nontraditional people in office occupations. Solicit cooperation of the business community prior to this activity.

Retaining students. Statistics show that there is a great attrition rate in the number of students who enter a nontraditional program and the number of those students who complete such a program. Once nontraditional students are enrolled in business, office, and distributive education classes, they need additional support and counseling programs to help them stay with the program and to help them maximize their potential in the program.

Business teachers and school counselors can help retain nontraditional students by doing such things as the following:

1. Using peer counseling. Peer counselors can give educational advice, provide information, develop friendships, and affect attitudes.

2. Scheduling monthly counseling sessions in which students discuss activities and feelings in their educational training.

3. Using telephone counseling. Have a period of time each week in which a counselor is available by phone for counseling sessions.

4. Giving nontraditional students leadership responsibilities if they have that potential.

5. Encouraging nontraditional students to participate in related clubs and organizations.

SUMMARY

It is the law that business, office, and distributive educators provide sex fair educational training—recruitment, learning, placement, and counseling. It is the educator's responsibility to present not only the utilitarian purposes of education—development/refinement of knowledge/skills for job entry— but also to meet society's economic needs—sufficient numbers of traditional and nontraditional entry-level workers.

To address the problems of providing sex fair educational programs and of graduating trained traditional/nontraditional workers, educators can (1) implement fully the laws and orders concerning sex equity, (2) change recruitment and admission practices and policies, (3) improve guidance and counseling efforts, (4) adapt and revise curricular materials and teaching practices, (5) work toward sex equity in male/female representations on the teaching staff, and (6) participate in research and development efforts to promote/develop sex fair vocational education.

SEX EQUITY RESOURCE MATERIALS

The following resources can provide bibliographies concerning sex equity, summaries of legislative acts and orders, guidelines for promoting sex equity in business/office/distributive education, and compilations of teaching strategies—activities and content information—to encourage sex equity in the classroom.

American Education Research Association
1126 16th Street, N.W.
Washington, DC 20036
202-223-9485

American Federation of Teachers
Human Rights & Community Relations
11 Dupont Circle, N.W.
Washington, DC 20036
202-737-4400

American Institute for Research
3301 New Mexico Avenue, N.W.
Washington, DC 20016
202-686-6800

American Vocational Association
1510 H Street, N.W.
Washington, DC 20056
202-737-3722

Education Commission of the States
Equal Rights for Women in Education
   Project
300 Lincoln Tower
1860 Lincoln Street
Denver, CO 80202
303-861-4917

National Advisory Council on
   Vocational Education
425 13 Street, N.W., Suite 412
Washington, DC 20004

National Center for Career Education
University of Montana
P.O. Box 7815
Missoula, MI 59801
406-243-5262

National Center for Research in
   Vocational Education
The Ohio State University
1960 Kenny Road
Columbus, OH 43210
614-486-3655

National Coalition for Sex Equity
   in Education (NCSEE)
P.O. Box 82
El Dorado Hills, CA 95630
916-322-7388

NEA Order Department
The Academic Building
Saw Mill Road
West Haven, CT 06516

National Foundation for the Improvement
   of Education (NFIE)
400 N. Capitol Street, Suite 379
Washington, DC 20001
202-833-5426

Office of Education
Department of Health, Education &
   Welfare
Title IV Civil Rights Act of 1964
400 Maryland Avenue, N.W., Room 2001
Washington, DC 20202
202-245-8484

Project on Equal Education Rights (PEER)
National Organization for Women
1029 Vermont Avenue, N.W., Suite 800
Washington, DC 20005
202-332-7337

Racism/Sexism Resource Center
Room 300, 1841 Broadway
New York, NY 10023

Resource Center on Sex Roles in Education
Council of Chief State School Offices
400 N. Capitol Street, Suite 379
Washington, DC 20001
202-833-5426

Superintendent of Documents
U.S. Government Printing Office
Washington, DC 20402

Title IX Coordinator and/or Sex Equity
   Coordinator (Vocational Education)
Your State Department of Education

Women's Educational Equity Act Program
Office of Education
400 Maryland Avenue, N.W., Room 2147
Washington, DC 20202
202-245-2182

Women's Educational Equity
   Communications Network
Far West Laboratory for Educational
   Research and Development
1855 Folsom Street
San Francisco, CA 94101
415-565-3032

Women's Equity Action League
Educational and Legal Defense Fund
805 15th Street, N.W., Suite 822
Washington, DC 20005
202-638-1961

214

CHAPTER 18

Broadening Content for Gifted Students

EUGENE P. WHITNEY

New York State Education Department, Albany

Business education at the secondary school level is traditionally geared to the average and below average student. Programs for gifted students are generally considered the domain of the math, science, and fine arts departments. However, the business education curriculum has much to offer the gifted student, and business education programs developed to meet the specific needs of this population have been and can continue to be highly successful and beneficial. The initial task for the business educator attempting to meet the needs of gifted students is to identify the specific gifted student populations that are to be served. Once the students are identified, their specific needs can be assessed and appropriate learning activities developed.

There are two general categories of gifted students. First, the classic group most often identified by educators as gifted are those students who demonstrate superior academic ability. The second group, which has more recently been officially recognized as gifted, is made up of those students who demonstrate outstanding ability to perform particular activities and functions. The first group has a unique universal need that is the primary responsibility of business educators; the second group has a variety of needs that can be administered to by specialized business education programs.

BUSINESS PROGRAMS FOR THE ACADEMICALLY GIFTED

The academically gifted students are the most easily identified, and they are the students least likely to be enrolled in the secondary business education program. Students with superior academic ability are generally guided into the college entrance program and are encouraged to take advance placement courses. This generally leaves little time in the school schedule for business education. A very small percentage of the current business education programs administer to the needs of this population.

It should be noted that most of the average academic ability students are also guided into the college entrance program. Consequently, from the business educator's perspective, all students cast into the college entrance track can be considered a target population to be served. Roughly 80 percent of the secondary school students across the country are guided into a college entrance program that contains little or no training in the areas of career exploration and personal business management. All students at some time or other in their lives will have to use basic personal business management skills to survive in our economically oriented society. Basic legal skills, recordkeeping skills, buying skills, and management skills cannot be attained at an effective level without some preparation and training. A personal business management course to assist these students in effectively managing their personal business affairs may be the greatest contribution that business education can make to this neglected population.

The Alpha Mu Study included a survey of some 10,000 graduating seniors in sample schools in selected states from Massachusetts to California and found that two-thirds of the graduates were grossly deficient in basic business survival skills.[1] The research committee conducting this survey recommended a personal business management course for all students before graduating from the secondary school program. The program suggested goes above and beyond the typical consumer economics program and is compatible with the "New Approach to Consumer Education" cited in the September-October 1979 issue of *Business Education World*.[2] A course of study to include the basic business survival skills essential for all could be condensed into a one semester offering to meet the needs of gifted students. A suggested list of objectives for such a course of study is presented below.

The key consideration for this program is the level at which the course is to be presented. The program must be a challenge to the above average, academically gifted student. Consequently, the course must be geared at a much higher academic level than the typical consumer education type course which is frequently used as a refuge for the lower ability student. It must be pertinent and practical and should not be a warmed-over version of the traditional offering. The content should be designed to give busy minds the basic guidelines to develop the necessary skills to effectively manage their personal business affairs.

Suggested Course Outline for a Personal Business Management Course To Complement the College Entrance Program for Academically Gifted Students

Introduction

1. Start the class with the concept that each person is in business to maintain his/her own financial livelihood. Everyone must develop and use effective business practices to achieve maximum success.

1. Average person makes nearly a half million dollars in a lifetime.

   Over half of advertising by newspapers, billboards, radio, and TV attempts to persuade people to buy things they don't need.

   Wise management of personal wealth can provide maximum comfort.

---

[1]Whitney, Eugene P. "A Report on the Survey of Basic Survival Skills." Alpha Mu Study. *Delta Pi Epsilon Journal* 21:1; January 1979.

[2]Whitney, Eugene P. "A New Approach to Consumer Education." *Business Education World* 60:1; September-October 1979.

Unit I. Understanding Your Paycheck

Students will be able to identify all deductions taken from their paycheck and to calculate the value of the fringe benefits they receive with their employment. They will further be able to determine their "real income" and their "real wealth."

1. Identify take home pay.

1. Actual cash after deductions

2. Identify deductions from paycheck.

2. Federal withholding taxes
   Social Security taxes
   State withholding taxes
   Union dues/purchases
   Other

3. Identify the benefits received through deductions.

3. Federal income taxes pay for maintenance of system that allows one to work and live in freedom.

   Social Security taxes provide retirement income as well as financial assistance for certain tragedies, etc.

4. Identify fringe benefits.

4. Unemployment insurance, hospitalization, etc.

5. Determine money value of fringe benefits.

5. Figure actual cost of these benefits if one were to purchase them on the open market.

6. Determine real income.

6. Add fringe benefits to gross salary.

7. Determine real wealth.

7. Make an inventory of things owned.

   Add value of fringe benefits (i.e. potential income from hospitalization benefits, unemployment insurance, etc.).

Unit II. Basic Legal Skills for Personal Business Management

Students will be able to identify the major factors to be considered to protect their rights when entering into a contract for goods and services. They will further be able to identify the advantages and disadvantages of the major methods of buying on credit.

1. Know your seller.

1. Reliability vs. legality
   Dealing with minors
   Receiving stolen goods

2. Warranties

2. Elements of a legal warranty

3. Protecting your rights

3. "An ounce of prevention is worth a pound of cure."

4. Enforcing your rights

4. Consumer protection agencies
   Better Business Bureau
   The courts (as a last resort)

5. Buying on credit

5. The conditional sales contract
   Home mortgages
   The charge account
   Bank credit cards
   Company credit cards
   Special agreements

217

| 6. The cost of credit | 6. Figure the costs of buying on credit in each type of purchase. |
| | Emphasize the wisdom in saving to purchase non-necessities. |

Unit III. Basic Recordkeeping Skills for Personal Business Management

Students will be able to identify a practical means for accounting for income and expenditures. They will further be able to maintain a personal checking account and reconcile the account balance with the periodic bank statement and file income tax forms.

1. Develop the importance of keeping records.	1. Records needed for income tax, to verify bills and charges, etc.
2. Using the bank as your personal auditor	2. Establishing a checking account
3. Choosing a bank	3. Compare checking account regulations and charges.
4. Using a checking account	4. Writing checks Making deposits Reconciling the bank statement
5. Identifying tax deductible items	5. Use a letter key with the check number to identify payments for medical expenses, M; contributions, C; interest, I; etc.
6. Completing tax forms	6. Use current federal and state tax forms.

Unit IV. Basic Decision-Making Skills for Personal Business Management

Students will be able to identify personal budget plans to maintain three different living levels. They will further be able to identify the practical aspects of choosing a standard of living.

1. Distinguish between necessities and desires.	1. Determine what is needed to exist; then what is needed to exist comfortably; then what is desired to meet expectations.
2. Examine your expectations.	2. Identify expectations that are for personal comfort, for status maintenance, and for conspicuous consumption.
	Objectively evaluate your expectations.
3. Prepare three budgets—one on existence level, one on comfort level, and one on expectations level.	3. Prioritize expectations level budget.

Unit V. Preparing for the Future

Students will be able to identify a means for protecting their personal wealth against risk of loss. They will further be able to identify means by which they can manage their resources to provide for future security.

218

1. Insurance	1. Identify contingencies. Categorize by insurable and uninsurable. Determine cost of insurable contingencies. Determine feasibility of insurance for each contingency.
2. Investment	2. Identify possible funds for investment if living at the existence level (with and without insurance), at the comfort level (with and without insurance), at the expectations level (with and without insurance). Determine investment possibilities and expected income one could acquire if living at existence level, at comfort level, and at expectation level.
3. Develop management plan.	3. Determine 1-year, 5-year, and 10-year plans considering possible postponement of comfort and/or expectations to realize greater future comfort and security.

Exploring business careers. Another business education program that would meet the specific needs of academically gifted students is a business careers course. Business careers in management, computer science, and accounting offer many rewards for the gifted. Quite often these students are neglected in the secondary school career exploratory program with the presumption that they will automatically go on to college and make a choice at a later time. A concrete goal established early could give an extra incentive to help these students achieve their maximum potential. A short minicourse to explore the opportunities available in the vast field of business occupations could be coordinated with exploratory courses in other occupational areas, or it could be self-contained.

Personal shorthand and personal typing. Two business education courses that are commonly used to enrich the educational training of academically gifted students heading for higher education are personal-use shorthand and personal typewriting. Both courses provide skills that are of great assistance to a college student when taking lecture notes and preparing assignments as well as for personal-use activities.

A unique personal-use shorthand course offered in a city public high school features dictation practice materials related directly to a first-year college psychology course given at a number of colleges in the immediate area. The teacher researched the problem areas encountered by first-year college students in that region and discovered that the vast amount of material covered in a particular first-year psychology course frequently resulted in failure. With the permission of the college professors involved, the shorthand teacher obtained lecture notes common to these classes and used the material for classroom assignments. Consequently, the course not only provided a basic note-taking skill but also gave students a familiarity with difficult material that many would encounter the following year at college.

The personal typewriting course is often enriched also to include particular manuscript and thesis requirements common to the colleges in surrounding areas. The key to the effectiveness of such a program is a dedicated teacher who will take the time to research specific needs and use the imagination and initiative required to develop content and classroom activities to meet these needs.

PROGRAMS FOR STUDENTS WITH GIFTED PERFORMANCE SKILLS

Students with gifted performance skills are less likely to be recognized and given an opportunity to develop their gifts than are those students who are academically gifted. However, they very often can be identified; and they can be given meaningful programs to fully develop their exceptional talents.

In vocational business education, a student with gifted performance skills could be one who demonstrates the ability to type at an unusually high rate of speed with exceptional accuracy. Another gifted student in business whose talents are more difficult to document might include the business law student with exceptional perception of legal concepts and their practical application. This category of gifted students could also include the accounting student with the exceptional ability to analyze a business transaction, or the management student with the exceptional ability to organize and manipulate human behavior to achieve a predetermined goal.

Students with gifted performance skills are not as readily and widely accepted as the academically gifted students, but these students can become directly involved with vocational business education. Programs for these students should be one of the top priorities for business educators.

Because of the relative difficulty in measuring gifted performance skills and the relatively short time that consideration has been focused on this facet of education, there are few, if any, large scale programs in operation. Experimentation in this area is fairly widespread, however, and a review of some of the more successful programs may be helpful to serve as a model for duplication or to stimulate creation of new programs.

Work experience programs. A work experience program that places students with exceptional talent in an identified area into an apprentice type position where that talent can develop and grow may prove to be as beneficial to the business as it is to the student exposed to the program. An example of such a program is the "Unique Work Experience Program" conducted by an area occupational center in upstate New York. Top academic students who have maintained superior scholastic standing are allowed to take a six-week block of time away from school in an appropriate business where they follow a regular business schedule and perform some of the basic related activities associated with the profession in which they are interested. The experience gives them the opportunity to see "first-hand" the actual environment associated with the selected profession and assists the students in gaining insights to help them better choose their career path. The identification of students in this program is determined basically by student interest; and superior academic achievement is admittedly a criteria for eligibility. However, with a means to identify specific gifted skills and a viable plan to recruit appropriate students, this program could provide a far-reaching business education program that could be adapted to a wide range of exceptional talents.

Advance placement courses. A number of progressive schools on Long Island offer an advance placement bookkeeping/accounting course for exceptionally gifted students that is recognized for advanced credit at most of the postsecondary institutions in that region. The course is accelerated to cover the typical two-year secondary school program of bookkeeping and accounting plus additional content suggested by the institutions of higher education that are involved with the program. The main ingredient for developing this type of program is an enthusiastic and ambitious teacher who will take the time and expend the effort to make contact with the appropriate colleges. The program must be developed to appeal to and meet the need of the specific group of gifted students involved.

Interest is a definite factor used to identify the enrollees in this program. However, identification is also made in the beginning bookkeeping courses by the classroom teacher who observes outstanding ability exhibited by students in performing accounting tasks. The teacher then counsels the student and recommends that consideration be given to the advance placement course available.

Other advance placement courses are offered by some secondary schools in business law, typewriting, and shorthand.

Competency-based typewriting. The New York State competency-based typewriting program offers a unique opportunity for students gifted in this area to demonstrate their talents and achieve superior competency as quickly as their talent will allow. The two-year state program is divided into seven levels with competency examinations developed for each level. After achieving the first level (keyboarding), students proceed at their own pace and ability. Some gifted students have mastered the first-year program in one term; whereas, exceptionally gifted students have mastered the two-year program in one year's time. Individual students can progress to whatever level of competency they choose as quickly as their talents permit. This program obviously also has many benefits for student populations other than the gifted.

Business operations. Junior Achievement programs offer an excellent opportunity for gifted students to gain a grasp of the concept of business organization and management. In these programs, students develop and operate an actual business enterprise for profit. They start with the legal process of incorporation and proceed through all of the operational functions of a business organization, finally concluding with the dissolution of the corporation and the distribution of profits. There are numerous variations of this program scattered across the country in innovative classrooms. One example is the "Cup Cake Company" operated by the gifted students in an introduction to business class in a Western New York State high school. The company was formed to channel the energies of advanced students who completed regular assignments far ahead of their peers. These students purchase cake mix, bake cupcakes, and sell them at school functions. The students keep detailed accounting and cost records as well as a complex market analysis. The profits are accumulated for an interesting, educational end-of-the-year field trip.

Business and society. A unique approach to business management and its relationship to society in a futuristic mode is suggested in the New York State publication *A Look to the Future.*[3] A course of study to consider the fundamentals of business enterprise and the expectations of business and societal behavior in the future could be a magnificent challenge to gifted students and teachers as well. Suggested content for a five-unit course of study in this area is presented below.

Suggested Content for the Consideration of
Future Behavior Patterns in Business and Society
for Gifted and Perceptive Students

I. Value Considerations
  (a) Quantity vs. quality
  (b) Independence vs. interdependence
  (c) Mastery over nature vs. living in harmony with nature
  (d) Expediency vs. integrity
  (e) Organization convenience vs. self-development of the individual
  (f) Working for vs. working with
  (g) Uniformity and centralization vs. diversity and pluralism
  (h) Work as an unavoidable duty vs. work as self-fulfillment
  (i) Private material needs vs. social wants

II. Fundamentals of Business Enterprise (Seven pillars of business)
  (a) Growth
  (b) Technology
  (c) Profit and the market system
  (d) Private property
  (e) Managerial authority
  (f) A day's work for a day's pay
  (g) Loyalty

III. Future Business Trends
  (a) More service oriented
  (b) More international
  (c) More public in its operation
  (d) More social goals oriented
  (e) More selective in its growth strategies
  (f) More conservation/recycling oriented
  (g) More concerned with human resources
  (h) More decentralized in its operation and management system
  (i) More participation in its governance

---

[3]Wilson, Ian H. "Business and the Future." *A Look to the Future.* Bulletin #213. Albany: New York State Education Department, 1978.

IV. Management of Human Behavior
    (a) Concept of personnel management
    (b) Fundamentals of human behavior
    (c) Developing attitudes
    (d) Changing attitudes
    (e) The image
    (f) Developing the image
    (g) Affecting human behavior through image and attitude
    (h) Negotiating human behavior
    (i) Systems approach to human behavior management
    (j) Techniques for managing human behavior

V. Practical Applications of Business Management
    (a) Developing a business structure for the future
        1. Purpose
        2. Governance
        3. Employee considerations
        4. Growth considerations
        5. Compatibility with nature
        6. Profit potential
        7. Social acceptability
    (b) Participation in the business structure
        1. Uninvolved employee
        2. Involved employee
        3. Public servant
        4. Independent contractor
        5. Business owner/manager

Youth leadership organizations. Youth leadership clubs such as FBLA offer an excellent opportunity to identify student leadership abilities and to further develop these abilities. The political process used to select student officers allows exceptional talents to develop and rise to recognition. Experience with these programs shows that overinvolvement of faculty advisers tends to diminish the effectiveness of the program. In order for student talent to progress to the fullest, advisers must play the role of "limited overseer."

Programs for gifted students can be as broad as the gifts involved and the imagination of educators to help develop these gifts. The limited material presented in this chapter only begins to scratch the surface of this emerging concern of secondary school educators. Business education has a prominent place in this movement, a place that will be determined for the most part by those in the front lines of business education, the business education classroom teachers.